SHOOT T...

Police accountal... ...ity, firearms and fatal force

Maurice Punch

LEARNING RESOURCES CENTRE

HAVERING COLLEGE

First published in Great Britain in 2011 by

The Policy Press
University of Bristol
Fourth Floor
Beacon House
Queen's Road
Bristol BS8 1QU
UK
t: +44 (0)117 331 4054
f: +44 (0)117 331 4093
tpp-info@bristol.ac.uk
www.policypress.co.uk

North American office:
The Policy Press
c/o International Specialized Books Services (ISBS)
920 NE 58th Avenue, Suite 300
Portland, OR 97213-3786, USA
t: +1 503 287 3093
f: +1 503 280 8832
info@isbs.com

© The Policy Press 2011

ISBN 978 1 84742 472 3 paperback
ISBN 978 1 84742 473 0 hardcover

British Library Cataloguing in Publication Data
A catalogue record for this book is available from the British Library.

Library of Congress Cataloging-in-Publication Data
A catalog record for this book has been requested.

The right of Maurice Punch to be identified as author of this work has been asserted by him in accordance with the 1988 Copyright, Designs and Patents Act.

The Policy Press uses environmentally responsible print partners.

Cover design by The Policy Press
Front cover: photograph kindly supplied by Getty Images
Printed and bound in Great Britain by TJ International, Padstow

For Jimmy Julio Michael Punch and his parents
George and Maria

Contents

Foreword and acknowledgements

This book arose directly from the resurfacing of the term 'shoot to kill' following the killing of an innocent man by the Metropolitan Police Service – colloquially referred to as the 'Met' – in London in 2005 at Stockwell Underground Station. My academic curiosity was aroused by that extraordinary event and the implications for British policing, but already before that affair I was interested in issues of operational and institutional accountability in policing. Recently, moreover, I began to pay attention to these crucial subjects in relation to the police use of firearms. This was for two main reasons.

First, I have often collaborated with police practitioners in my work and publications. In the age of smart cops the contribution of these 'reflective practitioners' brings valuable insights from insiders both about strategic and operational issues and especially about the predicament of the front-line officer at the delivery end of the most important government agency in society. We can, for instance, ruminate on firearms policy, but we must always consider the sometimes crude reality and acute dilemmas facing the officer confronting a gun, without a weapon or with a firearm. The latter carries the awesome responsibility of being able to take the life of a fellow citizen. The state has abolished the death penalty, but has delegated a form of 'capital punishment' to a law-enforcement officer low in the formal hierarchy.

My focus in this work draws, then, on the knowledge and experience of several reflective practitioners but especially that of Geoffrey Markham, who served in the Essex Police for over 40 years (1957–99). He became Assistant Chief Constable (ACC), was a member of the Association of Chief Police Officers (ACPO)[1] for 16 years and served on nine ACPO committees including the Joint Standing Committee on Police Use of Firearms. Geoffrey became an authority on firearms and contributed to *The Manual of Guidance on the Police Use of Firearms* (ACPO, 2001).[2] He has handled major incidents during a period of rapid and significant change in British policing. During his training in 1957, for example, there was no attention paid to firearms: 'They were only mentioned in relation to the law on weapons and licensing and also with regard to humane use against animals. But there was no thought given to weaponry at all, although there must have been an arsenal somewhere' (interview, Markham). Additionally the Essex Police became strongly committed to establishing accountability – setting up early audit trails on major policy matters and during large-scale incidents – and to a thorough professionalism on firearms.

We met in the late 1960s when Geoffrey attended Essex University and I was on the faculty.[3] On returning to the force in 1972 he became responsible for setting up the Force Support Unit (FSU) and developing the firearms capability, while later as ACC (Operations) he often acted as 'Gold Commander'[4] at a range of incidents including some with armed criminals. He participated in different capacities at three of the four aircraft hijacks experienced to date in the UK (in 1975, 1982 and 1996 at London Stansted Airport). Until recently Geoffrey lectured at Bramshill – formerly the Police Staff College, now part of Centrex, National Police Training – on accountability and critical incidents with particular reference to firearms. He also provided advice and evidence to both the Crown and the defence in the so-called 'Sussex' case when a police constable was prosecuted for murder after the shooting of an unarmed man, James Ashley, during a planned operation in 1998 (see Chapter One; also Squires and Kennison, 2010: 166–71). Since moving to the Netherlands in 1975 I kept in touch and we have regularly discussed diverse aspects of policing and collaborated on several publications around major incidents and accountability (Punch and Markham, 2000, 2004, 2006; Markham and Punch, 2007a, 2007b).

Another contact from that period is Ralph Crawshaw, who also studied at Essex University on secondment from the Essex Police, which he left as Chief Superintendent in 1989 after 30 years of service having worked in senior operational and staff functions. He then took a Masters in Human Rights Law at Essex and commenced a second career in the 'HR' field, which took him to umpteen law-enforcement and government agencies throughout the world and also led to several encyclopaedic publications on HR geared to policing

(Crawshaw and Holmström, 2006; Crawshaw et al, 2006). Ralph has frequently helped me and now especially on HR issues for this book.

Second, this topic tied into my long-term research interest on policing, police corruption and corporate crime with a strong focus on *organisational deviance* (Punch, 1985, 1996, 2009a, 2009b). Following the Stockwell shooting, moreover, I became intrigued by the 30 years of the 'Troubles' in Northern Ireland, from 1968 to 1998 (McKittrick and McVea, 2001), for it was then that the term 'shoot to kill' became widely used in debate, polemics and the media (Stalker, 1988; Urban, 1993). There were accusations about serious misuse of force by the police, the Royal Ulster Constabulary (RUC), and by military units including the Special Air Service Regiment (SAS). In that exceptional context of civil strife it was held that some people suspected of involvement in the Irish Republican Army (IRA) campaign of insurgency had been shot in abeyance of the rule of the law and in a manner amounting to summary execution (Stevens, 2003; Punch, 2009a: 143–56).[5]

Valuable input was provided by a number of British, American and Dutch academics and police officers whom I consulted. Some have particular expertise as former firearms officers, operational commanders or as academic researchers in this specific area. Several are 'crossovers' who were police officers who became academics.[6] The contributors include Otto Adang, Jyoti Belur, Piet Deelman, Auke van Dijk, Julian Dixon, Bob Golding, Bob Hoogenboom, Dave Klinger, Peter Moskos, Steve Savage, Philip Stenning, Jaap Timmer, Kees van der Vijver, Dermot Walsh and Ron Weitzer. A senior Met officer, Commander Ian Carter, was most helpful. Stan Gilmour (Thames Valley Police) read several drafts and provided many insightful comments. Peter Squires and Peter Kennison kindly sent me the draft of *Shooting to Kill?* (2010) prior to publication and we discussed its content at length. Jim Waddington, the acknowledged expert in the UK on this area as well as public order, was especially forthcoming with help and advice. I was loosely involved with the international 'Police Use of Force Group' (PUOF), led by Philip Stenning and Thomas Feltes, and benefited from several meetings and its comparative material. I am fortunate in London to have access to erudite and supportive colleagues including Ben Bowling, David

Downes, Janet Foster, Penny Green, Mercedes Hinton, Tim Newburn, Paddy Rawlinson, Paul Rock and Robert Reiner. I would like to thank all these colleagues and friends most warmly for their help. I hesitate to mention my veteran squash partner in Amsterdam, Derek Phillips, as he derides obsequious acknowledgements. I am grateful, too, for the professional but personal approach of my editor Karen Bowler and also of her colleagues at The Policy Press. This book is, however, solely my work and the views expressed in it are mine and mine alone. Should there be any mistakes in the text then they are my responsibility.

Finally, I have as ever received constant encouragement from my dear wife Corry and from Julio, Maria and George – and have been pleasantly distracted by grandson Jimmy – and from my extended family in the Netherlands, UK and US; this support is much appreciated.

Notes

[1] ACPO: 'The Association of Chief Police Officers is an independent, professionally led strategic body. In the public interest and, in equal and active partnership with government and the Association of Police Authorities, ACPO leads and coordinates the direction and development of the police service in England, Wales and Northern Ireland. In times of national need ACPO, on behalf of all chief officers, coordinates the strategic policing response. ACPO's 341 members are police officers of Assistant Chief Constable rank (Commanders in the Metropolitan Police and City of London Police) and above, and senior police staff managers, in the 44 forces in England, Wales and Northern Ireland, and other forces such as British Transport Police and States of Jersey Police' (from the website of ACPO, www.acpo.police.uk).

[2] This version was published after his retirement. The first ACPO *Manual on Police Use of Firearms* was brought out in 1983 and has been continually updated. It effectively lays down national guidelines; formally each chief constable is autonomous in his or her decision-making, but ACPO now works on the principle that firearms policy and practice need to be national.

[3] The Essex Police then operated a scheme allowing officers to take a degree full time (Lee and Punch, 2006).

[4] For major incidents and set-piece firearms operations there will normally be an accountability structure based on the Gold, Silver and Bronze command and control model (Punch and Markham, 2004). Gold is for the strategic role, Silver for tactical, operational command and Bronze is for implementation.

[5] The Provisional IRA, founded in 1969, was the main opponent of the security services in Northern Ireland and on mainland Britain. The armed republican movement has a long history and there were several republican paramilitary organisations involved in the Troubles, but by the IRA in that period I mean the Provisional IRA (English, 2004).

[6] One of these was responsible for a fatal shooting in his first year with the Los Angeles Police Department (LAPD) and subsequently become an academic with expertise on police use of firearms (Klinger, 2004).

Abbreviations/acronyms

ACC	Assistant Chief Constable
ACPO	Association of Chief Police Officers
AFO	Authorised Firearms Officer
ARV	Armed response vehicle
ASU	Active Service Unit (IRA)
CAD	Computer-aided dispatch
CID	Criminal Investigation Department
COBRA	Cabinet Office Briefing Room
CPS	Crown Prosecution Service
CQB	Close Quarter Battle
CRW	Counter Revolutionary Warfare
CT	Counter-terrorism
DPG	Diplomatic Protection Group (later Royal and Diplomatic Protection Service, RDPS)
DPP	Director of Public Prosecutions
DSI	Dienst Speciale Interventies (Unit of Special Interventions) (Netherlands)
DSO	Designated Senior Officer
EComHR	European Commission on Human Rights
ECHR	European Court of Human Rights
EConvHR	European Convention on Human Rights
FATS	Firearms Training System
FBI	Federal Bureau of Investigation
Federation	Police representative body for lower police ranks in England and Wales
FSU	Force Support Unit (Essex)
GMP	Greater Manchester Police
H&K	Heckler and Koch (firearm)
HEMS	Helicopter Emergency Service
HMIC	Her Majesty's Inspectorate of Constabulary
HOWG	Home Office Working Group (on firearms)
HR	Human rights
HRA	Human Rights Act

IPCC	Independent Police Complaints Commission
IRA	Irish Republican Army, here meaning 'Provisional' IRA
JIC	Joint Intelligence Committee
JSP	Jacketed soft-point bullet
LAPD	Los Angeles Police Department
MACP	Military Aid to the Civil Power
Merseyside	Police force for greater Liverpool area
Met	Metropolitan Police Service (also MPS)
MoD	Ministry of Defence
MPA	Metropolitan Police Authority
NDA	National Detective Agency (Netherlands)
NSY	New Scotland Yard, Headquarters of Metropolitan Police
NYPD	New York City Police Department
OPONI	Office of the Police Ombudsman for Northern Ireland
PCA	Police Complaints Authority
POU	Public Order Unit (US)
PPS	Public Prosecution Service (Netherlands)
PPU	Police Paramilitary Unit (US)
PSNI	Police Service of Northern Ireland (since 2001)
PUOF	Police Use of Force group
RCMP	Royal Canadian Mounted Police
RDPS	Royal and Diplomatic Protection Service
RUC	Royal Ulster Constabulary (until 2001)
SAS	Special Air Service (22 SAS Regiment, British Army)
SB	Special Branch, 'political' wing of British police
SFO	Specialist Firearms Officer
SLP	Self-loading pistol
SLR	Self-loading rifle
SO12	Met Special Branch
SO13	Met Anti-Terrorism Branch
SO15	New combined Special Branch and Anti-Terrorism Branch of Met

SO19	Met firearms unit; first D11, then PT17, later SO19 at time of Stockwell and currently CO19
SPG	Special Patrol Group (Met)
SWAT	Special Weapons and Tactics
TAG	Tactical Assistance Group
TVP	Thames Valley Police
WWI	World War One (1914–18)
WWII	World War Two (1939–45)

Timeline

1829	Met purchases flintlock pistols.
1869	Met buys revolvers; carried in risky areas.
1898	Hague Convention bans 'dum-dum' bullets in conventional warfare.
1911	Sydney Street siege in London's East End, police seen with rifles and shotguns; weapons made available at some stations in London.
1939–45	Police equipped with firearms for war duties in WWII.
1950s	Stockpiles of weapons for police in event of disorder following nuclear warfare.
1955	Armed diplomatic protection (DP) officers in London; later as RDPS, duties included protecting the Royal Family.
1961	Formation of Met's Special Patrol Group (SPG); some units later issued with firearms.
1965	HMIC finds chaotic situation in forces regarding firearms and Home Office issues report on 'Arms for Police in Peacetime' recommending standardisation of weapons, training and procedures.
1966	Harry Roberts with two accomplices shoots dead three unarmed officers in London.
1967	First official police training for firearms in Met with instructors writing their own manual; PC Slimon by chance encountered a bank robber, shot him dead and was himself wounded – this was the first fatal police shooting in 20 years; first 'SWAT' squad formed in Los Angeles (LAPD); Criminal Law Act 1967, section 3, establishes principle of 'reasonable force' when protecting life.
1968	Start of inter-community conflict in Northern Ireland and re-emergence of IRA.
1969	Provisional IRA starts campaign of violence in Northern Ireland; for some 25 years also threat of insurgent violence on mainland Britain; Home Office 'Working Party

on Firearms for Police Use in Peacetime' chaired by HMIC and aided by the 'Consultative Panel of Firearms Instructors' in 1971.

1970   First police sniper training; special counter-terrorism units developed in France (GIGN) and Germany (GSG9); SAS trains some police forces including GMP in 'fast-entry'; some SPG officers in Met are armed.

1972   Israeli athletes murdered at Munich Olympic Games.

1973   Two young men with replica weapons shot dead by members of SPG at the Indian Embassy in London.

1974   Attack on Princess Anne in her car; her protection officer is injured and his automatic pistol jams; partly in response to this, Met purchases 800 Smith and Wesson model .36 revolvers.[1] Army units with armoured cars sent with police to London Heathrow Airport.

1975   Spaghetti House and Balcombe Street sieges in London end without police violence although shots fired at police during latter; Home Office approved new Met anti-terrorist unit equipped with Browning SLPs, Heckler and Koch MP5s, shotguns and body armour. SAS had developed a Counter Revolutionary Wing (CRW) in the late 1960s, which became permanent in 1975.

1976   Armed officers in Met are ordered to keep weapons out of sight.

1977   ARVs (Armed Response Vehicles) introduced in Nottingham.

1979   Joint Standing Committee of ACPO on firearms; Home Office Guidelines on firearms.

1980   Iranian Embassy siege and SAS assault; five hostage-takers killed.

1981   First 'suicide by cop' reported in New York.

1983   Stephen Waldorf shot by mistake in London; *Dear Report on the Training and Selection of Authorised Firearms Officers*; first ACPO Firearms Manual.

1984   Global economic conference in London with substantial armed police presence carrying the H&K MP5K 9mm

	('sub-machine guns', according to the media) following US pressure regarding security of the American President.
1985	Terrorist attacks at Rome and Vienna airports; army and Met firearms units sent to London Heathrow Airport; Mrs Groce is shot and paralysed in London; a boy aged five is shot during a police raid on a house in Birmingham; an SO19 officer is charged with murder after shooting a man twice who tried to ram him with a car – the first officer to be charged with a murder while on duty.
1987	Hungerford massacre: 17 killed (including a police officer and the offender, who committed suicide), 12 wounded; Met firearms units permanent and visible at Heathrow Airport; HMIC strongly recommends national introduction of ARVs.
1988	On Gibraltar three-person ASU of IRA shot dead by SAS team; Firearms (Amendment) Act 1988 brings prohibitions on ownership of self-loading rifles and shotguns.
1990	International agreement in Havana on police use of ammunition with directive to avoid ammunition causing unwarranted injury and causing undue risk.
1991	ARVs introduced in Met; first official national guidelines on post-shooting care for officers.
1992	First 'suicide by cop' reported in UK; Home Office Review of ARVs.
1994	Home Office Guidelines on 'Issue and Use of Firearms by the Police'.
1995	First hostage-rescue capability in GMP.
1996	Dunblane massacre: 18 fatal victims, including the shooter, and 13 wounded.
1998	Legislation prohibits private ownership of handguns above .22 calibre.
–	Sussex shooting: officer shoots dead unarmed man, James Ashley, during a planned operation, is prosecuted for murder and acquitted.
1999	Harry Stanley shooting: two Met officers shoot dead a man carrying a table-leg.

2001	ACPO Working Group and 'Manual of Guidance on Police Use of Firearms'.
2004	IPCC operational and mandated to investigate police shootings; Highmoor Cross shooting incident in the Thames Valley Police (TVP) region; TVP criticised by IPCC for slow response and 'caution'.
2005	Four bombs explode in London on 7 July; on 21 July four further devices fail to explode in London; on 22 July Jean Charles de Menezes shot dead at Stockwell Underground Station by Met firearms officers from SO19.
2007	IPCC publishes 'Stockwell Two' report on communications by Met around shooting of Mr de Menezes and later 'Stockwell One' report on the shooting incident; CPS decides not to prosecute anyone regarding the shooting; Metropolitan Police prosecuted and convicted under health and safety law as a result of Stockwell shooting; two armed robbers shot dead at Chandler's Ford by Met officers in Hampshire.
2008	Mark Saunders shot dead in London after a siege at which police fire 11 rounds, hitting him five times.
2009	Coroner's report on Stockwell killing and inquest transcripts published.

Note

[1] The calibre of firearms mentioned in the book can be taken to be inches, as with .303 Lee Enfield, unless the calibre is metric in which case millimetres will be used, as with 9mm Browning.

Police ranks

Chief Constable
Deputy Chief Constable
Assistant Chief Constable
Chief Superintendent
Superintendent
Chief Inspector
Inspector
Sergeant
Constable

The first three are referred to as 'chief officers'; below that level officers serving in the Detective Branch have 'Detective' before their rank. At chief officer level the Metropolitan Police has the following ranks:

Commissioner
Deputy Commissioner
Assistant Commissioner
Commander

ONE

Police, state, fatal force and accountability

> ... for 150 years police use of force has been formally
> based upon notions of restraint, minimal force, the rule
> of law, *not setting out to kill the suspect*, discretion at the
> moment of firing for the officers involved and the legal
> responsibility of the individual officer. (Squires and
> Kennison, 2010: 1, emphasis added)

Policing and the gun

Most police officers in Britain will never hold a firearm, face a gun
or fire one. And the majority have consistently shown that they have
no desire to carry arms routinely. Furthermore, in the vast majority
of incidents where firearms are deployed in Britain no shots are
fired.[1] A highly experienced SO19 officer involved in the Stockwell
shooting had taken part in some 2,000 firearms operations yet had
never before fired at a person. One chief officer had granted around
4,000 authorisations for firearms use, but none had resulted in bullets
being fired. And on the very few occasions when police do open fire
more than half the bullets *will miss their target*. Then in the extremely
rare cases when people are unfortunate enough to be struck by a
police bullet, more than half will survive. The evidence is crystal clear;
whatever the intention, *most police shootings do not kill*.

That also holds for the Netherlands and, somewhat surprisingly, for
the United States. We may hold a stereotype of American officers as
being 'quick on the trigger' and expect a high mortality rate among
those shot by the police. But the overall data is in many respects not
that very different from Britain. For example, within the New York
Police Department (NYPD) – the largest US police department with

over 30,000 officers in a historically violent city – the vast majority of officers will not discharge a firearm during their entire career, according to a recent study by the Rand Corporation (Rostker et al, 2008). Furthermore, the detailed accounts of 80 American officers involved in over 100 firearms incidents analysed by Klinger (2004), reveal that they often exercised restraint for a wide range of reasons. They frequently managed not to shoot to kill even where they would have been perfectly within their rights in doing so. In real-life situations they hesitated, took risks and prevented a fatality and sometimes avoided deaths that would have been labelled unjustified and perhaps might have haunted them for years. The officers describe how everything seemed to slow down; they became highly focused, unconsciously filtering out noise and the wider context and became absorbed in the detail of the position of a hand, a facial expression or a tone of voice. They noticed the suspect was only a boy; the suspect did not place his finger on the trigger; the weapon looked plastic and was probably a toy; the suspect was intoxicated and just did not look like someone prepared to shoot an officer; they could empathise with the suspect and sensed he was responding to what they were saying, and so on, and they held back from shooting. The ballistic realists of the 'Dirty Harry'[2] school would doubtless abhor this neglect of self-preservation. But in practice many of these American officers did not open fire and managed to exercise restraint even in unusually stressful situations; in so doing they preserved life.

Embedded in this reticence is the ethos of 'civil policing', which leads to policy and practice based on the domain assumptions itemised above by Squires and Kennison; namely restraint, minimal force, legality, individual responsibility and, if at all possible, the preservation of life. Within that ethos the gun is not primarily an offensive weapon, but is more a symbol of resolve and a signal of last resort, intended to act as a deterrent. It is the ultimate negotiating gambit to persuade someone to desist. A firearms squad in full gear during a rapid entry or making a 'hard arrest', for instance, usually does so with much shouting, kicking and profanity; its members are playing a robust and abusive role to overwhelm the suspect into submission. Hailwood (2005: 14) describes the reasoning behind this tactic of surprise and controlled aggression:

I believe you should plan in all the advantages. It's not a game of cricket, you don't give the suspect a sporting chance – you have to fuck with his thought pattern, psychologically and physically dominate him. He needs to think this nutcase dressed like Robocop and shouting obscenities at him is mad enough to pull the trigger. His only option is to hit the deck and surrender – as fast as possible. In all my time as an armed officer, this tactic never failed.

In a sense, behind this technique, however excessively crude and ugly it may appear to the observer and especially to the blameless who are roughly treated, is the hope that it will not be necessary for the squad to use its firearms, and that the suspect will not be given the opportunity to use his, or will see the futility of even contemplating doing so. At yet another level reinforcing this is the awareness that in a firearms encounter the police must do their utmost to get it right and especially avoid getting it wrong. Indeed, among the range of critical incidents that police have to deal with, firearms are the ultimate in that beforehand it is known that there is *always* the possibility of a fatality. Greenwood (1972: 3) acknowledges this heavy burden of responsibility:

> In no field is the price of incompetence so high as in armed operations.... No subsequent action, no recrimination and no compensation can bring to life the innocent citizen or the police officer needlessly killed. Nothing will destroy confidence in the police more thoroughly than the apparently ill-trained and ill-disciplined policeman who kills or maims the innocent or who, through his incompetence, fails to protect the public from a dangerous offender.

But Greenwood focuses here very much on the individual failure model and omits to mention possible faults in the agency's leadership and 'command and control' of armed operations.[3]

In this book I will be exploring the police use of firearms, but I will also be using that topic to address two intimately related features of policing. One is the command and control dimension that Greenwood neglects and the other is the nature of accountability in major and critical incidents. All three elements are linked to the consideration in Chapter Five of the dramatic sea-change in police firearms use that abruptly emerged with the Stockwell shooting. In turn, this raises the key issue as to whether or not British policing is moving away from those domain assumptions underpinning that traditional ethos of civil policing to a new style closer to aggressive, proactive, paramilitary policing.

Police, state and fatal force

One of the most important decisions the state can make is to take the life of one of its own citizens. By implication the gravest judgement a police officer may have to make – on behalf of the state, but also of society – is to kill someone by shooting him or her dead.

That is why in a democracy the state's use of violence against citizens by its agents is embedded in checks and balances to ensure both legality and accountability. Clearly there are also societies where the state and state agencies employ extreme violence as a tool of repression (Ellis, 1988). There can be death squads, extra-legal violence, vigilantism, abduction and torture with simply no structure or culture of accountability; and police can kill with impunity (Huggins, 1991; Hinton and Newburn, 2009). For those who live in a free and open society such unaccountable violence in a totalitarian or 'failed' state is a horrifying scenario. Indeed, even when the rule of law is ostensibly in place it can be that state representatives, faced with an acute threat, resort to illicit force. The Deputy Safety and Security Minister in South Africa, for instance, engaged in dangerous rhetoric in responding to a violent crime wave when she exhorted the police, 'You must kill the bastards if they threaten you or the community. You must not worry about the regulations. That is my responsibility' (*Pretoria News*, 19 April 2008). Her message to the police at a community meeting, which elicited a standing ovation, could be interpreted as encouraging or even inciting extra-legal police shootings, which are common in a number of societies including India, Jamaica and Brazil (Penglase, 1996; Hinton, 2005; Belur, 2010; Bowling, 2010). In India, for example, it is not uncommon for the police to act as judge, jury and executioner in exercising a form of street capital punishment by shooting dangerous criminals and Maoist Naxalite insurgents in ambush situations either as a form of reprisal for their violence and/or because they have successfully evaded conviction (Belur, 2010).

This matter takes us into complex territory and it is the purpose of this book to examine the nature of police use of firearms and fatal force in relation to legality and accountability in a democracy. When an individual police officer aims his or her weapon at a fellow citizen, and has to decide whether or not to pull the trigger, that highly contextual and emotionally charged moment carries with it a raft of wider social, cultural, political and professional factors. These relate to training, selection of personnel, tactics and choice of weapons but, above all, to a philosophy of policing and its foundations in a culture and structure of accountability. This ensures the legitimacy and acceptance of the police and its legitimate use of force. In Britain this is related to the traditional 'policing by consent' paradigm (Waddington, 1991). This delicate and constantly negotiated 'contract' between police, citizens and the state has an influential litmus test in the application of fatal force. Indeed, I shall argue that there have been developments in the last decade that give cause for considerable concern about the balance in that contract relating to police use of fatal force in the UK.

One of the defining moments in the history of British policing has to be the shooting dead of Jean Charles de Menezes on an underground train at Stockwell Station in London in 2005, for the manner in which he was shot – with 'ammunition hitherto regarded as illegal and inappropriate, using tactics that verged on the brutal and excessive' (Waddington and Wright, 2007: 478) – raised a host of issues. These were not only around operational practice, but crucially also about policymaking, legality, transparency, accountability and above all legitimacy. In turn these reflected on the very future of British policing, which has long prided itself on being an essentially 'unarmed' and non-violent institution, highly restrained in the use of violence and fatal force. Yet in 2005 a concealed policy was suddenly exposed that can be delineated in one way, and one way only; it was without a shadow of a doubt 'shoot to kill' in the sense that the only possible outcome was set in advance – and that was death. It was unlike any police shooting ever before in Britain and effectively amounted to 'shoot to eliminate' (see next section).

Shoot to kill

The intricate and confused events on that fatal day in London in the summer of 2005, leading to the death of an innocent man going about his daily business, graphically illustrate some pivotal issues in policing. A specific incident is often taken to illuminate wider institutional and environmental pressures and deeper organisational fault lines in the area of crisis and disaster management (O'Hara, 2005; Alison and Crego, 2008).[4] My text draws on that material but also from sociological, criminological and organisational studies perspectives (Manning, 1977; Weick, 1979; Punch, 1983, 2008; Newburn, 2003, 2005). It is also consciously pitched at a broad audience. This is because one of the central tenets here is that the general public, and even parliamentarians, have been excluded for several decades from any meaningful debate around police use of firearms and the predictability of fatalities. Indeed, the policy 'ownership' of that crucial issue – when and how may the state kill its own citizens? – has been delegated, perhaps in a typically British fit of simulated absent-mindedness that cloaks what is really happening, largely to the police themselves.

In effect, the agency responsible for the deployment of fatal force, where every time a police weapon is drawn there will always be the possibility of a fatality, has also been made responsible not just for weaponry and ammunition, but also for policy on when and how those weapons will be fired. This contrasts, as we shall see, with other countries, including the Netherlands. It seems to come as a surprise, even to some social scientists, that societies differ and that people in them do things differently from one's own society. The British approach, with high policy devolvement and operational autonomy, may well be judged after due deliberation to be sound and desirable;

but the covert process of arriving at policy on firearms has patently lacked transparency and has scarcely been 'democratic'.

In addition, and most disturbingly, the British Police Service has for some 175 years investigated itself and this has included its own use of firearms and of fatal force. Almost perversely, then, the police as a vital institution of the state with the exceptional power to deprive citizens of their freedom and even of their lives, inspected and regulated itself and even investigated the deaths it had caused. Plainly this raises profound questions around the norms and standards of good governance and the adequacy of structures of accountability with regard to the police use of fatal force. It is quite conceivable that a police force investigating another police force, which is how external investigations were carried out in Britain, did so with professionalism, dedication, objectivity and acumen. But there always remained the fundamental principle that an institution should not police itself while there were often suspicions and allegations of favouritism and cover-up. The introduction of two external agencies to monitor police complaints, the Police Complaints Board (PCB) in 1976 and the Police Complaints Authority (PCA) in 1985, did not stem the criticism as they were both reactive, had no independent investigatory capacity and were reliant on the police to conduct the investigation (Smith, 2005). Both were much criticised and were often referred to in derogatory terms; the PCB was considered a 'complete waste of time' by Chris Mullin MP, while Ian Blair, the former Met Commissioner, remarked in his memoirs that it was an 'even more toothless tiger' than the PCA and the Independent Police Complaints Commission (IPCC) (Punch, 2009a: 205; Blair, 2009). It was only in 2004 that the IPCC, the successor to the PCA, became operational and provided for the first time an external, impartial, oversight agency with an independent investigatory capacity. In practice the IPCC still remains highly reliant on the police to conduct investigations on its behalf. And it was to receive a tough baptism of fire following that seriously flawed operation in London in July 2005 when it conducted a double investigation into the Metropolitan Police.

It was then in reaction to the Stockwell shooting that the emotive phrase 'shoot to kill' re-emerged in the policy and policing arena (Leppard, 2006). The term drew its strength from the notion that

–

the British police employed firearms reluctantly and with restraint and tried, if at all possible, not to kill an assailant or suspect. Here I wish to refer to four facets of police use of firearms arising from the debate on this matter.

Shoot to prevent

First, there is the long-standing, traditional interpretation of policy and practice that when a police officer deploys a firearm it is precisely *not* 'shooting to kill' but 'shooting to prevent'. In 2005 the then Home Secretary, Charles Clarke, explained this to a parliamentary committee following the Stockwell shooting:

> I think shoot to kill is not an appropriate phrase or description ... the purpose of operations involving firearms is the intention, in appropriate circumstances, to bring an end to an imminent threat to life or serious injury. Tactics are targeted at that.... Where a firearm was actually discharged of course death may result and has resulted absolutely tragically, *but that is not the objective.* (Quoted in Squires and Kennison, 2010: viii, emphasis added)

This reflects the standard position, which argues that the purpose of shooting is not specifically to kill; and in fact an officer should endeavour *not* to kill if at all possible.

Although we may think of US policing as espousing a forceful if not aggressive shooting policy based effectively on 'shoot to kill', Klinger (2004: 34–5) maintains that training is based on precisely the opposite:

> Another thing that recruits learn in the academy is that the purpose of deadly force in police work is not to kill, but rather to stop whomever officers are shooting at from accomplishing an illegal act.... Once the threat has passed or the felon halts, police must stop shooting.

Thus are police recruits disabused of the popular notion that police officers 'shoot to kill'.

This approach I shall refer to as *shoot to prevent*.

When we turn to current police operational practice in the UK it is based on firing a weapon in the full knowledge that the shooting may well kill. This pragmatic approach is not incompatible with 'shoot to prevent', but is more a realistic gloss on it. It teaches officers to aim at the body mass; not to try to 'shoot to wound', because hitting the suspect is too uncertain and it is too risky as the suspect can continue the threatening behaviour even when seriously wounded; and that the officer should assume that the shots may be fatal. Behind this is clearly the knowledge that many firearms incidents in which the officer is in immediate danger are unexpected, of very short duration, at close range and few shots are fired. Practice here recognises the vulnerability of the officer and the need for a swift reaction and reducing that response to absolute basics; the guideline is to aim for the body mass, not to hesitate by contemplating wounding the suspect and assume the shot will most likely be fatal. But even then this does not promulgate the deliberate *intent* to 'kill' although that may be the result. As Klinger (2004: 35) puts it, 'Death is a by-product, not the intended purpose, of police gunfire'. This is also the position taken by Waddington (1991: 79): 'the goal is not death but total and immediate incapacitation'; the person shot will probably die, he adds, but that is not inevitable.

In short, the explicit aim of killing people has never been part of democratic policing policy, but this should not obscure that police could always 'shoot to kill' as a tactical option during an operation: 'If I judge that the only way to stop someone from killing another person is by shooting him in the head, knowing that they will die, then I have the right to do it − it is a proportionate use of force' (personal communication: Gilmour).

Shoot to kill

Second, the debate and controversy on police shootings tends to revolve around a concern about moving from 'shoot to prevent' to 'shoot to kill', not as a tactical option, but in the sense of setting out operationally to adopt tactics that can almost only lead to death. In Britain there is a deep-rooted antipathy to the latter. The concern is now that the police have moved from restraint to a much too swift resort to proactive and aggressive shooting instead of employing alternatives.

This style is often associated with American policing as a negative reference point. And it is the case in the US that whatever the message is in training, the informal 'cop code' advises that when an officer draws a firearm he or she sets out to kill the suspect. An officer recalled that in the field training, officers mentoring recruits continually hammered home to them never to draw their weapon as a bluff; 'If you're going to pull the trigger, it's because you need to take a life, so don't pull it out unless you plan on using it' (Klinger, 2004: 47). This is based on the occupational common-sense notion: 'if you are not ready to shoot first you will probably be too late'.[5] It could also be taken as an adage to think before pulling a gun because of liability. In that sense it amounts to a double and potentially contradictory message effectively proclaiming 'because your shooting may kill the suspect or someone else you should be very sure of what you are doing before you take out your firearm', which implies time for consideration with possible restraint; but also 'when you take out your weapon you will shoot to kill'. Caution precedes decisiveness. That the former often wins is evident from the fact that in reality police frequently exercise restraint and successfully manage not to shoot to kill (Klinger, 2004).

Shoot to kill as murder

Third, the term had earlier in the 1980s been employed to convey the spectre of grave misuse of force by police and military units during the situation of near civil war in Northern Ireland (Mulcahy, 2006). In effect it implies illegal killings. In that turbulent and violence-ridden period it conveyed the suspicion that suspects of republican terrorist activity and others had been shot in abeyance of the stated rules of engagement and of the rule of law (Stalker, 1988). Some commentators even spoke of 'death squads', as found in a number of states with records of gross violence and low accountability. But these particular units, it was claimed, had been operating not in some rogue regime in South America, but closer to home, within the UK itself. In this emotive sense it suggests that there was no intention to apprehend the suspects; that the decision had been taken in advance to kill people whom had not been brought before a court and had never faced trial; and that this amounted to a form of *summary execution* by members of a state agency. This illicit use of fatal force in covert operations I shall refer to as *shoot to kill as murder*. In India, for example, the police construct opportunities to shoot criminals in 'encounters' that are effectively conspiratorial ambushes; but these illicit killings are widely accepted within the police force, by the media and by the general public, and are tolerated if not covertly encouraged by some politicians (Belur, 2010).

Shoot to eliminate

Fourth, there is a category where the fully conscious intent is not only to kill, but also to continue shooting until any possible danger – or chance of recovery – is eliminated. This is the approach used especially during covert, counter-insurgency operations, which may be legal or illegal; and in the latter they are effectively murder. Although this style is diametrically opposite to the traditional 'shoot to prevent' approach, there are occasions where it is sanctioned by the authorities and held to be legitimate and legal. Those occasions are typical of certain military or paramilitary operations with a high risk level against a dangerous and armed opponent, and which are conducted on behalf of the state. But the intention is clear and there can only be one possible outcome: there is no hope of recovery and death can be the only result. This is reflected in the 'military paradigm', which is dealt with in Chapter Five.

In 2005 the phrase 'shoot to kill' in the second sense emerged again with regard to the police fatal shooting at Stockwell Station by a firearms unit of the Metropolitan Police. This disturbing incident acutely raised the question as to who had determined that the victim should die in that particular fashion. Indeed, who has the power to define when 'police can kill'? I shall pay attention in tackling these

—

matters to how policy is forged regarding the police use of fatal force; and also how the police develop and deal with operational policy and practice on firearms use. Before turning to those areas in the following chapters I shall present two key cases. One relates to a police fatal shooting in Sussex in 1998 and the other to the killing by the SAS of three suspects of IRA insurgency on Gibraltar in 1988. Both cases present significant implications for the use of armed force and for accountability.

Sussex and Gibraltar: Fatal force and accountability

The Sussex shooting of James Ashley

Within the British accountability structure each individual officer is held legally accountable for his ('or her' understood) use of force. The right to apply fatal force is contained in two acts of parliament and common law and is recognised in human rights law. In practice the legal grounds for using a weapon against an assailant and afflicting injury or death rest typically on a self-defence plea under common law: namely, that the officer had 'an honestly held belief' of imminent danger and had to fire to preserve his life or that of others. This defence becomes questionable if not implausible if the victim of a police shooting was unarmed or was holding something that turns out not to be a firearm. The latter in turn depends on whether or not the instrument looked like a firearm, as certain toys and replicas are highly authentic, while some replica guns can even be rebuilt to fire a projectile (McLaglan, 2005).

A highly significant case for the British Police Service on leadership in firearms operations and on accountability in respect of firearms was based on an incident in East Sussex early on a January morning in 1998. Following a drugs enquiry and with the authority of the Deputy Chief Constable of Sussex, a team of 25 armed officers entered a block of flats in St Leonards in Hastings to arrest a number of suspects, one of whom was wanted on a charge of violence, and to recover drugs and also a firearm. This was a high-risk operation using the so-called 'Bermuda' technique for rapid intervention, where each officer took a different room to enter. Other forces were negative about using the technique for this purpose and afterwards its use in this case attracted strong criticism from experts (Squires and Kennison, 2010). Indeed, in retrospect the entire operation was judged to be seriously flawed in several ways related to intelligence, training, preparation and command, and it led to several inquiries and court cases (Davies, 2001a; *The Guardian*, 2001a, 2001b).

In particular there were several apartments to be searched and it was not known in which one the main suspect was residing. During the course of the raid another suspect, James Ashley, who was alleged to be violent, was awakened when the police noisily entered the flat. He had been asleep in bed but he stood up and moved forward in the dark. An officer suddenly confronted him in the light of the torch on his firearm and Ashley stretched out his arm; the officer instantly reacted by shooting him dead with a single round from his Heckler and Koch MP5 carbine. The bullet entered the man's arm and lodged in his heart. The suspect turned out to be naked and unarmed; there were no arms or drugs on the premises; and the main suspect was also not there. That put the conduct of the operation under critical scrutiny; and, importantly, placed the officer's self-defence justification in jeopardy.

The implications of the Sussex incident for operational policing were and still are profound, for in Sussex the officer who fired the fatal shot was taken to court in May 2001 on a *murder* charge. Formally it was his personal duty and responsibility, whatever the briefing conveyed, to assess the situation and make a threat assessment; and he was sent to arrest someone and not to stop him killing others. His defence was then that he thought the man was armed and dangerous and he feared for his life; the suspect's outstretched arm towards him made the officer think there was a weapon pointed at him. This prosecution clearly has implications for individual accountability and sent out a signal that an officer, in the course of his legal duty and under the command of superiors, could still be held to account individually for the most serious of offences. However, in instructing the jury to acquit him, the presiding judge, Justice Anne Rafferty, stated baldly that *those who should have been held accountable were not present in her court* (Hopkins, 2001).

Her words have monumental significance in relation to allocating accountability. She stated: 'Those having responsibility for implementing, seeing good compliance and monitoring good practice as to the use of firearms bear a heavy responsibility for the death' (Davies, 2001a). In effect, she was putting out the strong message that legal accountability should be drawn upwards in the organisation. This plainly echoes the thrust in the European Court of Human Rights (ECHR) *McCann* ruling, which I shall deal with next, as well as the new 'corporate manslaughter' legislation then under consideration (Gobert and Punch, 2003). Indeed, she may well have had these two measures in mind, although at that time a police force could not be prosecuted for corporate manslaughter. Her statement in court is absolutely fundamental to the swelling discourse on police accountability.

Furthermore, a superintendent and two inspectors from the Sussex Police were subsequently charged with misfeasance in public office in relation to the shooting incident. Continuing the 'vertical accountability' theme of Justice Rafferty in the first trial, the lead counsel for the Crown at the second trial lambasted the lack of training of the Gold Commander and the 'organisational state' of the Sussex Police. But the case collapsed when the prosecution offered no evidence (Hopkins and Davies, 2001). It can, then, happen that the personal and institutional repercussions of a 'bad' shooting reverberate for some considerable time. It was only 11 years after this calamitous incident that an out-of-court settlement was finally reached in the Ashley case with the Sussex Police admitting negligence, apologising and paying damages to relatives (Campbell, 2009). This shooting had not only led to the avoidable death of an unarmed man, but also drew inquiries by two other forces that, in a cloud of mutual recrimination, raised serious accusations about the conduct and competence of several senior officers including the Chief Constable (Davies, 2001b). Indeed, one of my police respondents said 'the Chief Constable should have stood in the dock next to that constable' on the grounds that senior officers should be prepared to take not only operational accountability, but also liability for institutional and command and control failures.

Deaths on the Rock: SAS, IRA and ECHR

A landmark human rights case with important implications for 'command and control' of operations and accountability is *McCann et al v The United Kingdom*. This arose from the killing of three suspected IRA insurgents by four soldiers of the SAS on Sunday, 6 March 1988 on Gibraltar. Although military personnel were deployed it was initially a *police* operation to arrest and detain the suspects. This will always be the case as the Army has no operational authority in British society in peacetime, unless martial law has been declared, and it only goes into action at the request of the civil authorities. In fact, arrest procedures had been practised by police and the soldiers and efforts had been made to find a suitable place to detain the suspects after their arrest. But the operation turned out to be quite different to what was formally and explicitly intended.

The operational mode actually adopted by the SAS unit on Gibraltar is an illustration of the 'military paradigm' in relation to tackling major incidents that will be further dealt with in Chapter Five and that adopts the 'shoot to eliminate' approach. But it is examined here for the considerable significance of the subsequent ECHR ruling for policing and the issue of accountability.

On Gibraltar in 1988 a plain-clothes SAS unit was trailing a three-person Active Service Unit (ASU) of the IRA. The ASU was thought to be preparing a remote-controlled explosion with a car bomb to coincide with a military parade on the 'Rock'. On 'signing over' to the military, the civil authorities and police made it clear that the purpose of the operation was to *apprehend* the suspects (Crawshaw and Holmström, 2006: 86–104). The SAS unit trailed the ASU, which had split into a male–female pair (Mairead Farrell and Danny McCann) and a single male (Sean Savage). At one stage the couple were alleged to have suddenly noticed the SAS unit trailing them and to have made a sudden movement. Both were shot and firing continued after they had fallen to the ground while the third member of the unit was shot shortly afterwards at a different location close by.

It turned out that all three were unarmed; had no remote-control device on them; the car used that day had no bomb in it; and there was no military parade planned for that day. Furthermore, witnesses maintained that no warnings were given, that the couple had first raised their arms and that firing continued after the IRA insurgents had been disabled and were on the ground. Mrs Farrell had been shot at a distance of only three feet and was shot in the face and back; McCann was shot in the head and back; Savage was hit by 16 bullets. The shots were carefully aimed to hit the brain and vital organs. Forensic evidence indicated that firing had continued after all three were on the ground and one expert spoke of a 'frenzy' of firing in relation to the multiple wounds inflicted on Savage (Waddington, 1991: 94). There was clearly no warning given and there was no attempt at an arrest.

The investigation into these highly controversial shootings was conducted by the miniscule Gibraltar police force. There were subsequently no prosecutions of the soldiers following the Gibraltar encounter. There had to be an inquest but this one had to cope with Public Immunity Certificates, which the government uses to limit – in the interests of national security – what can be said, discussed and revealed in public. At the inquest the soldiers, who were concealed from public view, maintained that they were informed in the briefing that this was a 'button-job', meaning causing an explosion with a remote-controlled device, and that they perceived the sudden movement of the couple as a sign of imminent danger requiring immediate use of fatal force.

Whatever the expressed intention of the operation it turned out to be more like a pre-planned assault. In this style of military action there is typically prior intelligence; the construction of a suitable location with the element of surprise (if not an ambush); no warning; no attempt to apprehend and no response to any efforts to surrender; multiple shots at the head and vital organs; and continued firing after the victim is disabled until he or she is effectively 'blown away' in a hail of bullets. This clearly typifies 'shoot to eliminate'. There is, moreover, often mention afterwards of a 'sudden movement' by the victim that justified the shooting by providing the element of immediate danger (Urban, 1993). In essence the status of the targets has been altered from suspects to be arrested to face trial in order to establish guilt to enemies on an active service mission who are caught in the act, are causing imminent danger and can be shot dead; or, in the eyes of some, 'executed' without trial. Indeed, if the ASU had detonated a bomb on Gibraltar leading to large loss of life and had subsequently been arrested, then under UK law its members could not have faced capital punishment if convicted.

This style of operating is a close-quarters combat model taken from special operations in an armed conflict and from counter-insurgency tactics; it is designed to eliminate a clearly defined enemy and is deeply alien to everyday law enforcement in a democracy.

ECHR ruling

In coming to its decision on the Gibraltar shootings, the ECHR in Strasbourg scrutinised carefully not only whether the force used by the soldiers was strictly proportionate to the aim of protecting persons against unlawful violence, but also whether the anti-terrorist operation was planned and controlled by the authorities so as to minimise – to the greatest extent possible – recourse to lethal force (Crawshaw and Holmström, 2006). The reasoning behind the Court's decision in this case is noteworthy, and hugely important to those planning and commanding and controlling operations involving the use of force. The Court placed the responsibility for violations of the right to life *squarely on those in command of the operation.*

Concerning the soldiers, the Court accepted that they honestly believed, in the light of the information they had been given, that it was necessary to shoot the suspects in order to prevent them from detonating a bomb and causing serious loss of life. The Court considered that the use of force by agents of the state, in pursuit of one of the aims delineated in Article 2 of the European Convention on Human Rights, might be justified under this provision where it was based on an honest belief, perceived for good reasons to be valid at the time, but which subsequently turned out to be mistaken. To hold otherwise would be to impose an unrealistic burden on the state and its law-enforcement personnel in the execution of their duty, perhaps to the detriment of their lives and those of others. It followed that having regard to the dilemma confronting the authorities in the circumstances of the case, the actions of the soldiers in the eyes of the judges did not in themselves give rise to a violation of Article 2.

The question arose, however, as to whether or not the anti-terrorist operation as a whole was controlled and organised in a manner that respected the requirements of Article 2. In addition the questioning pursued the point as to whether or not the information and instructions given to the soldiers, in effect rendering inevitable the use of lethal force, took adequately into consideration the right to life of the three suspects. In considering this question, the Court examined the various strategic and tactical decisions taken by the authorities prior to and during the anti-terrorist operation.

Concerning the briefing attended by the soldiers, the Court noted that it was considered likely that the attack would be by a large car bomb, and consequently a number of key assessments were made. In particular, it was thought that the bomb would be detonated by a radio-controlled device; that the detonation could be effected by the pressing of a button; that it was likely that the suspects would detonate the bomb if challenged; and that they would be armed and would be likely to use their arms defensively if confronted. In the event, all of these crucial assumptions, apart from the terrorists' intentions to carry out an attack at some stage, turned out to be erroneous. In fact, the Court observed, it appeared that insufficient allowances had been made for other assumptions than the ones made. For example, since the changing of the guard ceremony was not to take place until 8 March there was the possibility that the ASU was on a reconnaissance mission. While this was a factor that was briefly considered, it did not appear to have been regarded as a serious possibility. In the absence of sufficient allowances being made for alternative possibilities, what should have been working hypotheses to be examined were conveyed to the soldiers as certainties, thereby making the use of lethal force almost unavoidable. Furthermore, the Court observed, the failure to make provision for a margin of error also had to be considered in combination with the training of the soldiers to continue shooting once they opened fire until the suspect was clearly dead.

Against this background the authorities were bound by their obligation to respect the right to life of the suspects by exercising the greatest of care in evaluating the information at their disposal before transmitting it to soldiers whose use of firearms automatically involved shooting to kill. The soldiers' reflex action in this vital respect lacked the degree of caution in the use of firearms to be expected from law-enforcement personnel in a democratic society, even when dealing with dangerous terrorist suspects. It stood in marked contrast to the standard of care reflected in the instructions in the use of firearms by the police, which emphasised the legal responsibilities of the individual officer in the light of conditions prevailing at the moment of engagement. This failure by the authorities also suggested a lack of appropriate care in the control and organisation of the arrest operation.

In sum, the Court was not persuaded that the killing of the three suspects constituted the use of force not more than absolutely necessary in defence of persons from unlawful violence within the meaning of Article 2, paragraph 2(a), of the Convention. Accordingly, the Court held, by 10 votes to nine, that there had been a violation of Article 2 of the Convention.

Evading accountability?

But next to those dry judicial deliberations in Strasbourg there was also continuing controversy about the legitimacy and legality of the Gibraltar killings. Such incidents are open to dispute and to multiple interpretations. It has been convincingly put forward, for instance, that the ASU had from early on been trailed through Spain by Spanish police and security units cooperating with British police and intelligence officials. In fact Spanish officials not only confirmed this but also proudly reconstructed for a TV programme their shadowing operation of the ASU as they travelled through Spain (Thames Television, 1989). It is also known now from revelations during the last decade that the IRA was deeply infiltrated by British intelligence agencies.

All three ASU members had been allowed to pass into Gibraltar, with one travelling in a car that did not contain a bomb but was meant to occupy a parking space for a second vehicle with the explosive device that was left in Spain. Allegedly British intelligence knew that this was a reconnaissance mission because there was no bomb in the car driven into Gibraltar; there was never any military parade on that day of the week; and the IRA had never previously exploded a device in that manner. Later some experts maintained that a remote-controlled explosion from that distance and location was technically impossible. The interpretation from this journalistic material would suggest that this was an elaborate ambush and that the three British citizens were 'assassinated' in the name of the Crown (Thames Television, 1989; Williams, 1989). It was of especial interest in the testimony of some eye-witnesses interviewed by journalists that the first SAS team was said to have arrived at the scene in a police car, some said with a siren blaring, and that the soldiers in plain clothes rushed over to Farrell and McCann. The other SAS team on foot watched this happen and then pursued Savage. This would explain the sudden movement of the couple as one of startled surprise as they saw armed men rush at them rather than of offensive action to push the button or grasp a weapon. Also, if the aim was to arrest dangerous terrorists with a bomb then why arrive sounding a siren and lose the element of surprise?[6] There also seems to have been a degree of manipulation around the inquest, with dates being moved, some witnesses not being called (including no one from the Spanish police) and a campaign of disinformation about critical witnesses (Kitchin, 1988; Williams, 1989).

It could be offered that in Sussex a lone constable was prosecuted for murder for firing a single shot on a legitimate operation and at the behest of an ostensibly complete command and control structure. After Gibraltar no one was prosecuted for the fatal shooting by an SAS unit in a controversial if not dubious operation with the killing of three suspects without warning, using multiple shots and with the fully conscious purpose not just to kill them but to 'eliminate' them (Kitchin, 1988). This suggests two explanations. One is that when the military intervene there is a form of wilful suspension of legality. The other is that there rarely are any prosecutions or convictions for such incidents conducted on behalf of the state.

The most glaring illustration of this is the shooting dead of 13 innocent and unarmed civilians by British paratroopers during a civil rights demonstration in Derry on 'Bloody Sunday' in 1972 (and with a 14th victim dying later; Saville Report, 2010). This was like Amritsar, when soldiers opened fire on innocent civilians in India, but now on UK soil. It has not only taken 38 years for this to be established in a public inquiry (an earlier inquiry was a disgraceful whitewash), but no prosecutions have ever resulted from this massacre by the military (Saville Report, 2010). This is probably because the audit trail reaches high into the military and political establishment where it encounters an intransigent wall of deniability. The individual constable is subject to prosecution but the 'state', meaning the government in office, connives to evade accountability (Brodeur, 1981; Green and Ward, 2004).

Lessons for operations and for accountability

Both of these cases are key cornerstones in relation to command and control in organisations and to police use of fatal force. In the Sussex shooting the implication of the inquiries and court cases against officers was crystal clear. Senior officers and others should scrutinise policy, procedures, training, leadership, risk assessment, evaluation of intelligence, tactics and operational practice with regard to police use of firearms. This was reinforced by a journalist who closely followed the case and wrote that the evidence 'painted a picture of casual disregard for the rules which ring-fence the police use of firearms, a picture in which complacency and confusion conspired to jeopardise the lives of members of the public and of junior police officers alike'; there was a 'volley of error unleashed by just about every rank in Sussex Police' (Davies, 2001a). As a result of these developments the Chief Constable of Sussex reluctantly stepped down earlier than planned under pressure from the Home Secretary and the Deputy Chief Constable resigned (Allison, 2001a, 2001b).[7]

The luminous message emanating from the Sussex case was that deploying firearms in police operations must be embedded in competent leadership together with institutional accountability and liability and not just individual accountability. In short, in firearms operations where there is always the possibility of fatalities, the police simply have to do everything possible to get it right. And, crucially, Justice Rafferty was saying that the officer who pulled the trigger should not become the scapegoat for the command and control inadequacies and failures of senior officers.

Furthermore, the important *McCann* judgment has been cited subsequently in other cases where the planning and command and control of operations involving the use of lethal force have been an issue in right to life cases (Crawshaw et al, 2006). What the judgment did incisively was to take the responsibility from those who applied lethal force and place it squarely where it belonged – on those who planned, commanded and controlled the operation. The briefing of the soldiers, for example, had been crucial to the fatal outcome. Another key feature of the *McCann* case, moreover, was the observation by the ECHR that a general legal prohibition of arbitrary killings by the agents of the state would be ineffective if no procedure existed for reviewing the lawfulness of the use of lethal force by state authorities. The Court pointed out that the obligation to protect the right to life, read in conjunction with the state's general duty under the European Convention on Human Rights (EConvHR) to secure to everyone within its jurisdiction the rights and freedoms defined in the Convention, requires by implication that there should be some form of effective official investigation when individuals have been killed as a result of the use of force by agents of the state. Having reviewed the adequacy of the inquest proceedings in the *McCann* case, the Court concluded that there had been no violation of the right to life on this ground.

The combined import of these two cases pointed to the following:

- all firearms operations should be compliant with human rights law and Article 2 of the Convention;
- responsibility for failure leading to a fatality has to be sought among those who managed the operation;
- the nature of the briefing prior to deployment is crucial;
- operational alternatives needed to be given serious consideration prior to action;
- all incidents with fatalities as a result of use of firearms have to be properly investigated;
- and, significantly, that what was ostensibly an arrest operation to apprehend suspected terrorists was more appropriately handled by the police than by the military.

In essence these authoritative sources were making clear two essential standpoints. First, with regard to the police use of fatal force, the accountability trail had to lead up the hierarchy to senior officers. Second, the officer pulling the trigger in such operations should not be made a scapegoat carrying the liability for wider institutional failures. Both sources were powerfully indicating that *accountability should be drawn upwards.*

Implicitly they were also conveying that the police organisation simply had to put its house in order and start taking firearms as a literally deadly serious matter. Attention to major incidents involving firearms, and hence always with the possibility of fatalities, has had a considerable impact on policing. It forces the organisation to concentrate on the structure of command and control and the leadership competences needed to implement command; to see that tactics, training, choice of weaponry and selection of personnel receive the closest scrutiny; and to start taking accountability to be central to the policing of such incidents in preparation for the inevitable arrival of external stakeholders including oversight agencies. It is debatable, however, if these messages were swiftly absorbed in British policing.

Notes

[1] In the United Kingdom (UK) of Great Britain and Northern Ireland there used to be three separate police systems in three jurisdictions – in England and Wales, Scotland and Northern Ireland. The Royal Ulster Constabulary (RUC) in Northern Ireland was quite different because of the particular political and legal context of policing in a partitioned Ireland and the recurrent security situation (Mulcahy, 2006). The RUC was disbanded in 2001, and the Police Service for Northern Ireland (PSNI) was founded in that year and became included in policing under 'England, Wales and Northern Ireland'. There are now two police systems but Northern Ireland, like Scotland, has different laws from those of England and Wales. But as the RUC in Northern Ireland was armed since the early 1920s, and still is, as the PSNI, I shall refer largely to 'British' policing rather than UK policing while much of the data cited refers primarily to England and Wales.

[2] Clint Eastwood starred in a series of films based on the character 'Dirty Harry' Callahan, a detective in the Los Angeles Police Department (LAPD). Dirty Harry is the archetypical cynical cop who believes in the necessity of bending and breaking rules, with little hesitation in using violence, but in order to achieve 'deserved justice' against criminals; he has given his name to the 'Dirty Harry problem' (Klockars, 2005).

[3] Greenwood (1966) was a pioneer in the police use of firearms and has devoted his career to improving the quality of armed response in British policing.

[4] An excellent example of this is provided by the prolonged ramifications and repercussions of the police handling of the racist murder of Stephen Lawrence for both the Metropolitan Police in particular and the rest of the British police in general (Foster et al, 2005).

[5] Klinger (2004) had long experience with firearms including combat experience in Vietnam, but it sobered him considerably when, during a 'Firearms Training System' (FATS), he was confident that he had an armed assailant covered who looked about to surrender only to be 'shot' by him!

[6] Furthermore, if there had been a bomb in the car, it was asked, why not do something to keep people away from the area where the bomb was supposed to explode, as the ASU members had walked some distance from the car? And if Savage had carried the remote-control device and had heard the first shots then he could have set off the explosion before the second team got to him. There still remains a degree of uncertainty and confusion about the events and the veracity of accounts by witnesses (Asher, 2008: 473-80).

[7] Apparently what irked the Home Secretary and others was that he persisted in backing his officers and even promoted some of those whom, it was alleged, had conspicuously failed in the operation. The Home Secretary seemed to be using this case to exert his authority over chief constables as he and the government were keen to bring in legislation allowing them to remove chief constables (Blair, 2009).

TWO

Firearms in British and in Dutch policing

> In the very rare cases where arms had to be used the British police showed an almost endearing incompetence and seemed quite proud of a total unfamiliarity with their weapons and sensible methods of dealing with cases. (Greenwood, 1979)

Peel and benign Bobbies

Police violence, and especially police use of firearms, touches a highly sensitive nerve in Britain. This is because, from the commencement of modern policing in 1829 with the establishment of the Metropolitan Police (Met) by Sir Robert Peel, the British Police has operated on a policy and exuded an image that all its officers were unarmed (Ascoli, 1979). Furthermore, Peel's model for policing was that police officers would not carry firearms;[1] would not be given the military-style training typical of *Gendarmerie*-style forces on the Continent; would be restrained in the use of force; and would be directly answerable to the courts. This conveyed a powerful message. Peel was reassuring the public, and his political opponents, that in Britain the state was essentially benign and the citizen need not fear arbitrary violence from it. Indeed, the formation of the New Police by Peel drew partly on the failure of the military, which had proved incapable of maintaining public order without causing considerable casualties.[2]

For almost one and a half centuries, then, the iconic 'Great British Bobby', patrolling alone and with his truncheon concealed beneath his tunic, symbolised this aversion to the use of overt force in the policing of British society (Emsley, 2009). Indeed, Waddington (1991: 9) asserts that this 'policing by consent' paradigm of civilian policing – where Peel envisaged the Bobby as no more than a citizen in uniform – drew its authority and legitimacy from the 'benign, non-aggressive image that the British police institution has tried to cultivate'. This has meant that for many years Britain stood out as an exception to the practice in most forces throughout the world, including the relatively pacific Netherlands, of all officers routinely carrying guns. There are in fact few other forces in modern societies where the police are not armed, and typically in most forces abroad every police officer carries a weapon while specialised units can be heavily armed.

Taking the unarmed 'Bobby' of 1829 as a starting point, I shall now turn to the developments in the police use of firearms in the UK and also to how policy and practice in this area have been shaped.

Developments in firearms policy and practice

> A few senior officers ... found it hard to accede to their men carrying firearms under any circumstances.... For them *The Blue Lamp* provided the policing model to which their officers should adhere, and as guardians of the Dixon image,[3] their ludicrous solution was to issue firearms and then direct that they must not be loaded. In this way the senior officer could claim that his men were not really armed because the weapons were useless, at least until they had been loaded, thereby making possession of them virtually meaningless. (Waldren, 2007: 29)

That initial decision of Sir Robert Peel in 1829 not to routinely arm the Metropolitan Police was a conscious political gambit to make the 'New Police' more acceptable to a highly sceptical parliament with an aversion to Continental, paramilitary policing. However, although the British Police Service has operated as an essentially unarmed agency until comparatively recently, it has always had direct or indirect access to firearms and other weapons (Miller, 1977; Waldren, 2007).[4] Some policing units before 1829 were armed, including those run by the Fieldings from Bow Street, and on several occasions during the 19th century proposals to provide officers with firearms – and even light artillery! – were given serious attention (Emsley, 1996). This was partly related to the persistent fear of major public disturbances and the habit of recruiting former military men to lead police forces. It could even be argued that Peel's initial pragmatic balancing act, if not sleight of hand, designed to save his proposals from yet another parliamentary defeat, saddled British policing with a myth that cloaked the reality. And that this myth has dogged the Police Service until quite recently.

It is obvious that Peel had no personal, moral or ideological objection to arming the police. Indeed, as Secretary of State for Ireland Peel had earlier in 1816 shaped an armed, paramilitary police force, which evolved into the Royal Irish Constabulary (RIC). This became the model for British colonial police forces in a range of countries. Later the Royal Ulster Constabulary (RUC) emerged from the RIC after the partition of Ireland in the early 1920s (Ryder, 2000). This meant that for many years there was an armed police force in one part of the UK, but not on mainland Britain. Indeed, during the emergency situation of the Troubles (1968–98) there was extensive use of firearms in that part of the UK. And an attempt to disarm the RUC in the early 1970s, and to operate on the unarmed model of the mainland, had to be reversed in the face of violence aimed especially at the police (Waldren, 2007). This use of firearms in Northern Ireland included the police at one stage randomly firing heavy machine guns mounted on armoured cars. This is something that has never occurred in the history of policing in Great Britain and it is almost unthinkable in the British context.[5] Indeed, there was great political and public consternation when armoured military vehicles appeared together with police at Heathrow Airport in 1974.

In practice, however, the British police on the mainland operated largely as an unarmed service for some 150 years although ironically armed policing was exported to the colonies (Anderson and Killingray, 1991). There the police played multiple roles including one of maintaining order against indigenous populations by force of arms if necessary. But for a number of reasons it is the case that in recent decades the British police has become routinely 'semi-armed'. However, this occurred through the back door and almost by stealth, for this crucial development was accomplished without any public debate and without passing any legislation.

The explicit operational policy and practice with regard to the employment of potentially fatal force was, however, always firmly *rooted in restraint* in the use of firearms and of *avoiding the death* of the person involved in the incident if at all possible (interviews, Golding, Markham and Waddington). Almost everyone emphasises that philosophy and practice was conservative, risk-averse, 'cautious not cavalier' and based on restraint, negotiation, containment and use of fatal force only *in extremis*, when all else had failed (Waddington, 1991). In scrutinising these matters I shall divide policy and practice on the police use of firearms since the Second World War (WWII) into five overlapping phases.

Phase one: Hazardous amateurism

The picture of post WWII police use of firearms in Britain is one of cannon-like revolvers, a few old army–surplus Lee Enfield .303 rifles, little or no training on firearms use and tactics, and an apparent determination not to attend seriously to the matter.[6] On some occasions officers were issued with firearms but ordered not to load them until they went into action or were simply told not to use them. There were no holsters and weapons were carried in a pocket with the spare ammunition in another pocket. If there was any training it was pitiful if not a near-farcical ritual. Some officers fired a few perfunctory rounds at an army range and were instantly certified to carry arms; they were then sent out on armed patrol the very same day! In London, moreover, the routine arming of diplomatic protection (DP) officers had commenced already in 1955: (This Diplomatic Protection Group was later known as the 'RDPS', or Royal and Diplomatic Protection Service.) They were issued a 1934 model Beretta without a holster. One such DP officer of the early days could not recall any training at all; his previous military experience was considered sufficient (Waldren, 2007: 6). Then some officers in London in the late 1960s began to carry guns during the Christmas period when there was often a spate of armed robberies. That meant being issued with a revolver ostensibly loaded with six rounds and with the six spare rounds loose in a pocket; but then being told not to load the gun.

—

It goes without saying, in the modern light of practice on firearms use, that this attitude and these practices were highly dangerous for the officer with the gun, and for bystanders, and likely to be hopelessly ineffective in the face of an armed criminal. In retrospect it can be seen as highly irresponsible in putting lives at risk on the basis of a kind of determined, myopic amateurism that was hazardous if not deadly dangerous for the poorly equipped, poorly trained and poorly led officer with a gun.

This phase can perhaps best be summed up by two responses to a most serious incident, which forms one of the key moments in British police history. The Police Service and much of the public were deeply shocked by the shooting of three unarmed officers in 1966 in London by the gangster Harry Roberts and his accomplices. Some commentators drew attention to the fact that capital punishment had been abolished the year before and that those convicted of capital offences would no longer face execution. Roberts then went into hiding and there were sightings of him all over the country. Photos appeared in the newspapers of officers with Lee Enfield rifles and Webley revolvers searching for him. Then at one stage he was reported to be in a flat in Basildon in Essex and a former officer recalls how the Essex Police reacted: 'There was no real armed response available. Three of us were issued with an old Webley [revolver] in two parts; two of us had a part each and the third had the ammunition in an envelope. These were only to be put together at the scene. As I was a sergeant with the most recent experience in National Service, I was told I could return fire *but only if I was fired at first*' (interview, Markham, emphasis added). This response was clearly clumsy, inadequate and unsafe for the officers involved.

Following another supposed sighting of Roberts, a Met officer with military experience was also issued with a revolver and told to look for him on Ham Common:

> The sergeant got this Webley out. It was in a cardboard box, wrapped in greaseproof paper. It had never been issued, never been cleaned, nothing. I clearly remember his instructions … 'Don't you load it whatever you do, but most importantly don't you bloody well use it on

anybody. You just go out there and arrest this bloke and bring that thing back to me and I'll put it away'. I sat in the van with this 'thing' sitting on my knees in its box like it was red hot. When we got to the Common the blokes said: 'Don't get out Tony – we'll do it. You just sit there with that and then we'll take it back and give it to the sergeant'. (Waldren, 2007: 180)

Roberts was not there, otherwise there could have been several more dead policemen thanks to an incompetent if not negligent institution that was plainly putting officers' lives at risk.

But the Roberts shooting did foster a number of changes. This illustrates the incident-driven nature of policy changes in this area (see Squires and Kennison, 2010). Indeed, Waddington (1991), who is an authority both on police use of firearms and public order, maintains that 1966 can be taken as a watershed in policing Britain in both these areas. Faced by a number of public order confrontations in the 1960s the Police Service started to move towards mobile response units to back up routine policing and to provide training for public order. These had varying names: in the Met it was the Special Patrol Group, or SPG (which attracted some notoriety: Rollo, 1980), in Essex the Force Support Unit (FSU) and in Greater Manchester the Tactical Assistance Group (TAG). Also the reaction to the increasing number of firearms incidents, with the Roberts shooting as a traumatic event, meant that 1966 'marked a fundamental change in the approach of the police to armed operations' (Waddington, 1991: 13).

Phase two: 1966 and all that: Armed denial

In the late 1960s and early 1970s there was then a move to arming some officers on a regular basis. The first formal training course for the Met was at Lippitts Hill in 1967, with sniper training following in 1971. This shift also became influenced by the appearance of domestic terrorism and the rise of international terrorism. And yet the Police Service itself proved reluctant to acknowledge this and functioned with an element of denial about this increasing use of firearms. Indeed, police leaders and politicians seemed petrified of being accused of arming the police 'though a process of stealth', as one Labour MP cautioned (Waldren, 2007: 38). This was of course precisely what was happening. It took yet another searing incident at Hungerford in 1987, amplified by developments abroad, to move the police into the next phase of employing firearms on a routine basis throughout the country.

The armed struggle in Northern Ireland commenced in 1969 and there was an IRA threat on the mainland from the early 1970s. In the 1973–82 period, for example, London experienced over 250 bomb-related incidents and 19 shootings connected with the IRA, which caused 56 deaths and over 800 injuries (McNee, 1983: 73–82). Although the IRA mainland campaign was geared mostly to bombings, and the IRA typically did not attempt armed attacks on police officers as was the case in Northern Ireland, their ASUs were normally armed and prepared to shoot if necessary.[7] This was evident in the Balcombe Street siege of 1975, when an armed ASU fired at the police before running into a flat and taking an elderly couple hostage. The flat was surrounded by visibly armed police. The public and televised surrender of the ASU was successfully concluded without shots being fired or blood being shed (Moysey, 2007). This was a triumph for patience and negotiation and for the re-trained 'British way'.

Internationally, however, there was a rash of terrorist incidents with shootings, bombings and skyjackings, including the horrendous murder of Israeli athletes at the Munich Olympic Games of 1972. Responding to the increasing threat of terrorism, a military unit with armoured cars accompanied by armed police was despatched to London Heathrow Airport in 1974. A decade later in 1985 there were attacks on passengers for El Al flights at Rome and Vienna airports resulting in many casualties. Army and Met firearms units were once more despatched to London Heathrow Airport and El Al flights into UK airports were subsequently even more heavily guarded by armed police. Met firearms units were permanently stationed at Heathrow Airport and exceptionally they patrolled visibly armed.

These international developments also led to an expansion of armed officers on diplomatic protection in London and elsewhere. PC Trevor Lock with his hidden revolver at the Iranian Embassy siege in 1980, as we shall see in Chapter Five, was one such officer. There was also increased protection for the Royal Family, which clearly emerged when Princess Anne was attacked in her car in The Mall; her armed protection officer was injured in the encounter after his self-loading weapon had jammed. It had also become evident earlier, following the fatal shooting at the Indian Embassy in 1973, when two of three apparently armed intruders were killed, that some units of the Met's SPG were carrying firearms. The somewhat primitive reality of that process was delineated by Gray (2000: 39), who served in the SPG:

> The security of central London was often the group's posting. That meant that any bomb, terrorist or firearms' call in the city centre was going to be our problem. A pragmatic approach to matters was adopted in those days. Only an inspector's authority was required for an authorized 'shot' – that is, an ordinary duty police officer trained in fundamental firearms tactics and authorized to carry firearms – to take out a revolver. The SPG interpretation of such matters was hardly clinical. They would book out a big box of revolvers and, if you were authorized, you took one. It would be stretching things to say that, if someone needed shooting, well, you just shot them, but it was not so very far from the truth.

But on reading the Commissioner's Annual Report (1974) on the Met for 1973 one would almost think that no one carried weapons, because they are scarcely mentioned. Among all the statistics in the report on every aspect of policing there is not a word on the issuing of firearms, how often they were used or any hint of policy in relation to them. The Indian Embassy incident is mentioned briefly but it is almost as if the gun has been paint-brushed out of that incident and even out of policing London in the early 1970s. This represents a wider wish to preserve the traditional image of an unarmed police while virtually denying that more police were carrying arms on a permanent basis.

For instance, when photos emerged in the press of officers plainly wearing side arms there were immediate denials that this indicated any change in policy. This happened in 1967 and when a senior officer was asked on TV, 'Does this mean a change of policy; that more policemen are carrying firearms these days?', he curtly replied, 'No, none at all. No change at all' (Waldren, 2007: 24). Then in 1973 the Home Office released a statement that the Home Secretary had 'emphasised in Parliament that the increased frequency with which firearms have been issued is a response to the more frequent circumstances in which this has been necessary and that there has been no change in policy.... The Home Secretary is anxious to ensure that the increase in the number of occasions when it is necessary to issue firearms should not result in issue coming to be regarded as in any sense routine' (Waldren, 2007: 44). Indeed, in some forces, including Greater Manchester, officers were ordered not to display their weapons and to keep them concealed from public gaze (Hailwood, 2005: 112). Met Force Instructions in 1976 also ordered that the 'holstered handgun will be carried out of sight'. The then Met Commissioner, McNee, considered it embarrassing that officers were photographed with their firearms visible and let it be known 'that it is still the policy of this force to maintain an unarmed traditional image and the unnecessary display of firearms is contrary to this policy' (Waldren, 2007: 68).

The Police Service, however, was in practice and largely of its own volition developing its firearms capacity. In Essex, for example, there was in the early 1970s a perceived need for a firearms response on a call-out basis to deal with armed robberies and other incidents with guns (this section draws on the interview with Markham). In his 16 years as Assistant Chief Constable (ACC), Markham issued some 4,000 authorisations for firearms use. This high number is because provincial forces have a limited number of chief officers for authorisation compared to the larger, metropolitan forces and one or two officers can play a prominent role. This could also mean that the selection of personnel, choice of weapons, deliberations on tactics and ownership of the audit trail were in the hands of a few people for a considerable period of time with benefits in continuity, oversight and institutional memory.

A part of the Force Support Unit (FSU) was trained to use, and issued with, the Smith and Wesson .38 Special revolver, an adapted 7.62 mm military rifle with telescopic sights and high-velocity ammunition for sniping and with shotguns with a variety of ammunition (then principally for use against animals).

What is clear is that although there were Home Office guidelines on weapons and ammunition, Essex, like each individual force, was free to pursue its own search for the most appropriate weaponry. However, the experience of firearms teams was shared informally via ACPO and this stimulated the shift from revolvers to semi-automatic pistols. Essex adopted the Beretta handgun, which was considered the best side arm available at that time, but did not refer this choice to the Home Office. The firearms committee at Essex also engaged in a lot of experimentation.[8] There was much debate there on the strengths and shortcomings of specific weapons; but its members 'never once looked at the US', which was considered a negative reference point for police firearms use. Given the proximity of Stansted Airport, the preferred airport in the UK for skyjackings, Essex officers had good relations with the military, and visited the SAS in Hereford, and armed Essex officers conducted joint exercises with the SAS at Stansted. The force then adopted the Heckler and Koch (H&K) shoulder-fired MP5 carbine with a 9 mm round. The H&K is the weapon used in various versions by the SAS and many other special forces units as well as police forces in numerous countries.

The Essex experience mirrors broader developments that brought about improved equipment and training. What the Police Service was beginning to implement was a mobile, armed response to firearms incidents. The Met SPG was an early example in the 1970s and can be seen as a forerunner of what later became known as 'Armed Response Vehicles' (ARVs). ARVs are patrolling vehicles containing a secure armoury; they have a crew of well-trained officers who are on call to respond to incidents where firearms are suspected or known to be involved or where police use of firearms may be deemed necessary.[9] The first specifically mentioned ARVs were deployed in 1977 in Nottingham. The Association of County Councils had taken note of this development and had recommended something along those lines to ACPO for wider diffusion. But there was no support from the Police Chiefs for further implementation of ARVs at that stage. Hence it was not until 1991 that they were formally introduced in the Met, while there was typically substantial diversity in implementation throughout the nation's forces. Indeed, in 1986 the Home Office Working Group (HOWG) on police firearms pronounced on ARVs and did not see 'any reason to commend the practice to chief officers' (Home Office, 1986; Waldren, 2007: 138).

This reveals the inbred conservative mindset of the time at the highest levels of policymaking with strong reluctance to face up to the reality of police firearms use. There was a need to take this matter seriously while setting national standards instead of accepting if not colluding in piecemeal and patchy implementation. As so often happens with policy shifts on firearms, it took a truly traumatic event to concentrate the minds at ACPO and in other elevated regions of policymaking.

Phase three: Semi-armed with national provision: Hungerford and 'ARVs'

In August 1987 Michael Ryan shot dead 17 people including himself and injured 15 others in the small town of Hungerford in Berkshire (Hilliard, 1987). Among the dead victims was an unarmed police officer. It took some time to mobilise an armed unit and the shooting lasted several hours, ending with Ryan's suicide. Ryan, a local man, started a shooting spree outside the town, which included killing his mother and some domestic pets, setting his house on fire and had him coolly firing at anyone in his path with a Beretta pistol and two high-powered rifles. After a couple of hours besieged in an empty school building Ryan shot himself (Josephs, 1993).

In a small, peaceful market town like Hungerford no one ever contemplated a massacre on this scale, and a mass shooting was unprecedented in Britain. The events unfolded rapidly and almost no force in the world could have coped with such an unexpected scenario in a peaceful, rural setting. Most of the victims were shot within an hour and those fatally injured died within 15 minutes. It is unlikely that any unit could have deployed in time to save them unless, by good fortune, there was a fully mobilised, highly experienced and well-led firearms unit on the spot. Even then its members would have needed armoured vehicles, heavy-duty body armour and high-powered rifles. This is true of nearly all massacres, but Hungerford painfully exposed the fact that in a largely unarmed system the local police force, Thames Valley, had difficulty in swiftly mobilising its limited armed response to combat a dangerous and determined suspect with powerful weapons in an unanticipated location. But that would have been true for every police force in Britain.

This was still the case in the recent Cumbria massacre of June 2010. In this idyllic, rural county beloved by tourists, Derrick Bird killed 12 people, wounded 25 and shot himself. Unusually for a shooting rampage, which are typically at one location, he moved around rapidly covering some 30 locations over a distance of some 45 miles, which made it especially difficult for the police to keep track of him and to deal with multiple casualties in many different places and to preserve the 30 crime scenes (*Reuters*, 2010). His shooting spree started with killing his twin brother and several acquaintances but then he calmly shot at people at random; on several occasions he was pursued by unarmed officers and once he aimed his shotgun at two unarmed officers in a van but did not open fire. Inevitably questions were raised about the speed of the police response and the availability of armed officers. But in a spontaneous, fast-moving incident in a rural county it took time to mobilise the roughly 40 armed officers available and to try and locate the suspect. He had shot himself before police could catch up with him. It would also have been folly for any unarmed officers to approach Bird, who was clearly prepared to kill people without hesitation (*The Guardian*, 2010).

The trauma of Hungerford served as a dramatic wake-up call for the entire British Police Service (Edwards, 1988). In the aftermath of this gruesome incident an important, and national, policy repercussion was that the initial response to firearms incidents by ARVs became standard throughout the country. This followed the recommendations in the McLachlan Report (1988), which examined the police response to the Hungerford massacre and which recommended the purchase of armoured vehicles and the introduction of ARVs (Mason, 1988). Its author was the Chief Constable of Nottingham who had a decade earlier in 1977 introduced ARVs and who had been highly critical of the 1986 HOWG report. His own report was followed by a pressing recommendation from Her Majesty's Inspector of Constabulary supporting the introduction of ARVs. The HMIC could not formally tell the forces what to do but it powerfully pushed for conformity. 'There was lots of pressure to conform on this', to the extent that it effectively amounted to 'a binding policy directive', according to one chief officer (interview, Markham).

With no public debate, then, the British Police Service had silently abandoned its traditional unarmed position and became effectively 'semi-armed', with for the first time the nationwide ability to rapidly deploy lethal force. These developments were, however, largely at the practical, operational level geared to skills, tactics and equipment but they required a corresponding shift to cope with this at the 'command and control' level. Waddington (1991: 55), however, somewhat ominously noted at the beginning of the 1990s:

> Increasing specialisation has increased the 'professionalism' of the officers who are called upon to carry guns. Unfortunately, the same cannot be said of the senior officers who might be placed in command of a firearms incident. Command, it seems, remains the bastion of the tradition of 'amateurism'.

Phase four: Almost professional

From the late 1980s onwards there was a discernible move to taking firearms seriously in relation to equipment, training, tactics and infrastructure. And from the early 1990s there were periodic calls for heavier weapons for a larger number of patrol officers in the face of rising gun crime (Leppard, 1994; Leppard and Prescott, 1994). The headlines proclaimed, 'Police Chiefs seek more firepower', 'Police step up gun patrols to protect London officers' and 'Armed patrols loom' (Tendler, 1994a, 1994b, 1994c, 1994d; Travis, 1994). When an agency goes down this road it means both continued institutional commitment in the face of competing demands and investing significant sums of money. For instance, four ARVs deployed on a 24/7 basis require 60 officers to operate them. Developing a firearms capacity is, then, an expensive business. Officers have to be selected and trained; they need first-class weaponry, equipment and vehicles, some of which need to be armoured; and there have to be purpose-built indoor and outdoor training facilities, which are all-weather and which provide buildings to be used for siege management and hostage-rescue exercises. The officers have to train regularly, be physically fit and be in a constant process of learning from incidents they have dealt with and from experience elsewhere (Collins, 1998). Above all, firing ability is a skill that requires constant practice. In the larger forces in particular there were generally developments at two levels.

First, the initial response to firearms calls was by the ARVs providing 24-hour cover with trained firearms officers in a patrolling vehicle with a locked armoury containing weapons and body armour. In some forces with sporadic firearms incidents these officers often carried out general patrol or traffic duties. But this meant they could be involved in dealing with an incident when the call to respond to a firearms-related incident was received. In some forces, such as the Met, the ARVs became dedicated to firearms incidents simply because the volume of work could justify this (Gray, 2000).

Second, forces started to set up special units with extensive training and equipment and with a broad range of skills. It should be borne in mind that the ECHR had, following the Gibraltar shooting, recommended not using the military for arrests that could also be conducted by the police. There had further been an agreement between the SAS, police and the relevant ministries not to call in the military except for a highly limited type of counter-terrorist operation (Waldren, 2007: 146). This meant that special police units had to become multi-skilled, take on most of the highly serious operations themselves and develop a hostage-rescue capacity (Hailwood, 2005).

In relation to these developments there were two further features that are crystal clear from the insider accounts of firearms practitioners (Collins, 1998; Gray, 2000; Hailwood, 2005). First, firearms facilities and training went from utterly primitive to being highly sophisticated and tailor-made; the teams were receiving the best of weapons; and the tactical acumen of firearms teams also developed rapidly with experience and with the exchange of best practice from home and abroad. This improvement, from the days of no holster and loose spare rounds in a pocket, is depicted in the photos in Collins (1998). In one photo there are the 4.5 stones (28 kilos) of personal equipment worn by an SFO (Specialist Firearms Officer) team member. This includes body armour, ballistic helmet, respirator and goggles, coveralls, ear defenders, torches, abseil harness, a Heckler and Koch MP5 (A3) carbine and a Glock SLP (self-loading pistol). The weaponry available consists of a Steyer 7.62 mm sniper rifle, various Heckler and Koch rifles (for sniping, with silencer, with fixed stock and retraceable stock), an L67 baton gun, two types of Remington 870 12-bore shotgun (one with a sawn-off barrel for 'Hatton' rounds to blow open doors), a CS launcher and the Glock 9 mm SLP.

Peel must have been turning, or grinning, in his grave. Any traditional image of the Bobby is dispelled by the sight of fully tooled-up firearms officers who are now nearly identical to Special Forces soldiers in appearance. And they are well-equipped, well-trained and capable of tackling nearly all of the most challenging encounters within the policing remit. Even then they simply cannot emulate the intensity of training and of demanding exercises undertaken by Special Forces; police units exercise every few weeks but the SAS exercise almost every day (interview, Commander Carter).

But, second, those insider accounts are replete with disparaging remarks about senior officers. This is almost universally par for the course in police circles, but here the disdain is particularly sharp against 'buffoons with rank', 'incompetents' and a 'shiny arse admin wank'. These are from the particularly acerbic Hailwood (2005: 7), who laments, 'at times you felt you had two adversaries; the criminal himself and certain senior managers, some of whom would run a mile at the sight of an angry man'. Firearms officers are, moreover, a special kind of warrior caste, very much at the sharp end of policing and its members typically have negative stereotypes of the desk-bound bureaucrats above them. They form a kind of bolshie democracy where rank is not important, but performing at the sharp end is; and where speaking one's mind is vital to learning from mistakes because mistakes can be deadly. The roots of this sour friction can be traced for convenience to the introduction of ARVs. Again that early situation reflected the in-built reluctance to admit that police firearms were routinely available on the streets. The desire to control and restrict firearms use was as such justifiable and understandable. But this was at times operationally cumbersome, if not unworkable, while on occasion the practitioners' immediate needs met a distant, uncomprehending and unresponsive senior officer. Gray (2000: 1) comments that in 1991 with the introduction of ARVs in the Met, 'the degree of caution exercised by the Establishment was so great as to be stifling'.

The ARV usually had a crew of two or three officers and it contained a locked armoury with carbines, handguns and body armour. The crew could not carry the weapons or holsters on their person and could only unlock the armoury on the authorisation of a senior officer. At one stage in 1983 this was set at ACPO rank, but in practice lower ranks could grant an authorisation in an emergency (Waldren, 2007: 94). The exception was an incident in progress when lives were in immediate danger and the officers themselves authorised the firearms deployment. But even if it was acute the crew still had to unlock the armoury, load the weapons and put on their body armour. Some crews apparently 'armed up' on the way to the incident and then waited in the car for authorisation. In London, moreover, the highest-ranking officer on operational firearms duty for the entire Met at night was at one stage effectively a sergeant; normally there was one for North London and one for South London. Yet on occasion Gray (2000) carried responsibility for the whole city, which almost beggars belief. For authorisation to mobilise the weapons in an ARV out of office hours Gray had to phone a chief inspector who had to phone his boss who was probably in bed asleep. The quality of response of a senior officer woken in the middle of the night, who may well have had an exhausting day before, can only be guessed at. This does not sound like an adequate measure to elicit vital decisions on possibly life or death matters.

It could also happen that a call from the public or from unarmed officers went first to the force 'CAD' (Computer Aided Dispatch room or 'control room'), where the duty officer had no experience with firearms and was also distracted by having to respond to a range of other calls. This was simply one element in revealing that the

Achilles heel of authorisation, however well organised and however swift the response, was the lack of experience on firearms and other major incidents among supervisory officers. To the great frustration of firearms officers engaged in an ongoing operation it could occur that authorisation was withheld on procedural grounds. Also in a fast-flowing action that crossed force boundaries it might happen that a senior officer in one force gave authorisation, but the senior officer of the neighbouring force refused it. This occurred when a Met unit was involved in an operation that originated in Hertfordshire, but when the action moved to the London area the Met officer in charge flatly refused to grant authorisation. In pre-planned operations, moreover, it was not unknown that those involved in a firearms operation would delay a request for authorisation until a particular senior officer came on duty who was known to be decisive and reliable in granting authorisation, rather than approach an officer who was notoriously timorous in granting authorisation.[10] Similarly, in the CAD room duty officers became 'quite adept at identifying' officers who would grant authorisation and would not even bother to phone others. Rather they would leave it to the ARV crew in an emergency to take the decision (Waldren, 2007: 179).

This lacuna in command and control generally – of senior officers largely working office hours and of their lack of command and control experience – was exposed during the Highmoor Cross shooting (dealt with in Chapter Three; IPCC Press Release, 2004b). Three women were shot by a man with a shotgun and when the calls from distraught neighbours came in to the CAD room, it took the duty officer some time to contact a Silver Commander and to mobilise a firearms team. The tardiness of the police response was strongly criticised in the IPCC supervised report (IPCC, 2004) on the incident. The policy and operational reaction of the Thames Valley force following this appraisal was to have two Silver Commanders with firearms experience available on a 24-hour basis in vehicles equipped as mobile communication centres. While this was a sound response to filling the immediate command vacuum, it should be said that the Essex Police had already been operating this system for some years, since 1998, which is an indicator of how each force had its own style and there was little uniformity in implementation. In general, however, in a firearms-related incident it has now become common that an ARV will be dispatched to the scene by the officer in charge of the CAD room; a Silver Commander in a mobile control centre will be responsible for authorisation to deploy weapons and also to provide command support; and the duty Gold Commander will be informed and will turn out if necessary.

But there remains an underlying friction representing a significant culture clash. Firearms officers are often of a certain social type and are culturally not unlike front-line, combat soldiers (Asher, 2008). A former senior officer said of armed teams that 'you have to keep on top of them continually and be wary of a sort of over-professionalism when they start to push the boundaries' (interview, Golding). One should be wary of stereotypes but by most accounts they tend to be macho, action-oriented, dedicated to their craft, a-theoretical, blasphemous, rabidly jocular and tightly bound to their peers. The flavour of their memoirs can be conveyed by Hailwood (2005: 99) when describing a 'dynamic entry' raid with the GMP: 'I was 23 years of age, my arsehole was tight enough to extract the tops of beer bottles. My stomach was in knots, but I was enjoying myself'. In practice they can be faced with demanding situations where they have to take quick decisions that are formally way above the responsibility that is supposed to go with rank. And at times they face an organisation that is only nominally geared to 24/7 operations.

They have two natural enemies. One is, surprisingly, other officers in the unit who either do not pull their weight or are not professional enough and can even be unreliable. Hailwood (2005: 169) speaks of the 'enemy within' in referring to 'lazy, jealous, destructive' colleagues. The other is the stereotypically well-groomed, well-educated senior officer who either does not comprehend the sort of situation he or she is in or, worse, is reluctant to take a decision. While this kind of 'management cops versus street cops' dichotomy runs though many front-line organisations where the practitioners mistrust the 'theoreticians' (Reuss-Ianni, 1983), this is particularly strong where you have to deal with danger, put your life on the line and face taking someone else's. This problem of command and control mobilisation and lack of operational experience among senior officers will be considered further in Chapter Four.

Phase five: Stockwell and beyond

To summarise the developments sketched earlier it could be argued that it took the British Police Service and the associated policy community several decades to start taking firearms seriously and to wake up to the implications of having firearms as a permanent and constant capability. At times the practitioners were moving faster than the policymakers and opinion leaders. But then there was always the traditional independence of the individual chiefs, which was defended fiercely, so that at the top there was rarely unanimity while any implementation was likely to be patchy. Some of the accounts of firearms practitioners are replete with references to colleagues and senior officers within their own force who were either not supportive or who actively opposed the firearms branch (Collins, 1998; Gray, 2000). From the late 1960s onwards, however, there is an escalating tendency to foster increased consistency and professionalism regarding firearms.

That tendency came from specific individuals and within certain segments of the service. The first attempt at a firearms manual was unofficial and was penned by a serving officer, Greenwood (1966). Sometimes the Met was in the lead but not always; the large metropolitan forces of Merseyside, Greater Manchester and West Yorkshire also developed early on a firearms capacity. At other times provincial forces were innovative, with Nottingham claiming that it first introduced ARVs in 1977, some 14 years before the Met did so. Essex was providing 24-hour, mobile cover at the Silver Commander level several years before Thames Valley did so following the Highmoor Cross shooting. Also West Mercia Police took the role within ACPO of coordinating the production of the firearms manuals and overseeing expertise on police use of firearms.[11] But behind all this there was also a stream of reports and initiatives.

In this process the Home Office, HMIC and ACPO played important roles. In the early 1970s, for instance, firearms training was painfully inadequate, but a number of HMIC workshops led to recommending new weapons and also aided 'in changing the face of British firearms training' (Waldren, 2007: 34). The Home Office set up a 'Working Party on Firearms for Police Use in Peacetime' as well as a 'Consultative Panel of Firearms Instructors'. Later there was the 'Home Office Working Group on Police Use of Firearms' (HOWG) and ACPO introduced a Joint Standing Committee on the topic in 1979 and the ACPO Working Group on Police Use of Force was formed in 2002 (Waldren, 2007: 59f). The first official 'Manual on Police Use of Firearms' was published by ACPO in 1983 and has been continually updated with parts of it now publicly available from the ACPO website (ACPO, 2006). The Home Office produced 'Guidelines on the Issue and Use of Firearms by the Police' and made these public in 1983. There were publications by the Police Complaints Authority (PCA) and later the IPCC that influenced policy and practice and a number of reports arising from incidents had a considerable impact, as with the 'Dear Report' (1983), which followed the Waldorf shooting in London (see Chapter Three).

Much of this material was confined within the Police Service and its immediate policy community, but some of it was in the public domain. What this all led to by the first decade of this century was well-trained and well-equipped firearms teams with a sound grasp of tactics and with purpose-built facilities. The new training complex of the Met at Gravesend cost more than £55 million to complete and was considered world-class (Waldren, 2007: 215). But as we shall see later, British firearms practices became rooted – through a policing philosophy, court cases and deliberations on weapons, ammunition and tactics – in a particular style of reticence and restraint.

As I shall make clear in Chapter Five, that long-standing tradition, style and reticence evaporated on one day in London in July 2005. The manner of shooting at Stockwell was completely new and seemingly ushered in a far more aggressive style of policing. Will this fundamentally alter that traditional British police philosophy and practice in the future? This brings me to look at how weapons have been deployed in Britain and how that philosophy and practice of restraint emerged.

Deployment of firearms in Britain

Compared to police forces where all officers are routinely armed, those officers using firearms in Britain are selected and trained to 'marksman' level, meaning a high level of competence with constant practice. In reality British police officers infrequently fire their weapons 'in anger' and rarely kill anyone in shooting incidents. One reason for the high survival rate is simply that officers miss more often than they hit the target.

The police use of firearms has attracted two valuable pieces of research. The first is *A Review of the Discharge of Firearms by Police in England and Wales 1991–1993* by Burrows (1996). This work was conducted in consultation with the PCA (Police Complaints Authority). The second is a review by the PCA itself of shootings by police in England and Wales between 1998 and 2001. The first report is a comprehensive review of every occasion that police officers opened fire in England and Wales during 1991, 1992 and 1993. Some 23 cases were included in the review; five occurred in 1991, 12 in 1992 and six in 1993. Significantly for those considering accountability, police officers fired a total of 100 rounds in the 23 incidents and hit their intended targets 44 times, resulting in seven deaths. *They missed their targets, then, on more than 50% of occasions.* And the second report does not fundamentally alter this conclusion.

To maintain perspective, firearms were issued to police on 5,625 occasions in 1992 and discharged at only 12 incidents or roughly once in 450 incidents. Burrows classified the incidents reviewed into: robberies or attempted robberies; domestic incidents; and other incidents. The categories are self-explanatory with the exception of 'other incidents' – these mainly involved 'disturbed individuals who had obtained possession of a firearm and were placing life at risk'. Significantly, ARVs were more often deployed at the sudden incidents covered in the 'other' and 'domestic' categories than they were in 'robbery' incidents – because many of these are pre-planned deployments based on 'slow-time' police reactions to previously acquired intelligence.

Then in January 2003 the PCA reviewed shootings by police in England and Wales from 1998 to 2001. It examined a total of 23 incidents referred to the PCA (eight of which were fatal): 'In terms of the number of incidents dealt with each year, the police use of firearms is a generally successful policing strategy. The total number of shots fired and the number of armed incidents which result in a discharge of a police weapon, is a tiny fraction of both the number of operations for which firearms are issued and the number of ARV operations' (PCA, 2003: 2). However, there was no improvement on the relatively low 'hit rate' reported by Burrows although, in the PCA review, incidents where the police fired but scored no hits were excluded.

Prior to Burrows' work many officers anticipated high accuracy rates, which are usually reflected in training results on the firing range. Consequently, 'over-penetration' became the initial major topic of concern bringing with it fears for innocent bystanders caught in the line of fire. After Burrows, *accuracy* became and still remains a central issue. The accuracy rates itemised by Burrows are not unusual and it is unlikely that more training, higher standards or different weapons will significantly improve accuracy.

More recently, the Home Office statistics for 2006/07 reported that firearms were authorised on over 18,000 occasions, but these led to only nine shootings. This is a rate of one firing in 2,000 encounters; however, five people were killed and two were injured. Furthermore, between 1985 and 2007 an average of nine shots annually were fired by police resulting in 2.3 fatalities and 2.7 injuries (Squires and Kennison, 2010). An extreme contrast to this pattern is found in Brazil, where the police shoot dead around 3,500 people each year; and then 'mostly in the back'.[12] But in essence it is *highly unusual for a British firearms officer to fire a weapon at another person during his or her operational career.*

When it does occur against a human target officers in Britain are trained to aim for the body mass because it forms the most prominent target; this is also standard practice in the US and many other countries. The reality of using weapons is that mistakes will be made; in a 10-year period, for instance, 41 people were shot by police in Britain who turned out not to be carrying a firearm, and 15 of them died (Davies, 2001a). Fourteen had replica guns and 14 had some other form of weapon; but seven had no sort of weapon at all. In addition, as we have seen, at least half the bullets fired by police in Britain miss their target. With over-penetration of bullets going though the body and stray bullets, this makes it hazardous to be in the vicinity of officers firing weapons. In recognition of these factors, policy is based on firing at the largest part of the body rather than firing a warning shot or aiming at the limbs as happens in some other societies, including the Netherlands (see the section on the Netherlands later).[13] This firing at the body mass may well result in the death of the person hit, but as mentioned in the previous chapter there is some ambivalence about the explicit level of intent with regard to causing death. Clearly if an officer aims for the body he or she is likely to kill the suspect. But people do recover from several shots to the body, and even sometimes to the head, providing that no vital organs have been hit and medical aid is swiftly on the scene. In fact with a speedy emergency response and modern trauma surgery in a well-equipped hospital, lives are now saved in cases where the injuries would have certainly proved fatal in earlier periods.

The key factor in the decision to employ firearms is the perception of danger being caused by someone to the officers and/or others ,and the elimination of that danger. The use of force is then covered in statute law and by the common law governing self-defence. In reality, and in contrast to media portrayals, many firearms incidents involve direct confrontations not with armed criminals or terrorists using or threatening to use firearms, but rather with people who are under the influence of drugs or drink, are deeply emotionally upset or are having a psychotic episode. These people will probably have some kind of weapon or instrument that is used threateningly and appears to form a danger to officers or others. Under these circumstances the police are expected to exhaust all efforts at calming the person and at de-escalating the situation before the decision is taken to resort to firearms. If at all possible, depending on how rapidly the situation develops, police will identify themselves and will issue warnings about the possible use of force. In principle *single shots* will be fired, but officers are primed to fire a second time if required: 'The terminology used was always "a pair of carefully aimed shots" and the colloquialism "double tap" seemed to be something from the Army and was never used in training and actively discouraged elsewhere. The idea was that if you didn't get a reaction from your first shot you were prepared for the second, but you had to account for the second shot on the same grounds as the first' (personal communication, Gilmour). I shall explain later why that important policy decision for single shots was adopted.

A different scenario emerges if shots are fired or guns are aimed at the police and the officers are in imminent danger as in an armed robbery, sudden violent incident or set-piece confrontation with assailants carrying firearms or other offensive weapons. During the police response to a raid on a Post Office in Harrow in North London, for example, some 30 rounds were fired at the officers involved in the operation. Under these extreme and deadly dangerous circumstances police officers may fire continually and aim at any part of the body until the suspect is perceived to be fully incapacitated and no longer a danger; the likelihood of fatalities is then clearly very high. In fact one officer fired 15 rounds from his SLP during the Harrow incident, which is exceptional. However the officers would still have to justify the level of force used and whether or not it was possible to apprehend the assailants at any time during the operation. This is clearly defined in the Criminal Law Act 1967 (section 3), which specifies that the police should employ *minimum force* when violence is deemed appropriate. Minimum force is not defined and it is one of those elastic, weasel terms beloved by legislators but 15 rounds fired by one officer in responding to armed robbers in Harrow might be adjudicated as 'minimum force', whereas in another incident it might be a single round.

Furthermore, in Britain officers were previously trained to fire two rounds at a time; this is known as 'double tap' firing. But then there was the prosecution of a police officer for murder in 1995 having fired two shots at a man trying to knock him down with a car; he was acquitted but was asked at the trial to account for the use of a second shot when the first had proved fatal. Hence the policy became that officers would have to account for all rounds fired with a 'separate test of necessity' for each shot (Squires and Kennison, 2010). In some cases a single shot – and snipers always fire single shots – might be sufficient while with multiple shots each one has to be justified. This issue had earlier emerged with the conviction in 1993 of the British soldier Private Clegg for murder in Northern Ireland. He had fired at teenagers in a hijacked car who drove through a roadblock manned by soldiers who then opened fire on the rapidly disappearing vehicle.

—

Two of the car's occupants were killed and one of them, a young woman, was hit by the fourth bullet fired by Clegg (McKittrick and McVea, 2001: 297). The court clearly took into account the application of minimal force given the diminishing danger to the soldiers as the car drove away while there was no indication of any shooting from the vehicle; its occupants proved later to be unarmed. Although Clegg was a soldier his conviction and other court cases have subsequently had an impact on ACPO's firearms policy and practice. In the ACPO *Code of Practice on the Police Use of Firearms and Less Lethal Weapons* – the manual that has been revised on a number of occasions since its first edition in 1983 – this was formulated as, 'Individual officers are accountable and responsible for all rounds they fire and must be in a position to justify them in the light of their legal responsibilities and powers' (ACPO, 2003: para 3.1).

In Britain an officer using a firearm has, then, at the moment of firing to consider the necessity of each round discharged and will subsequently be held accountable for *each individual shot* fired. For that reason weapons are generally not on automatic fire but on semi-automatic for single shots. One AFO (Authorised Firearms Officer) I spoke to had never experienced anything other than using weapons configured for single-shot firing. But it is possible for some weapons to be reconfigured to fire bursts of three or five bullets or to be put on fully automatic. The Glock pistol is never on fully automatic. Firing bursts on fully automatic would only be for SFOs on major counter-terrorist operations or in dealing with the most serious forms of violent organised crime (interview, Waddington).

Next to that restriction it has generally been accepted that no one can give a direct order to an officer to fire his or her weapon. This was made explicit in writing in 1972 in the Met when 'district rifle officers' were introduced:

> At the scene of an incident they would come under the command of the senior officer present, although it was emphasised that 'it must be left to the discretion of the specialist officers whether to fire or not'. This is the first mention in writing of the principle that a police

officer, whether armed with a rifle or a shotgun, cannot
be ordered to shoot. (Waldren, 2007: 34)

In Essex it was even stated in Force Orders that any officer could at
any time abort an operation if he or she was not satisfied with their
role in it or the manner in which the operation was developing.

This style of reticence is exemplified in the first manual of firearms
guidelines in Britain, written unofficially by a serving officer who
remarked, 'in a police operation *the only acceptable casualty rate is
zero*' (Greenwood, 1979: 59, emphasis added). It is paradoxical, but
'success' for a highly trained firearms unit is to attend an incident
and leave without having used its weapons and maybe with no one
even being aware of its presence. In the literature there are, moreover,
a number of cases where armed units were in direct danger, with a
clear justification to open fire, but they persisted in negotiations that
fortunately resolved the incident without bloodshed (Gray, 2000:
225). This demanded not only restraint but first-rate negotiating
skills and professional coolness.

Implementation of policy and practice were hence geared to
employing highly trained, well-screened, specialist officers who
utilised restraint in the use of their weapons and in the number of
bullets fired when they were confronted with danger. The mantras
of policy were founded on controlling the situation through
containment, negotiation, intelligence and surrender. Importantly,
even where extreme circumstances are encountered involving
considerable danger and much use of firepower and where the
operation has been approved and run by senior officers, every officer
is still held *individually* responsible for his or her actions and may
face criminal charges in a court of law resulting from his or her
conduct. This long-standing tradition of reticence and avoidance of
violence has not only fed into policy and practice, but also explains
why many politicians – and police officers – in Britain are strongly
against routinely arming the police.[14]

Indeed, following a number of controversial incidents, including
the Waldorf shooting in London that led to the Dear Report (1983),
the number of AFOs *fell by around 50%* in the period 1983–92.[15]
This indicates a move towards professionalism, careful selection and

extended training. Although the debate on crime and firearms by some police representatives, politicians and the media often produced proponents of having more if not all officers armed, the policy and practice that emerged was precisely the opposite. It led to a considerable *reduction* in the number of officers carrying weapons.

The key concepts guiding practice have become professionalism, restraint, minimisation of risk, public safety, individual discretion, preservation of life wherever possible and internal and external accountability.

The Netherlands: Shoot to live[16]

> The Police Chief and the Chief Public Prosecutor from a Dutch police region were visiting the LAPD and took part in a shooting exercise where the 'FATS'-screen[17] showed a highly aggressive man in a domestic dispute who was threatening his family and then the police. Following Dutch practice the Police Chief waited until he felt he had no alternative but to shoot; he was then roundly criticized for this and told he should have fired much earlier. The Public Prosecutor with no firearms training or experience got worked up and fired almost straight away. He was applauded for 'getting it right'. (interview, Deelman)[18]

The Netherlands is a society with relatively low levels of violence yet where all police officers are routinely armed. It can serve as a useful comparison to Anglo-American experience in this area. For instance compared to the UK and the US, but like many Continental European countries, the central government plays a key role in both formulating policy on police use of force and even in taking operational decisions.

It first needs explaining that a Police Chief in the Netherlands does not have the operational autonomy on major decisions that has accrued to British chief constables under the philosophy of constabulary independence. Traditionally he ('or she' understood) had two 'bosses', the Mayor of the municipality (for 'public order') and the Chief Public Prosecutor for the judicial district (for 'crime enforcement and investigations'). This has remained the case since 1994 when the Dutch police was reorganised into 25 regional forces and one national, central force (Ministry of Home Affairs, 2007). All 26 forces fall primarily under the responsibility of the Ministry of Home Affairs for most matters, but for issues related to crime, investigations, shootings and terrorism, the responsibility shifts to the Minister of Justice; so people speak of the two 'police ministers'. This dualism is reflected in the control structure of the regional forces. The formal head of a regional force is the mayor of the largest municipality in the region, who is referred to as the 'Force Manager'; he or she is not an elected official and is not answerable to any elected body but ultimately to the Ministry of Home Affairs.[19] The Chief Public Prosecutor of a region is formally responsible for the investigation of crime by the police; he or she comes under the authority of the Ministry of Justice. The Police Chief's appointment is through recommendation by the Force Manager to the Minister of Home Affairs. All three regional officials are formally appointed by the Queen, who in a constitutional monarchy is the head of the government, on the recommendation of one of the two police ministers; all three enjoy security of tenure. The mayor effectively becomes a local government official on appointment and is expected not to display a party political line in decision-making (if he or she has a political background).

Important policy decisions on policing – but also major *operational* decisions – are taken in the 'triangular consultation' mechanism at the regional level that involves the Force Manager, the Chief Public Prosecutor and the Police Chief. The Police Chief may be deferred to for his or her professional expertise on operational matters, as a kind of tactical adviser, but strictly he or she is subordinate to the other two for major decisions.

The essential legal contours of the police use of force are embodied in law, namely the Police Act of 1993. The Minister of Home Affairs is, furthermore, responsible for the guidelines on the police use of force and on the choice of firearms and ammunition, known as 'Regulations and Instructions on the Police Use of Weapons' and the 'Regulations on Police Equipment', respectively, both from

1994 (Timmer, 2005). The two sets of regulations are debated in parliament, except for a number of confidential matters that fall under 'national security'. Political opinion is considered and can influence policy, while parliament must be regularly informed about the actual police use of force especially regarding death or serious injury. These formal regulations are a ministerial responsibility, however, and do not formally require parliamentary approval. In the Dutch system the government does not sit in parliament, it implements a policy forged by the coalition partners after the election and, although it is ultimately responsible to parliament, it operates with far more autonomy than in the UK. The views of the police through expert committees and trade unions will also weigh heavily in ministerial deliberations, but there is no question of the police deciding on the purchase of weapons, choice of ammunition or guidelines on use; all weapons are centrally approved and purchased by the government.

The law enacts that all police use of force needs to be judged on four criteria: proportionality, subsidiarity (meaning all options have been considered), reasonableness and moderation. The assumption is that all incidents involving use of firearms, including potentially those against suicide bombers involving head shots, can be judged within these four existing criteria (interview, Adang).

There is an important article in the criminal law covering liability. A police officer can claim that he or she is following a legitimate instruction from a superior. This is not meant as a blind 'orders are orders' guideline, for the officer is expected not to carry out an order that is clearly not authorised and legal. He or she can be prosecuted for offences as a result of a shooting, as in the UK, but can plead this extenuating 'legitimate instruction' defence. This measure of cover for liability contrasts with the UK, where the 'following orders' defence is not acceptable in law; and this clearly has its roots in the judgments at the Nuremberg trials where the standard defence of most Nazi defendants – 'I was only following orders' – was not accepted by the judges (Nollkaemper and van der Wilt, 2009).

Also of importance is that the law and the regulations explicitly comply with the Dutch Constitution, which promises protection of a citizen's bodily integrity. This in turn relates to the Hague Convention (1899) on the wartime use of weapons and ammunition, and with UN and European human rights law expressing the 'right to life' principle. For example, requests at one stage from the police for a bullet with more 'stopping power' than the full-jacketed ammunition with high penetration then in use, were rejected by the cabinet precisely on the grounds of the need for compliance with the restrictions of the Hague Convention (Timmer, 2005). This sort of bullet – including the Action 1 Nobel Dynamit adopted by special units in Germany and proposed at one stage for standard police use in the Netherlands – was further objected to because of the injuries it causes by a number of agencies including the Red Cross, the German Police Union and Interpol (see Timmer, 2005). Its proposed use, recommended by the technical committee on police use of firearms equipment and ammunition, encountered strong opposition in the Dutch parliament. The Dutch adoption of the Action 3 Dynamit Nobel bullet in 1990 was seen as 10 years in advance of other European forces because it combined relatively low penetration with not particularly excessive injuries (it was not likely to break up inside the body and to cause undue damage to bones). In rejecting proposals to adopt the Action 1, the Dutch government argued that it was inhumane and unacceptable to adopt it in peacetime. In brief, the lead-head of the bullet of the Action 1 forms a kind of mushroom shape after emission and can cause large entry wounds; the Action 3 also flattens out on emission, but is designed not to extend beyond the parameters of the shell. The Dutch police have recently moved to the Action Direct bullet, which has more 'stopping power' than the Action 3 in that it forms a rounded, almost mushroom shape rather like the Action 1 yet staying within the parameters of the shell.

The Dutch maintain that the police use of force is clearly and tightly regulated in the law and in the instructions/guidelines on the use of firearms and other weapons.[20] Along with this espoused clarity for practitioners is the fact that in some operational situations the responsibility is taken by regional officials, a minister or even at cabinet level. For instance in 1981 a dangerous and armed German criminal crossed the border into the Netherlands and took a Dutch army officer hostage as he was getting into his car. They drove around Arnhem for a while until the police became suspicious about the vehicle. When the members of the 'policy-triangle' were warned about the hostage-taking a police special firearms unit was called up.[21] But *before* that unit could even leave its barracks and before it could fire a potentially fatal shot, it had to have the permission of the Minister of Justice. Before mobilising the unit, then, the Chief Public Prosecutor had to go through his superior, the Procurator General, to reach the minister for a decision giving permission both for the unit to go into action and to make a 'shoot to kill' shot if appropriate. Nowadays the special units can mobilise when responding to an emergency, but they still have to await a decision from the minister before they are authorised to use fatal force.

In turning to operational practice there has been a similar development to that in the UK from amateurism with largely old-fashioned military equipment and rudimentary tactics to increasing sophistication in choice of weapons, development of tactics and specialisation. In my first contacts with the Dutch police in the mid-1970s, for example, the police were still using the Winchester M1 carbine dating from WWII and a Browning FN 7.65 mm pistol, which dated originally from the 1920s. The officers derided their pistol as a 'pea-shooter' compared to the heavy weaponry carried by criminals (Punch, 1979). For over 20 years the standard firearm has been the Walther P5 pistol, which has remained in production exclusively for the Netherlands, but is due to be replaced shortly. Special units have a number of versions of the Heckler and Koch MP5 and other weapons including sniping rifles, shotguns and guns capable of firing CS and tear-gas grenades (Timmer, 2005).

All regional forces have a specially trained 'AT' (Arrest Team), which is meant to tackle any serious incident that is seen to fall within the police mandate. They are similar to a SWAT (Special Weapons and Tactics) team in the US or a British specialist squad like CO19 in the Met. If there is any question of an incident that exceeds their capabilities then they can call on a number of specialised military units from the *Marechaussee*, the Marines or the army. The *Marechaussee*, a form of military police or 'Gendarmerie', performs a number of police-related tasks and has a special unit for firearms and arrests; the Marine Commandos have the equivalent of a Special Forces unit for close-combat intervention that is available for policing purposes; and the army has a special unit of snipers. There have been a number of terrorist threats against parliament, Schiphol Airport and Amsterdam Central Station and in 2002 there was a siege situation with suspected Muslim terrorists in The Hague. They were members of the so-called 'Hofstad Group' and they resisted an attack by a police arrest unit by throwing hand grenades, which wounded several officers; but the men eventually surrendered. In the light of that experience it was decided to form a combined military–police unit for serious interventions, known as 'DSI' (*Dienst Speciale Interventies*), or Unit for Special Interventions, but it has to date not been employed operationally.

It was partly due to dissatisfaction with how the siege was handled, and partly to combine the skills of the diverse units from the police and the military that it was decided to form the new unit for the toughest assignments. It is almost certain that these diverse units have special types of ammunition, but that is covered by confidentiality. I have been informed by the two leading scholars in this area and a former Police Chief that there probably is not an explicit policy like Kratos in the UK (see Chapter Five) to deal with suicide bombers. But the units involved would almost certainly have considered tactical options, such as head shots at a distance, having isolated the bomber, and will have trained certain officers with suitable ammunition to do that.

For a major operation the national crisis centre would be opened with the Ministers of Justice, Home Affairs, Defence and probably even the Prime Minister present. This means that in a serious situation involving firearms and likely fatalities a member of the central government would grant permission for the use of fatal force, which would then be implemented under the specific circumstances prevailing on the ground. In that sense the minister is a kind of 'Platinum' Commander with the regional policy triangle as 'Gold' and the senior operational police officer as 'Silver'. When I discussed the Stockwell case with a Dutch expert on police violence, moreover, he said that it would be 'unthinkable' in the Netherlands that the police alone would take the responsibility for the decision to shoot to kill someone except in an emergency requiring immediate action because of serious danger. The minister would have to give permission for such an operation and would be accountable for that decision (interview, Adang).

Everyone I spoke to on this matter expressed revulsion at the idea of using multiple hollow-point bullets fired at close range to the head, and felt that this went against the philosophy of firearms use in Dutch policing, but did not rule out that the DSI would use this tactic. They further maintained that it would be preferable that the DSI or a military unit carried this out rather than one of the regional police AT units.

Indeed, what is perhaps most significant in the Dutch example is that infusing policy and practice is a philosophy about the police use of violence that draws on a widespread societal aversion to violence, extremism and repression. It is worth recalling that the Netherlands was occupied for five years (1940–45) by the Nazis in WWII. Its population experienced a violent and repressive regime, which included collaborative Dutch police officers who rounded up Jewish citizens on a large scale to be murdered in the camps. German forces indulged in the open murder of citizens selected at random during reprisals, leaving their dead bodies on display in the streets as a warning (Moore, 1997). Members of the resistance were summarily executed with 'shot while attempting to escape' as the ritual expression justifying this. This indelible experience reinforced the historical background of a largely non-militaristic nation, with a long period of political neutrality and almost no legacy of domestic political violence, and which abolished capital punishment in 1870.[22] This has doubtless influenced Dutch political culture in recent decades with regard to the state's exercise of force.

In the 1970s, for example, there were two prolonged train sieges where armed Malaccans took hostages.[23] The first siege, which lasted 13 days and in which three people were killed by the hostage-takers, was ended by negotiations. The second siege lasted 20 days and, although no one was killed, negotiations broke down and the armed insurgents repeated their threats about killing hostages. Apparently, the cabinet, with a socialist prime minister deeply averse to violence, agonised about the decision, but eventually Marine Commandos launched an attack with overwhelming firepower – some 4,000 rounds were fired at the train – killing the six insurgents and two passengers (Bootsma, 2001). This exemplified 'The Dutch Way' of negotiation and conflict-avoidance whereas in most societies there would doubtless have been a much swifter intervention to end the siege and free the hostages.

This reflects the cultural and ideological values that cause Dutch governments and Dutch police officers to typically function on the principle that violence is a last resort when all other options have proved unsuccessful. A police shooting is almost viewed as a personal if not institutional *failure*. Procedure and practice are based on negotiation, verbal warnings, a warning shot and then aiming for the limbs (where appropriate). The explicit purpose is not to kill, but to incapacitate in order to apprehend. There has also been a concerted attempt to learn from cases and to use the lessons from them to train officers in how to deal with serious incidents, but especially those involving violence.

There can be a downside to policing a society where there are not only low levels of violence, but also where the police are expected – culturally, legally and institutionally – to exercise restraint and avoid fatalities, for this can even make them vulnerable when confronted with an armed opponent. For instance, two police officers were sent into the busy town centre of Enschede near the German border during the daytime because of reported drug-dealing. They approached a suspected dealer, a German man, and asked him to come with them to a quieter spot away from the crowds where they could conduct the search and take him in for questioning. They saw it as a routine control and without any danger, but the man suddenly pulled out a gun and fatally shot one of the officers and ran off between the shoppers. He was cornered near a busy school playground where he opened fire again hitting another officer in the head (who survived). Even then he was not shot by the police who did return fire, but he was cornered and persuaded to surrender. He turned out to be a highly dangerous criminal with a long record of violence in Germany, but the Dutch police were unaware he was operating in the Netherlands. The police were perfectly entitled to shoot him under those circumstances and yet they still exercised restraint. It could even be argued that policy and practice made a victim of that first officer; that Dutch policing should perhaps be far more stringent in searching and handcuffing suspects. But routine, complacency and context meant the Dutch officer saw no danger and no risk at that time and in that place; and when he was surprised by a violent criminal pulling a gun, the officer and his colleague had no chance to use their weapons (interview, Deelman).

With regard to accountability for firearms use, it is policy that all police violence which cause death or injury, hence including shootings, will automatically be investigated by the National Detective Agency (NDA). The NDA detectives are police officers with a special status who are directed by the Public Prosecution Service to investigate crimes by government officials. This does insure that all shootings leading to death or injury are investigated by an ostensibly independent external agency. However, in practice there can be delays due to non-reporting, tardy reporting or prolonged decision-making internally involving the 'triangle'. The chief prosecutor also has to decide if an officer has possibly committed a criminal offence. It used to be the case that an officer under investigation was routinely approached as a suspect, in fact to give him the rights of a suspect (such as choosing to remain silent), but nowadays he is treated as a witness unless the chief prosecutor decides otherwise.

The philosophy of reticence and of violence as a last resort that has fostered warning shots and aiming for the limbs would not be accepted in other countries where policy is geared to eliminating the danger (as a wounded person can still carry on firing), aiming for the torso to make hitting the target easier and to avoid ricochets, and putting the safety of the officer first. Warning shots are generally seen as inherently hazardous, and are not permitted in the UK, while it is surprising that the Dutch police are allowed to shoot at vehicles as this is widely discouraged elsewhere (although this practice has diminished considerably in recent years).

But that the philosophy and policy 'works' can be shown by the fact that the increasing use of firearms against the police has been met by a *reduction* in the police use of firearms; and, crucially, the percentage of people hit by police bullets who survive is estimated at 84% (Timmer, 2005: 26). In some countries the reverse holds, with that being the percentage who do *not* survive in Guyana (Mars, 2002).

An excellent illustration of the influence of policy, philosophy and training on practice was given following the murder of Theo van Gogh, the film-maker and journalist, in Amsterdam on 2 November

2004. He was cycling into Amsterdam when he was attacked by a young man, Mohamed Bouyeri. Bouyeri was born in the Netherlands to Moroccan parents and had become a radical Muslim as a young adult; he felt that van Gogh had insulted the Prophet Mohammed and deserved to die. He fired eight shots at van Gogh and then cut his throat several times as if he intended to decapitate him. He then calmly walked at a normal pace into a nearby park. Police officers had begun to arrive from different directions and Bouyeri fired deliberately at a police van, narrowly missing two officers who ducked behind the dashboard, and slightly wounded an officer on a motorbike. He reloaded his pistol, made no effort to escape and continued firing. He was then wounded in the leg and apprehended. The officer who shot him said it never occurred to him to fire at the suspect's body and he followed the standard instructions not to apply deadly force if, by firing at the limbs, the suspect can be apprehended.

It was clear from a note Bouyeri had pinned to the victim's body with a knife that he had hoped to die as a martyr (*de Volkskrant*, 2005). This was plainly a situation where in almost any other society Bouyeri would have been shot straightaway and killed with multiple bullets. He was firing directly at officers, so the element of danger and the self-defence factor were indisputable. Indeed, under Dutch law this action would have been perfectly acceptable in this situation. But the police argument later was that they did not end up with a second death on their hands; did not grant Bouyeri his wish to become a martyr for his *jihad* through 'suicide by cop'; and brought a murderer to trial where, in the presence of van Gogh's family and friends, he was convicted and sentenced to life imprisonment (Cramphorn and Punch, 2007). In a sudden and totally unexpected situation an Amsterdam police officer had not only kept cool but, not unimportantly, had also avoided having to live with the death of a fellow citizen even if that death had been fully justified. Dutch police officers are programmed to avoid fatal force if at all possible.

In analysing shootings generally there is often attention paid to individual, contextual and organisational values; but the wider social and cultural environment is also important. It could be argued, for instance, that Dutch policy and practice on police use of force mirror societal values (Timmer et al, 1996). They also draw on the 'luxury' of a low murder rate, very low rates of legal gun ownership and infrequent killings of officers. In 25 years, 1978–2002, police shootings led to 69 fatalities and 357 injuries or three deaths and 14 wounded per annum. That may not seem to be many, but proportionally in relation to population it is in fact fairly high within much of Europe. There is a 64% hit rate, but of concern is that 16% of the deaths were by unintentional shootings. Dutch officers have to go to the range four times a year and take a test twice a year, but audits show that roughly 20% have not fulfilled that requirement at any one time. There is some evidence that a number of officers involved in dubious shootings were not particularly proficient and/or had not kept to their training obligations. Following check-ups on compliance with range practice it often happens that officers have to surrender their firearm and are confined to the station or put on non-executive duties until they have completed the requirements. In the past there was a degree of nonchalance about their firearms, and during my fieldwork in the 1970s it was noticeable that some community beat officers and detectives would routinely go out without their weapon. Now, however, everyone on executive duty must carry their pistol.

It is rare that officers are killed while on duty. In the 1970s, for instance, six officers died and in the 1990s two officers were killed (Timmer, 2005: 526). Bulletproof vests have certainly saved the lives of a number of officers in recent years. In a number of those deaths, carrying a firearm was no protection because the incident occurred unexpectedly and rapidly as happened with the fatal shooting of the officer in Enschede. The sudden direct confrontation between a police officer and an armed and dangerous opponent is most unusual; the great majority of the incidents where the police draw their weapons are pre-planned routine operations that pass without a shot being fired (Timmer, 2005).

Then, out of the blue, there was a recent incident that dramatically formed the exception to the rule. A large, free pop concert and party organised by a beach pavilion on the coast at Hoek of Holland, which attracted far too many people and had weak safety precautions, was disrupted by a group of aggressive 'hooligans' from Rotterdam. These are hard-core, self-proclaimed hooligans who began causing trouble around football matches, but now seek violence at large-scale events with a low police presence. They started fights and when four plain-clothed officers moved in they were recognised and became surrounded by an aggressive crowd; they drew their weapons and fired warning shots. Due to poor command and control and a lack of back-up, the confrontation got out of hand. The under-strength group of uniformed officers – no support from the riot squad had been arranged – were driven into the sand dunes where they drew their weapons in self-protection. Some 70 rounds were fired and a youth was killed by a police bullet. This incident is currently under investigation but that level of firearm use is extreme and unprecedented by Dutch standards (Muller et al, 2009).

In summary, the main points derived from the Dutch experience are as follows.

- There is a high measure of legal clarity through the four criteria on the police use of force in the Police Act.
- Most regulations, except for some confidential ones applying to special units, are debated in parliament and political opinion is taken into account. The minister must inform parliament regularly on this area, but has a high measure of discretion in setting policy and guidelines.
- Legislation and regulation is compliant with international treaties and human rights conventions.
- The police are consulted on legislation, regulations, equipment and tactics, but do not have a deciding voice on equipment and instructions about violence.
- Police Chiefs are formally not primarily responsible for operational decisions at major incidents. Although they may be deferred to in practice, they function within a 'triangular consultation' with their civil and judicial superiors at the regional level. For major incidents responsibility may shift to the ministerial or even cabinet level (there is a select group within the cabinet for this role).
- Operational police officers following a legitimate order can use this as a defence in a criminal investigation and prosecution or in other forms of inquiry, or can argue that they had no reason to believe that it was not legitimate if that turns out to be the case.

- All police shootings involving death or injury are automatically investigated by the NDA but this can take place weeks or even months after the incident.

In brief, the policy, practice and philosophy on the use of force and firearms is based on violence as a last resort, verbal warnings, warning shots, aiming for the limbs if possible and avoiding fatalities by the Dutch 'shoot to live' approach.

This contrasts strongly with policy and practice in other countries including the US, where at times policing is likened to 'going to war' (Bayley and Skolnick, 1988). In my 30 years of contact with the Dutch police I have never felt that policing in the Netherlands could be likened to going to war and I have never observed the obsession with the gun that Crank (1998) speaks of in US police culture. That contrast between the US and the Netherlands serves to illustrate that societies differ for a range of reasons in styles of policing and in philosophies, policies and practices with regard to police use of force and to potentially fatal force through firearms.

The British way: Restraint and 'playing it long'

Finally what I wish to convey is that police firearms policy and practice in Britain has traditionally been based in most situations, and until early in the last decade, on the following:

- an emphasis on containment, risk assessment, negotiation and de-escalation leading to surrender; one officer referred to this as 'playing it long';
- the use of force as a last resort;
- the justifiable application of minimal and proportional force;
- the necessity to justify each single round fired;
- the personal responsibility of each individual officer operationally and judicially;
- that officers cannot be given a direct order to shoot; and crucially
- *not employing fatal force against someone if at all possible.*

Underpinning this 'restraint paradigm' are, moreover, two vital domain assumptions. The first is that the authority attributed to someone holding the office of constable is 'original, not delegated, and is exercised at his own discretion by virtue of his office'. Hence a constable is answerable only to the law and not to any other authority; he/she 'is accountable to no-one, and subject to no-one's orders' (Royal Commission on the Police, 1962: para 89).This common-law doctrine with deep historical roots applied to individuals; but there was also 'constabulary independence' for Police Chiefs as established in the tripartite structure that was formalised after the same Royal Commission (Reiner, 2010).

The second domain assumption was that the police had been granted a high measure of autonomy, far more than in most other police systems, and in reciprocation the police would not interfere in any way with politics and would remain politically impartial. In theory politicians would not meddle in operational decision-making and in return the police would not 'meddle' in politics. Perhaps this impartiality was something of a myth, as policing is inherently a 'political' activity and some Police Chiefs have taken strong positions on certain social and policing issues,[24] but the balance seems to have more or less worked for about 20 years. From the 1980s onwards, however, there has been intense pressure from central government on the police. One might even say that not only has constabulary independence all but disappeared – and there is a de facto national police agency (Reiner, 2010) – but also that the rights embedded in the office of constable have been eroded.These factors may well have proved highly significant in the developments that culminated in the Stockwell shooting in London in 2005 where the restraint paradigm gave way to playing it very 'short' indeed.

Notes

[1] Firearms were always available since 1829 (Waldren, 2007). In the early decades of the Met, moreover, senior officers in tough areas could carry side arms, and other ranks a cutlass (Miller, 1977).Then in photos taken during the Sydney Street siege in London in 1911 police officers can be seen somewhat gingerly holding rifles and shotguns, some taken

from a nearby gun shop, during a shoot-out with well-armed anarchists. The then Home Secretary, Winston Churchill, eventually called out the Scots Guard (Allason, 1983).

[2] In the 'Peterloo Massacre' the army's intervention in an illegal demonstration in Manchester in 1819 led to 11 deaths and some 400 injuries of which about 100 were to women (Critchley, 1978: 115–17).

[3] Constable Dixon first appeared as a police officer in a film *The Blue Lamp* in 1950 in which ironically he was shot dead by a criminal. But the character played by Jack Warner was resurrected in the long-running and highly popular TV series *Dixon of Dock Green*, which made Dixon a household name synonymous with the traditional image of the avuncular, common-sense, non-violent, British Bobby whose best weapon was his tongue.

[4] Behind the Commissioner's desk in the Met there are two cutlasses on the wall; cutlasses were taken on patrol in tough areas in the Victorian period and were also issued during public order incidents. Perhaps he now retains them for self-defence.

[5] During disturbances in the Catholic area of Belfast in 1969 Browning machine guns were mounted on three RUC Shorland armoured cars and fire was indiscriminately opened on the Divis Flats killing a nine-year-old boy lying in bed when a bullet burst through the wall and hit him in the head (Ryder, 2000: 113).

[6] At an inspection in the Met in 1952 it was found that among the revolvers 94 failed to fire, 21 malfunctioned and 54 were considered unsafe when loaded (Squires and Kennison, 2010: 60). The legendary Lee Enfield .303 rifle was in use in the British Armed Forces during a period of nearly 60 years (1895-1956), and for much longer in many Commonwealth countries, and an estimated 17 million were manufactured.

[7] PC Tibble was shot dead in London while chasing an IRA suspect in 1975.

[8] More out of curiosity than anything else, they even tried out the legendary .44 Smith and Wesson 'Magnum' of Dirty Harry fame. Its use in Britain would doubtless have caused an almighty stink.

[9] In some forces the ARV was a 'liveried' patrol car identifiable as a police car and with officers, usually in uniform, performing routine

duties between firearms incidents, whereas in others it was a dedicated firearms unit in an unmarked vehicle.

[10] One hears of situations, perhaps occupational myths (or perhaps not), where the duty officer in the control room did not phone a senior officer because he was well known for being deep in his cups before retiring to bed.

[11] 'West Mercia Police hosts the secretariat serving the Association of Chief Police Officers' Working Group on Armed Policing.... Responsibilities include the maintenance of the ACPO Manual of Guidance on the Management, Command and Deployment of Armed Officers and the National Police Firearms Training Curriculum' (from the current West Mercia Police website, www.westmercia.police.uk).

[12] According to Paes Machado, one of the Brazilian members of the Police Use of Force (PUOF) Group, who stated this in a presentation to Dutch firearms instructors in 2006. In Venezuela in 2009 there were 13,000 murders of which 20% were said to have been committed by the police (interview, Stenning).

[13] Standard firearms policy in the Netherlands is to use a weapon only as a means of last resort, to issue a verbal warning if possible and/or to fire a warning shot and, where considered appropriate, to aim for the limbs and not for the body mass (Timmer, 2005).

[14] Squires and Kennison (2010) review in detail the debates and diverse opinion surveys on police officers' views on arming the police and show that the majority of the Police Service remains opposed to universal arming (Bennetto, 1995).

[15] Early in this decade there were some 5,766 AFOs among 127,000 officers in England and Wales (Waldren, 2007: 222).

[16] This section draws on the expertise of the two leading authorities in the Netherlands on police use of force and firearms – Otto Adang and Jaap Timmer. Much detail is drawn from Dr Timmer's PhD thesis (2005), which is in Dutch but contains a summary in English. I also interviewed a former chief of the Twente Police, Piet Deelman, and Bob Hoogenboom, who is a specialist on policing and security.

[17] FATS is a video-simulated 'Firearms Training System'.

[18] The Met invited a group of crime reporters to their firearms training facility at Gravesend and allowed them to take part in the FATS

simulation; 'they all shot the wrong person' (interview, Commander Carter).

[19] The Force Manager is the mayor of the largest municipality in the region and is answerable to the town council of that municipality, but at the regional level there is no such organ for the Force Manager to report to so people speak of the 'democratic gap' in the regional structure since 1994.

[20] But then they say that about everything!

[21] Unfortunately one of the 'sharpshooters', as they were called then, fired at the by now stationary car from about 50 metres when he saw some movement inside and killed the army officer and not the hostage-taker. This illustrates how difficult accuracy can be under real, tense circumstances as opposed to practice on the range.

[22] The murder of the politician Pim Fortuyn in 2002 was the first political murder in the country in 300 years (Cramphorn and Punch, 2007).

[23] This was a protest at continual Dutch failure to support independence for the Malaccans from the former Dutch colony of Indonesia after its independence in 1950. The pro-Dutch Malaccans were evacuated to the Netherlands, which they viewed as a 'temporary' displacement, and were given a Dutch 'promise' that they would later return to their own independent country. Subsequently radical young Malaccans carried out several violent attacks in the 1970s.

[24] At one time the statements to influence policy and provision were very much in relation to law and order and weaknesses in the criminal justice system and in the early 1990s the then Met Commissioner, Condon, spoke out with others regarding more firearms for the police during routine patrolling (Bennetto, 1994; Campbell, 1994b; Campbell and Travis, 1994).

THREE

Police use of firearms: Deadly guns, scenarios and 'mistakes'

> A former Met firearms officer recounts a high-risk encounter with a gunman holding a hostage in which the officer then shot and killed the gunman who had just badly wounded a fellow officer. 'I was prepared to die…. Some people have said to me I was lucky to be involved in a real gun-fight. They are so stupid. You tell them that I was afraid. That I pissed myself. Tell them that it is a dirty, filthy, horrible business.' (Gray, 2000: 298)

Throughout this work I wish to convey that while there is a truism – 'it's not guns that are a problem but people' – it is clearly the case from much data that *guns are a problem*. They will always be a problem because they are intrinsically deadly instruments that become a social problem in relation to the widespread production and commercial promotion of weapons by the gun industry leading to public possession of guns for sport, hunting and self-defence; by the weaknesses in the legislation, licensing and regulation of firearms; and by the ease of access to legal or illegal weapons for criminal purposes (McLaglan, 2005).

In interpreting this material I shall hold that context and culture are pivotal in determining policy and practice (Waddington et al, 2009). And I shall have in mind primarily three societies – the UK, the US and the Netherlands – with three contrasting approaches to police use of force and of firearms. Throughout, I also have in mind that the Police Service is an emergency agency that responds to many mundane things but also to challenging incidents; some of these will require the mobilisation of potentially fatal force with the use of firearms. The chance of fatalities raises these incidents to the most important that police institutions will encounter and officers will have to deal with in their careers. And the police too can be victims of violence. For example, funerals for slain officers, or for officers killed on duty through accidents, are often strongly ritualised and highly emotional events (Manning, 1977; Crank, 1998).[1] Police funerals are ritually rather like military ones for soldiers fallen in action except that the dead officer was killed while doing his job by a fellow citizen in his own society in peacetime.

This leads me in this chapter to touch on the nature of firearms and the damage they can do; on massacres with legal weapons; on the diverse scenarios in policing for the use of guns; on the tension and emotion of firing at humans in conflict situations; and on police mistakes and accidents with weapons. All of these feed into considerations on policy and practice on police use of firearms and fatal force. But first I shall raise the policy issue of 'to arm or not to arm?'.

To arm or not to arm?

There is a meta-issue as to whether or not police officers should be routinely armed. Most police forces are in fact fully armed except for a few countries – including the UK, New Zealand, Norway and the Republic of Ireland (Waddington, 1999). But there is a general point to be raised: 'Should the police be armed in the first place?' and 'Why, then, is it necessary to routinely arm *all* police officers?'.

In the Netherlands, for example, every operational officer carries a gun. This is in a visible, easy-draw holster and the pistol is primed for immediate use. The great majority of Dutch officers, however, will never during their entire career draw their weapon out of its holster, and if they do, they will not fire it. In Amsterdam the chance that an officer will merely draw his or her gun operationally is estimated at once in 40 years, and the chance that they will ever come face-to-face with an angry man brandishing a weapon – on a 'wet night down a dark alley' as the saying goes – is miniscule. It could even be asked if they are technically competent to use a firearm in a conflict situation. They do train at a range four times a year but this is in contrast to a person joining a gun club in the Netherlands where she or he has to practise *16 times a year* otherwise the permit is rescinded. So to shoot at a target on a practice range as a civilian one has to exercise 16 times a year to prove proficiency, but to use a weapon on the streets as a police officer against a citizen one only has to practise four times a year. Indeed, one of the two main Dutch experts on police use of force and firearms admits that this level of firearms training is insufficient (interview, Timmer). And yet some 40,000 executive officers are carrying a deadly weapon on duty that most of them are not particularly adept at using.

But to withdraw firearms from routine policing would be simply unacceptable; the statistics on their use, or non-use, founder on the psychology that officers never know when they may face sudden danger. Consequently they feel more secure with a weapon on their belt despite the fact that they will almost certainly never use it; the 'almost' is, however, crucial. Indeed a central tenet of the police occupational culture everywhere rests on the perception that danger is an inherent part of the police officer's world; and that it is unpredictable where and when an officer may face violence – and from whom (Skolnick, 1966).

It may even be that the suddenness of a confrontation with danger means that the officer has no time to pull his or her weapon; in some circumstances being armed makes no difference to getting wounded or killed. There have been occasions where three or four armed officers have been killed by one or two armed men who took the initiative and surprised them; those who are willing and prepared to kill will always have an advantage over officers who at that moment are not geared to danger and not emotionally prepared for the likelihood of shooting.[2] Routine, the specific context, the local culture and complacency can kill – whether one carries a firearm or not.

Nevertheless, and quite understandably, the almost universal occupational culture and work-related psychology of officers remains fixated on the very rare moment when possessing a gun can or does make a difference; as when saving oneself, another officer or a citizen from death or serious injury. This can be during a violence-prone encounter with a criminal who is holding or even pointing a gun, or with a highly disturbed citizen, say wielding an axe over his terrified family, or when shooting a mad dog savagely mauling a young child.

—

In brief, arming the police is one matter, but disarming an already armed police would clearly be another matter altogether.[3] Of interest is that in the UK there has always been a clear majority of police officers *against* routinely arming the police (Nicholl, 1994; Travis, 1995; Waldren, 2007). This has been the response in a number of surveys at different times even in periods when some politicians and populist parts of the media were insistently arguing for a general arming of the police in the face of violent crime and/or terrorism. There are, moreover, some British officers who are vehemently opposed to arming the police, with a minority who say they would refuse to carry a firearm even if it meant leaving the police (Squires and Kennison, 2010).

A particularly tough conundrum arises from this. *First*, with an unarmed police there is likely to be less use of criminal violence, less armed violence against the police and obviously fewer police mistakes with weapons. This conclusion can be drawn from the data confirming this pattern with regard to the contrast between the largely unarmed Norwegian Police and the neighbouring but routinely armed Swedish Police (Squires and Kennison, 2010: 6–7). But the downside is that there will be occasions when police officers become victims of armed violence in situations when they are vulnerable to a ruthless or desperate criminal or a disturbed person who is not open to reason or negotiation. The prime example in the UK was when a hardened criminal, Harry Roberts, and an accomplice gunned down three unarmed officers in London in 1966.[4] It is always grim news to hear of an unarmed officer attending a routine call and being shot; and police and public consider it particularly poignant if it concerns a female officer. A West Yorkshire officer, Sharon Beshenivsky, was shot dead when she attended an alarm at a travel agency in Bradford in 2005. Three members of a criminal gang from London were attempting to rob the agency and they came out of the building shooting, fatally wounding Beshenivsky and injuring another female officer with her (Norfolk, 2007).[5] The two officers did not stand a chance against a vicious and unanticipated attack; but that would probably also have been the case even if they had been armed.

Second, routinely arming the police is likely to lead to fatal police accidents involving 'friendly-fire' from other officers and to fatal errors of judgement leading to the needless death and injury of suspects and citizens. In some circumstances the firearm is a crude and unforgiving instrument that is used to kill inappropriately. Also, police use of fatal force is always an emotive issue and especially if it is associated with race, discrimination, lack of due care, the failure to seek alternatives or seemingly excessive violence.

To express the two sides of the conundrum starkly; in the former the price paid for an unarmed police is that some officers will die who might have lived if they had been armed, and in the latter the price paid for an armed police is that some people will needlessly die because of accidents and 'mistakes'. The question is – which is the price society is prepared to pay and officers are ready to accept?

In pondering this balance, and the choice to be made at the system or state level, consideration and deliberation has to be given to the nature of the weapons available to the police and others. Policy and practice have to be geared to the sorts of guns and other weapons available and what they are capable of doing when fired defensively or offensively during activities that lead to police involvement. For instance, it may almost seem superfluous but it cannot be emphasised enough: firearms are predominantly *designed to kill*. Even weapons made ostensibly only for 'sport' or display can be used to kill.

This conveys that by definition firearms are inherently dangerous and *always potentially fatal* instruments, whoever uses them. Outside of the warfare for which most of them are developed and produced, they are dangerous and can cause death and injury in civil society when used by law-enforcement officials legally or illegally during the performance of their duty or when off-duty; and by criminals in the pursuit of crime and employing them against civilians, law-enforcement officials, private security personnel and against other criminals. Indeed, the media imagery tends to be dominated by the threat from, and fear of, criminals with firearms and of their violence when committing crimes. Yet a great deal of police activity in relation to firearms has little to do with ongoing, violent crime committed by criminals with illegal weapons.

Indeed, what tends to be neglected in the public perception and debate is the death and injury caused not by armed criminals but by the *legal owners* of weapons authorised by the police. In the UK, for instance, two appalling massacres were committed by citizens with no criminal records and with legally registered weapons. Both had a considerable impact on public opinion, in the media and on policy; but it is too early to discern what influence the recent shootings in Cumbria in June 2010 (discussed in Chapter Two), which now form the third massacre in Britain after Hungerford and Dunblane, will have on policy and perhaps legislation.

Legally held firearms and massacres: Dunblane and Hungerford

Every now and then, and out of the blue, police forces are confronted with mass shootings not by armed criminals, but by seemingly ordinary and law-abiding people and often with legally held weapons. Poignantly, several massacres have been at schools or colleges with many young victims. There have been examples in the US (University of Texas at Austin, Columbine High School, Concordia University and Georgia Tech), Germany and Finland. Generally it is easy to enter the building; the killers are students or others familiar with the layout; there are typically few or no armed guards; and there are defenceless students trapped in their classrooms. It is almost impossible for educational and police authorities in an open society to cater for and cope with such sudden, unanticipated violence. Above all the perpetrators typically have no criminal record, possess the weapons legally and any signals of violence they might have given are not picked up or are not taken seriously until it is too late. Public buildings and recreational facilities are also particularly vulnerable as they often have low security and a high concentration of people. Although the US tends to attract the most attention for shooting sprees, with 32 victims killed at Georgia Tech, the worst massacre was in Australia when Martin Bryant shot and killed 35 people at the Port Arthur heritage site in Tasmania in 1999 (North, 2000: 153).

In Great Britain there have been two particular massacres, one at Hungerford and one at a school in Dunblane, which not only posed severe problems for policing in terms of an adequate response, but also acutely raised the issue of the authorisation and licensing of firearms by the police. Both Hungerford (Millward, 1994) and Dunblane (North, 2000) also had a major impact on public opinion, policy and legislation.

The massacre at Dunblane in Scotland in March 1996 was particularly heart-rending because most of the victims were very young children (Cullen Report, 1998). Thomas Hamilton walked unimpeded into a primary school and started to fire at buildings, at children and staff at a distance and then entered the gym where a first-year class of five- and six-year-olds were starting the day with PE. He started shooting at random at the group; then he left and re-entered the gym, reloading his guns, deliberately shooting some of the wounded so that most victims had multiple, horrendous wounds. One young girl, lying wounded, could distinctly recall the logo on his boot as he walked up to her and shot her again in the back; she survived. Hamilton then shot himself. He had killed 16 young children and one teacher; another staff member and 12 children were wounded. The scene in the gym confronting other teachers, police and emergency workers was simply indescribable.

Hamilton was a notorious complainer who easily carried grudges. One of these was apparently focused on slights done to him by people associated with Dunblane. There was also a long history of complaints against him related to the diverse youth camps he ran; and some people, including several police officers and members of the shooting clubs he joined, were perturbed by his obsession with guns and his unorthodox way of handling them. These red warning flags, so glaring when revealed in the public inquiry after the tragedy, never prevented the police from automatically endorsing his firearms licence and never prompted any shooting club to bar him from membership. One police officer had written to his superiors:

> I am firmly of the opinion that Hamilton is an unsavoury character and unstable personality ... I respectfully request that serious consideration is given to withdrawing this man's firearms certificate as a precautionary measure, as it is my opinion that he is a scheming, devious and

deceitful individual who is not to be trusted. (North, 2000: 51)

Yet no action was taken; this warning and request was also not even filed in Hamilton's dossier. On the grounds that none of this had ever led to criminal charges, the renewal of his certificate was rubber-stamped.

This enabled him to purchase a small arsenal of guns and a wealth of ammunition in pursuit of his 'sport'. When he entered the school he was carrying four handguns, two 9 mm Browning pistols and two .357 Smith and Wesson revolvers, and he was in possession of over 700 rounds of ammunition. He fired well over 100 rounds hitting his 17 fatal victims 58 times; Mick North's five-year-old daughter, Sophie, was hit five times (North, 2000: 51). Starting in 1977 Hamilton had begun to purchase, on one occasion by mail order, a number of weapons starting with a .22 target pistol and moving on to revolvers, semi-automatic pistols and rifles; and they were of increasingly larger calibre. Early on he had purchased in a two-year period 13,300 rounds of ammunition and later in 1992 he was authorised to keep up to 7,500 rounds of ammunition at home, some of which comprised so-called 'soft-headed' bullets that can cause massive injury if used against a human being. Why does someone need, it was later asked, a high-powered, heavy calibre weapon for target practice, and so much ammunition, some of which is inappropriate for use in a shooting club? All of this potentially devastating weaponry was ostensibly for 'sport' at Home Office-registered clubs (Sampson and Crow, 1997).

Similar questions on licensing had already been raised at the time of Hungerford, which had left 17 people dead and 15 wounded (see Chapter Two for more detail). The man responsible, Ryan, was a 'loner' like Hamilton, but unlike Hamilton he was known only to the police as 'well-dressed, of good behaviour, courteous and quiet'. He legally possessed a number of guns, which he kept at his home. He owned two shotguns, two semi-automatic 9 mm pistols and two high-velocity rifles, a Chinese clone of the renowned Kalashnikov AK47 and a special version of the M1 Carbine (North, 2000: 16, 144). Ryan had no criminal record and no history of mental illness; this meant that the police had no reason not to grant him a licence.

—

Both cases raised the issue of the regulation of firearm possession and what weapons are acceptable for a citizen to possess in his or her home. Furthermore, the police response to such unanticipated attacks on vulnerable targets will always be reactive and inadequate, irrespective of whether the police are armed or not. After Hungerford, for example, the British Police Service widely implemented the deployment of ARVs (see also Chapter Two). But a report into the Hungerford massacre maintains that if an ARV had been sent to Hungerford, it would probably only have added to the casualties; the crew would have been 'outgunned' by Ryan firing aggressively with multiple rounds from high-powered weapons (Waddington, 1991: 116). Indeed, this knowledge later played a role in another shooting incident, which, like Hungerford, occurred in the Thames Valley Police (TVP) area. The loss of an officer at Hungerford was in the institutional memory when TVP responded to the incident which arose at Highmoor Cross in 2004 (interview, Gilmour; and see later in the 'Scenarios for armed policing' section).

Police use of firearms and weaponry

The history of firearms shows that in the last two centuries, but particularly in recent decades, such weapons have increased in sophistication, firepower, accuracy, reliability, range, ease of use and, above all, ability to cause death and injury. In general, police forces that arm their officers will have adopted revolvers, pistols, carbines, rifles and machine guns, which are also used or have been used by the military (see the Appendix for the diverse types of weapons). This was doubtless the case in the 19th century, when most police forces were first developed as paramilitary formations carrying arms; and then after the two World Wars when a large surplus of military firearms became available. Almost certainly little thought was given to providing a weapon and ammunition specifically geared to the needs of civilian policing. Indeed, in Britain after WWII (1939–45) those police forces possessing an arsenal usually had a motley collection of old military guns, mostly revolvers (Squires and Kennison, 2010).

In recent decades, however, police forces in many countries have become equipped with a variety of modern weapons including specialised rifles (for example, for sniping), assault rifles, shotguns, semi-automatic or automatic handguns, carbines, sub-machine guns and machine guns. The firepower of 'light' arms for the military has increased tremendously and the continually improving technology of the industry has led to hand-held guns that can fire a large number of bullets rapidly. Some modern versions of these weapons can fire at the rate of 1,000 rounds per minute or more. Many of these weapons designed primarily for military use have become potentially available for law-enforcement purposes, for legal purchase to civilians for 'sport' or 'self-protection' and for those with evil intent.

In short, the firearms industry has become capable of producing a vast array of different weaponry and a bewildering range of ammunition for all sorts of specialised purposes (as a visit to their glossy and upbeat websites and to weapons fairs demonstrates). Both police and criminals make use of a selection of this arsenal, which brings considerable destructiveness on to the streets. The so-called 'street-sweeper', a short-barrelled shotgun with a 20-round drum is a formidable firearm at close range. The Ingram Mac10 .45 machine-pistol is an especially ferocious weapon that can fire 1,200 rounds per minute; it is a devastating device to have to face in law enforcement. There is also a combined double-barrelled shotgun with a rifle used in game hunting; an officer might be lulled into thinking both shotgun barrels have been fired only to discover there is still a loaded rifle to contend with in an encounter.

What sort of weaponry is available legally or illegally will vary across societies. In certain post-conflict situations as in South Africa and the Balkans there is a high volume of illegal weapons in circulation because these were obtained during or after the conflict (Ellis, 1998; Glenny, 2009). The IRA insurgents in Northern Ireland, for instance, were soon able to purchase or obtain modern weapons from a variety of sources, with the Armalite rifle as the weapon of choice for sniping at police and British soldiers (English, 2004).[6] There are also societies, such as Switzerland and Israel, with 'citizen-armies', where a high proportion of the male population routinely keep a military firearm at home for many years because of the annual training stints they are required to take. Interestingly, the wide availability of guns at home as in Switzerland does not necessarily translate into a pattern of violence with firearms (Clinard, 1978).

Turning to British forces, since the early 1990s these have replaced the traditional police revolver with 'self-loading' weapons. Revolvers are reliable but require pulling the trigger for each shot, have a limited number of rounds (typically six but can be up to 10) and usually require time-consuming reloading. They also tend to be heavy and bulky and not easy to conceal so that they are not appropriate for some forms of police work. The self-loading pistol is flatter, usually lighter and easier to conceal, and an officer with, say, an 18-round magazine can change a magazine and have 36 rounds available compared to the six of a revolver with its longer reloading time. In Europe and the US many forces have adopted 9mm Glock pistols and Heckler and Koch MP5 carbines or similar modern and reliable weapons.

Weapons and violence: The US

It is difficult to generalise about policy and practice on police use of force in the US because there is no national police 'system'. There is a myriad of law-enforcement agencies and generally policy is set locally.[7] The federal government can promulgate guidelines and stimulate best practice through funding, but it has little to say on policy in the 50 states and the many local communities with regard to weapons, training and instructions on shootings. What can be said is that the US is frequently viewed as the extreme among Western societies because the American police have to respond to the widespread possession of firearms in a society with a strong gun culture and high levels of violence (Crank, 1998).[8] The stereotypical imagery of the officers' response to this was conveyed in the 1970s by the long barrel of the 'Magnum' revolver in the poster for the 'Dirty Harry' films with Clint Eastwood.[9] His portrayal of Detective Callahan fitted into the popular American genre of the 'righteous cop' who feels justified in using illicit means and gross violence against the 'bad guys' in the face of a deficient justice system, pusillanimous senior officers and devious, vacillating, media-obsessed politicians.

—

Something like 50% of American households have one or more weapons. The number of weapons in the hands of citizens is astronomical, making the US the world leader with an estimate of around *220 million* guns in private hands, and the majority of murders are committed by a firearm, which in 1999 meant 13,552 criminal fatalities by guns (Karmen, 2000: 64–5; North, 2000: 286; Timmer, 2005: 55). Indeed, in the 1990s, of the 644 officers killed during duty the majority were killed with a firearm and mostly with a handgun (Klinger, 2004: 11). Furthermore, it is well known that in the US a vast range of weaponry can be purchased legally over the counter or by mail order with minimal controls, depending on the state, and that the percentage of the population owning a firearm for diverse purposes is high compared to other societies where the sale of weapons is severely restricted.[10] This means that criminals can easily obtain weapons by purchase or by theft, while ordinary citizens may have relatively high-powered weapons in their possession that might be used against intruders or against others including the police in a conflict situation. It also implies that weapons can readily be purchased on illegal markets, say from gangs that have stolen weapons from shops or have received illicit consignments from dodgy suppliers within the industry. Merchants also sometimes sell guns illegally at weapons fairs.

Although America may be the extreme in terms of citizen-held weapons, in most Western societies it is the case that serious criminals can usually acquire an arsenal of modern and highly lethal weapons, judging by the range of guns used during criminal activities and by the weapons seized in police raids. Regarding Britain, McLagan (2005) speaks of gang members buying guns with all the ease of purchasing a toothbrush.

However, the gun has indisputably played a significant role in urban crime in the US. Speaking of Baltimore in the late 1980s, for instance, Simon (2009: 537) reflects that even then teenagers were sporting 'automatics tucked into their sweatpants. Smith and Wesson, Glock, Baretta, Sig Sauer …'; and one cop lamented, 'Even the dickheads of the world are carrying quality weapons'. Furthermore, in the drug wars during the crack-cocaine epidemic of the 1980s in New York, the players 'tooled up' with 'fully automatic pistols, machine guns, military assault weapons, silencers and body armor' (Karmen, 2000: 173).[11] And there is no doubt that some American cities have experienced high levels of violence. Baltimore has had at times almost one murder a day (Simon, 2009). Chicago has been the 'murder capital' of America on a number of occasions: in the early 1990s it was averaging around 900 murders a year or roughly two and a half a day in a population of three million. New York for about 20 years was experiencing some 1,600 murders a year, with the peak in 1990 at a staggering 2,245 violent deaths, in a population close to eight million. Karmen (2000), for instance, dedicates his book on murders in the 'Big Apple' to the *32,600* New Yorkers killed in the period 1978–98. Even then New York was not the country's leader in 1990, but merely the tenth in line in relation to murders per population with Detroit, New Orleans and Washington DC as the front-runners.

The imagery of how American officers respond to this environment of guns and violence was provided by the two leading scholars of policing in the US, Skolnick and Bayley. They describe officers getting ready for duty in Denver (1988: 141–2):

> Three times a day in countless locker rooms across the land, large men and a growing number of women carefully arm and armor themselves for the day's events. They begin by strapping on flak-jackets, designed to stop most bullets, under their regulation blue, white, or brown shirts. Then they pick up a wide, heavy, black leather belt and hang around it the tools of their trade: gun, mace, handcuffs, bullets. When it is fully loaded, they swing the belt around their hips with the same practiced motion of the gunfighter in Western movies, snugging it down and buckling it in front. They fasten it to their trousers with leather loops....
>
> In every sense of the word, going on duty as a police officer day after day is 'heavy'. Heavy physically, heavy in anticipation, heavy in meaning. What is striking and more than a little frightening is that the people going to this peculiar kind of war are very often hardly more than kids.

And they further comment, 'Policing in the United States is very much *like going to war*' (emphasis added). Given the huge variety of policing environments in the US, with many being rural and peaceful, this picture is unlikely to be universal and is doubtless more applicable to some parts of certain large cities. Boulder is in the same state as Denver (Colorado) but has perhaps just one murder a year. Also, Geller and Scott (1992: 449) estimated that for Jacksonville (Florida), which was a busy town with a fairly high crime-rate, an officer would have to work 139 years before being involved in a fatal shooting, 42 years for a non-fatal shooting and 10 years for discharging his or her weapon in some other circumstances. In New York, police were held to have used their guns in some way five times per 1,762 encounters (Crank, 1998: 92).[12]

In Denver, Skolnick and Bayley (1988) further noted that in addition to the standard equipment, the officer might also take small-calibre gun as a back-up in case of losing the regulation weapon in a conflict situation. In some forces this is standard and formally allowed. Furthermore, some officers have been known to take a so-called 'gypsy gun' with them; this is a non-traceable weapon to be planted on an unarmed suspect who has been shot by the police so that the shooting can be justified as 'self-defence'. Writing of Philadelphia in the early 1970s, Rubinstein (1973: 287–9) noted that officers were known to have loaded their weapons with self-made, illegal ammunition.[13] Even an academic researcher, John Van Maanen (1988: 88–9), took a number of illicit weapons with him while on patrol during his fieldwork. These included a 'two-incher' second gun in case he became disarmed and a .357 'Magnum' revolver, neither of which conformed to departmental regulations. The illicit revolver was presented to him on graduating from the Police Academy in full view of the police hierarchy, cadets' families and local television cameras. Presumably the Research Ethics Committee were not watching the broadcast!

The revolver remained the primary personnel side arm in American policing up to the 1970s and they are still in use in some forces and very often in private security. Typically police forces are now equipped with a variety of weapons depending on the local preference for certain types of rifles, semi-automatic or automatic handguns and shotguns.[14] This adoption of a rich arsenal of weapons in US policing is often openly visible in a rack behind the front seats in the patrol cars. The standard training adopted in much of the US – but again the length of training will vary widely from minimal to extensive – is based on 'double-tap' and 'point shooting'. The former means two rounds at a time aimed in the direction of the chest; the latter means that rather than taking careful aim, the weapon is simply pointed in the middle of the body mass. Earlier it was noted that Klinger (2004) stated that recruits were trained not to 'shoot to kill'; this might be driven more by considerations of legality and liability than by humanity. Other sources, in contrast, convey that when an officer shoots the intention is to kill (Rubinstein, 1973; Crank, 1998). FBI training, for instance, speaks of 'threat elimination' by continual firing, which with a change of magazines could mean an officer firing 36 bullets (Waddington, 1991: 95). This is clearly geared to high-threat situations where the conventional wisdom is to take cover and then 'spray and pray'. This policy recommendation arose from a prolonged shoot-out at Sunniland in Miami in 1986, when two suspected bank robbers opened fire killing two FBI agents. But the suspects continued to shoot even when severely injured; one should have been to all intents and purposes 'dead', having taken a lethal shot to his heart early in the confrontation, yet remained active for some 15 minutes still returning fire before collapsing (Simons, 2009: 408). Given this style of shooting it is surprising that some two thirds of those shot by the police in the US still survive their injuries (Timmer, 2005).

However, it is also the case that some forces have invested substantially in firearms training in an effort to reduce unnecessary deaths. The NYPD, for instance, has engaged in a thorough review of firearms training and use, with the help of the Rand Corporation (Rostker et al, 2008). One finding was that it was possible from records to locate officers who appear to have problems with the use of force; indeed, the extent of computerised data on officer performance can also be used to construct 'early warning' systems to identify such officers and offer them remedial training or bring disciplinary or criminal charges, whichever is appropriate (Walker, 2005).

The American police have at times, but particularly in the 1960s, faced intense urban unrest with extensive rioting and looting in a number of major cities. This often stretched the capacity of the police to respond, leading to asking the State Governor to call in the National Guard to restore order. One response to such incidents during which the police came under fire from snipers and faced massive looting and pillage was to create specially trained and equipped squads. These could also be used in siege situations and for forced entry. This style of specialised policing has become associated with a growing tendency towards the *militarisation* of policing in the US (Kraska and Kappeler, 1997).

Militarisation

Kraska (1999, 2001) in particular has traced this militarisation trend, noting an increase in recent decades in specially trained and heavily equipped paramilitary units. The first such squad was formed in Los Angeles in 1967. These units had various names – in Baltimore there was the 'Quick Response Team' (Simon, 2009) – but increasingly they were referred to as 'SWAT' squads, for 'Special Weapons and Tactics'. More often these days they are called 'Public Order Units' (POUs) to convey their role at large-scale events and demonstrations. In smaller departments they tend to be called 'PPUs' for 'Police Paramilitary Units' (Kraska and Cubellis, 1997) and on grounds of cost these are increasingly shared by several departments (interview, Klinger). The military is often keen to dispense of surplus weapons and police forces are eager purchasers at bargain prices or even receive weaponry for free. Indeed, after the North Hollywood shoot-out (see later in the 'Scenarios for armed policing' section) the LAPD was given 600 army surplus M16 automatic rifles by the federal government. The members of such special units tend to dress in combat gear, carry powerful weapons and train for critical incidents. However, as Kraska (2001) argues, they are an expensive resource that needs to be employed so they are frequently also used for routine police operations (drug raids, searches, public order). Especially since the terrorist attacks of '9/11' in the US there has been an emphasis on 'heavy' security measures and on federal funding for powerful equipment, including armoured cars, assault rifles and grenade launchers.

In recent years, moreover, in violent confrontations with demonstrators at international gatherings in a number of countries – as in Seattle, Genoa and Gothenburg – the media conveyed images of paramilitary-style police in full riot gear using tear gas, batons and brandishing weapons in the face of demonstrators. Even in the generally peaceful Netherlands, people were shocked in 2001 to see on television images of heavily armoured, paramilitary units with their faces concealed by masks. In armoured cars and with machine guns and sniper rifles they had taken control of strategic locations, following a warning of terrorist activity, and were assertively stopping dismayed motorists at the point of a gun. Such units had never before been visible to the public in this manner.

The weapons in such special units – and in SWAT squads in the USA – are typically modern, high-velocity (HV) guns, including sub-machine guns designed for the battlefield. A major reason why US police forces adopted this capacity was not just in response to major incidents like the urban riots of the 1960s, but also because the Constitution forbids the use of the military in conventional law enforcement; to do so without federal authorisation, as was granted during the urban riots of the 1960s, would be to commit a felony (interview, Klinger). This was an important external factor pushing the police towards developing their own heavily armed, paramilitary units.

Firearms: Injury and death

Almost any instrument used by the police can cause serious injury or death. For the police this can be a regulation truncheon, baton-round ('rubber-bullet'), taser ('stun-gun'), mace/CS gas/tear gas or any instrument, legal or otherwise, used offensively – such as a hand-held radio, knuckleduster, torch, a hard projectile replacing the baton-round, a non-regulation truncheon and so on.[15] There has been a move away from firearms use in some situations and towards alternative so-called 'non-fatal' weapons such as beanbags, plugs from shotguns, and tasers. In practice, though, there are no 'non-fatal weapons' and any instrument can kill in certain circumstances and by use on certain people. This was graphically illustrated when Royal Canadian Mounted Police (RCMP) officers used a taser five times on a disturbed man at Vancouver Airport leading to his death. His dying paroxysms, which had been caught on a mobile-phone camera by a bystander, have been widely communicated through *You Tube* (Goldsmith, 2009; *Ottawa Citizen*, 2010). However, the risk of injury and death is clearly enhanced by firearms or anything firing a projectile.

The wounding and killing power of firearms depends on a number of factors such as muzzle velocity, shape and weight of the bullet, the movement of the bullet in the air, the entry wound and what the bullet does within the body. A full-jacketed round is capable of going right through someone, causing a relatively clean entry and exit wound and, providing it does not hit a vital organ, that person will probably survive. Some people have even survived several, severe wounds including shots to the head (Waddington, 1991; Klinger, 2004).[16] It all depends on the shock of the impact, loss of blood and which organs or which part of the brain are hit. It can also depend on the speed of getting medical attention and the quality of medical provision; providing modern, well-equipped shock-trauma emergency facilities has saved lives – and reduced murder rates (Karmen, 2000).

A bullet will incapacitate someone for two main reasons: either it hits the 'brain, brainstem or spinal cord, causing immediate damage to the central nervous system'; or else it damages 'enough of the cardiovascular system to cause massive blood loss to the brain and eventual collapse' (Simon, 2009: 408). A bullet that has 'yawed' in flight will cause a larger entry wound than one with a smoother flight. After entry the bullet can be deflected within the body, hitting bone and organs; some bullets fragment and leave a number of twisted bits of lead and copper casing inside the body. The reason so-called 'dum-dum' bullets were banned by the Hague Convention (1899) is that they were deformed beforehand and/or expanded in flight causing gaping and jagged entry wounds. Formally the Convention applies only to the armies of the signatory countries during officially proclaimed warfare. That ban at the end of the 19th century has been reiterated by later non-binding directives from a range of institutions,[17] but the developments in weaponry and in the huge variety of bullets available means that many modern guns can do considerable damage anyway. The American M16 and similar high-velocity weapons, for example, are capable of creating large surface wounds and causing considerable if not fatal shock on impact without using special ammunition. Its predecessor the AR15 had the tendency for its bullets to topple in flight so that they 'scythed through people causing devastating wounds' (interview, Waddington). Importantly the Hague Convention of 1899 does not apply to law enforcement, although it is often taken as the standard on the acceptability of certain ammunition including 'hollow-point' bullets. Such hollow-point bullets were employed in the Stockwell shooting (see Chapter Five).

Death and injury depends greatly on the sort of wound caused by differential velocity, type of bullet, calibre of weapon, number of hits and distance from the weapon. Some people take multiple hits and survive whereas others are killed by a single round, but even low-calibre weapons, air-guns and 'BB-guns' can cause serious injury or even prove lethal. A .22 firearm, a calibre associated with target shooting as in Olympic competition, proved sufficient in the assassinations of Robert Kennedy and Yitzhak Rabin (North, 2000: 179). As Simon (2009: 209) wryly comments:

> Out on the street [in Baltimore in the late 1980s], the big guns – the .38s, .44s and .45s – still get the greatest respect, but the lowly .22 pistol has acquired a reputation all its own. Any West Baltimore homeboy can tell you that when a .22 round-nose gets under a man's skin, it bounces around like a pin-ball. And every pathologist seems to have a story about a .22 slug that entered the lower left back, clipped both lungs, the aorta and the liver, then cracked a rib or two before finding its way out the upper right shoulder. It's true that a man who gets hit with a .45 bullet has to worry about a larger piece of lead cleaving through him, but with a good .22 round, he has to worry that the little bugger is in there for the grand tour.

A female officer miraculously survived a serious shooting after a bullet went though her 'front rib cage; fragmented and nicked the stomach, liver and intestines; cut some veins and arteries; shattered the spleen; and hit the diaphragm, while the main part of it passed through the base of my heart and cracked a rib as it went out my back' (Klinger, 2004: 119).

In short, all weapons used by the police and others are dangerous and potentially lethal. Firearms are always potentially lethal and some of the modern police weapons are able to fire a variety of ammunition at high velocity with a high rate of fire, which can easily cause severe injury or death. Clearly this also holds true for criminals and at times they can obtain high-powered and heavy calibre weaponry that 'outguns' standard police weapons. This makes it difficult to know what an appropriate standard firearm is in forces where officers are routinely armed, as that weapon is primarily for immediate self-defence. There are times in the US when officers demand larger and more powerful weapons to match those of the armed 'villains' they encounter on the streets. Some police departments possess assault rifles as well as military-style armoured personnel carriers and grenade launchers, while one Texas department sought federal funding to buy a drone aircraft! In 2009 police in Boston planned to buy 200 M16 semi-automatic assault rifles with 'lite-brite penetrating ammunition' for specialist units in case of terrorist attacks as in Mumbai; but the Mayor turned this down (*Boston Globe*, 2009). This can lead to a form of 'arms race' where serious criminals are nearly always in the advantage because they are not confined by rules and regulations or budget restrictions, whereas the police are confined on weapons and ammunition and are inevitably cast in catch-up mode.

With the police much will depend on the nature of the encounter, the risk assessment and the appropriate weapons and special unit, if any, involved. Some useful examples with insights into the demands placed on the police can be gleaned from the accounts of officers who have served in firearms units (Collins, 1998; Gray, 2000; Klinger, 2004; Hailwood, 2005). At times police are faced with highly dangerous and challenging situations requiring intense physical exertion, rapid tactical thinking, continual reassessment of risk, and clear communications, leadership and decisiveness. The experts say there is no typical firearms incident and they display great diversity.

I shall touch on a number of scenarios that can be expected and that will require a firearms presence and possible active response.

Scenarios for armed policing

One can think, for instance, of police involvement in the following categories or scenarios that police officers may have to face, or at least have to contemplate, in their risk assessments:

- **'Mega'-incident.** These are by definition likely to be infrequent and the chance of encountering such an incident will depend on the size and nature of the force and the likelihood of threats. They can be in relation to attacks on high-profile government buildings, embassies, airfields, ports, tunnels, bridges, transport systems, industrial and off-shore installations, politicians and dignitaries and so on. Many forces will never have to deal with a mega-incident, but a few forces are far more likely to face one or several. They could be in the form of an attack on an embassy (as in the Iranian Embassy siege in London in 1980), a plane hijack (there have been three at London Stansted Airport, for example) or a terrorist unit active in the UK (as with the Balcombe Street siege in 1975).[18] The recent insurgent attack in Mumbai where a determined, well-armed group entered the city centre and stormed several buildings including hotels, opening fire and causing explosions, presented the authorities with an instantaneous mega-incident of near-nightmare proportions. The planning, resourcefulness, tactics, firepower and ferocity of the Mumbai group suggests prolonged training to near Special Forces level, according to the Mumbai police chief (in a conversation with Waddington). One can only speculate what that would mean in an assault on a major Western city. Much will depend on the police and emergency services pre-planning for such events and the capability of responding rapidly by opening the major incident control centre, mobilising armed units and calling up the other emergency services. These can be highly complex affairs requiring discussions at government and intergovernmental level, police negotiators, specialist firearms units

---

(snipers and a unit trained for forced entry) and many officers for other duties.

- **Major sieges and the military.** Major incidents can turn into siege situations. This is one of the most taxing scenarios. A lot will depend on the nature of the siege, on the presence of hostages and the weaponry involved. In the Balcombe Street siege in London, three armed IRA members ran into a flat more or less at random while trying to evade the police; the police played a waiting game and successfully negotiated their surrender. The Met did not require the assistance of the military although the SAS may have been in reserve. In the Iranian Embassy siege, on the other hand, where the hostage-takers had killed a hostage and were threatening to kill again, there was almost no other option than armed intervention requiring a forced entry leading to a close-combat situation while also taking the hostages into consideration.[19] On such severe occasions, then, there may be the need to ask for the cooperation of the military with political agreement on this at a high level (see Chapter Five).

- **Other sorts of sieges.** Police can be confronted with sieges during a robbery or in a household where someone has taken hostages and is threatening their lives. These may be successfully dealt with through negotiation, or can become complicated and taxing, as in one case where a man barricaded the entry of his house, possessed a gun, had his children with him and also set the house on fire (Gray, 2000: 94–104).

- **Suicide bombers.** As we shall see in Chapter Five, this new threat changed the landscape of firearms policy and practice in the UK (Kennedy, 2006). Certain police forces are far more likely to have to face this extreme challenge than others.

- **Shoot-outs: large-scale encounters between police and criminals or other groups.** There are occasions when police and criminals, or some other group, end up in an extensive fire-fight. An extreme example of this was the North Hollywood shoot-out in 1997 when two armed robbers with masks and guns were seen entering a bank by police officers in a patrol car. The criminals were heavily armed with 3,000 rounds of ammunition and five modified high-performance assault rifles – three were

Romanian clones of the formidable AK47 Kalishnikov assault rifle fitted with 100-round drum magazines – as well as two automatic Beretta pistols; the men also wore heavy body armour. They seem to have been prepared to take on the police as they had walked openly from their car with weapons drawn. Having intimidated all those in the bank by firing multiple shots into the walls and ceilings they left the bank with their takings. On leaving the bank the robbers were confronted with a cordon of police vehicles that had responded to the first car's emergency call and they immediately opened fire on the police. It would have been a far more difficult incident to resolve if they had returned to the bank where they would have had cover as well as a group of hostages, but the criminals stood their ground and started firing aggressively at anything that moved including civilians and even the TV news helicopters hovering above and transmitting the events direct to the viewing public. The two men fired over 1,200 rounds and used armour-piercing bullets that went though protective vests, wooden buildings, brick walls and patrol cars used as shields. Eventually the police response reached some 300 officers including a SWAT squad, and the police fired about 650 rounds, although only 1% of the latter came anywhere close to hitting the intended targets. In the fire-fight 10 officers and seven bystanders were wounded and it is surprising that there were no fatalities except for the assailants. Both robbers continued to return fire despite being wounded several times. Indeed, in a number of shoot-outs, seriously injured criminals have managed to carry on firing for some time (Klinger, 2004; Collins, 2008). Eventually one of them seems to have committed suicide; the other robber tried to escape in a car but was hit and apprehended.[20]

- **Large-scale, set-piece operations.** This could be a major event involving the Royal Family, the visit of a foreign head of state (say the President of the US), a high-level intergovernmental global G20 or EU conference or a major international sporting event (such as the Olympic Games). There will be a risk analysis made of the places to be visited and diverse sorts of firearms officers will be on duty (snipers, others for close protection and so on).[21]

- **Diplomatic and personal protection.** Armed officers are deployed to protect certain buildings and to provide close personal protection for significant officials and dignitaries. Some of the first routine arming of officers in Britain was for diplomatic protection in London in the 1950s.
- **Major set-piece, pre-planned operations in relation to robberies/raids.** Such operations will be based on prior information about a forthcoming armed robbery or other form of raid. The consideration is whether or not to arrest the criminal gang en route – and charge its members with conspiracy and other charges – or to allow it to attempt the raid. There are considerations about starting a shoot-out with possible innocent casualties (private security personnel, bank employees or members of the public) and also about the eventuality of a siege situation developing. This makes these high-risk incidents for the police as they may be accused of negligence if someone besides the offenders and officers gets hurt or of being 'trigger-happy' if they shoot several of the robbers. Whether or not to be 'proactive' was raised by the police response to an armed raid on a security van at an abattoir in Plumstead in 1987. Acting on information, a Met firearms squad was in place when the raid took place. The robbers refused to surrender; one pointed his weapon at the van driver, and the other two aimed their guns at the police but did not open fire. Two of them were shot dead and one was wounded. To the police present the shooting was legitimate and necessary, but critical questions were raised in the media about this 'ambush' with the point that it would have been possible to arrest the gang before the raid took place (Waddington, 1991: 24; Squires and Kennison, 2010: 80).
- **Spontaneous reaction to an 'across the pavement' robbery in progress.** This carries some of the risks of the previous category, but without the prior knowledge, as it is a reaction to a crime in progress. There may be protocols that the first officers on the scene form a cordon at a distance and await reinforcements, perhaps from a special unit in the hope that the robbers will leave the premises and this will avoid a siege situation.

- **Raid on a house to arrest one or more armed suspects.** This is also a high-risk type of operation that depends on good intelligence, sound information about the premises, an experienced and well-equipped team and the element of surprise to avoid armed resistance. As already described in Chapter One (see 'The Sussex shooting of James Ashley' section), such a raid went badly wrong in Sussex in 1998 with fatal consequences. In a raid in Birmingham in 1985 a five-year-old boy was shot and killed by mistake.
- **Domestic disputes and disturbed people.** These can be very awkward situations for the police. They are not dealing with criminals, but with ordinary citizens who are emotionally wrought or psychologically disturbed. Disputes within families can lead to dangerous situations where various instruments may be used as weapons and where the aggression can turn on the police. Officers in the US are generally wary of 'domestic disputes' as they are seen as inherently volatile given the high possession of gun ownership and the number of casualties suffered by police officers in these incidents. Equally taxing are situations involving vulnerable people who are under the influence of alcohol or drugs and/or are experiencing a psychotic episode. They may be threatening others with some sort of instrument used as a weapon and be impervious to instructions and negotiation. Another scenario is where a psychotic person creates a siege situation with his family or others whom he is threatening. Such a person is sick and requiring treatment and yet he or she may be shot because the police feel there is no alternative to save lives and prevent injury; but others may later demand why alternative, non-fatal methods were not employed. Fatalities with the non-criminal and the vulnerable raise particularly sharp criticism (see the later section on 'mistakes' and their significance).
- **Suicide by cop.** A subcategory of the previous scenario involves those who refuse to desist and virtually goad the police to shoot; this is colloquially referred to as 'suicide by cop'. The first report specifying this phenomenon emerged from New York in 1981 and the term was used for the first time in the UK in 1992.

- **Routine arrests and escorts.** A fair amount of armed police work concerns largely unproblematic and basically routine arrests, where the firearms are a precautionary measure, or when escorting certain categories of high-risk suspects or prisoners.
- **Miscellaneous ('believed armed') and animals.** Many, if not most, 'bread-and-butter' calls for an armed response in daily policing outside of high-crime areas with a prominent gun culture arise from reports of 'shots heard' or of a person 'believed armed' from members of the public who have allegedly seen someone with a weapon. Frequently these turn out to be unfounded, but they can have tragic consequences (as in the Stanley case in London; see the later section on '"Mistakes" and their significance'). People can pass on a suspicion in good faith or maliciously that can end with a fatality. Also falling under the 'miscellaneous' category is the shooting of dangerous animals that have attacked other animals or humans or are out of control. This category could also perhaps include the American officer who faced a stolen army tank! The tank drove down a city street crushing cars, knocking over telegraph poles and hitting hydrants and streetlights; the officer climbed on to it, opened the hatch and shot the driver, who would not respond to his warnings, in the shoulder (Klinger, 2004: 105–10).
- **Disturbed, dangerous and 'mega': Northumberland (2010).** Firearms officers frequently state that there are no standard scenarios or neat categories while there are often surprising and unanticipated elements in many incidents. This was true of an extreme example of the 'disturbed and dangerous' category in Northumberland in July 2010 which became effectively a 'mega-incident' for this largely rural, county force. A man, Raoul Moat, was released from prison and a warning was sent by the prison service to the local constabulary that he had threatened his former partner. However, the police did not take preventive measures, and Moat shot and wounded his former partner and shot dead her new partner; subsequently he seriously wounded a police officer. He then took off across the countryside and hid out for a week, evading capture despite a massive man-hunt, which included RAF helicopters. At one stage he took several

—

people hostage, and apparently he was also helped by a number of people. Eventually he was spotted on a river bank near the town of Rothbury. Moat was surrounded by armed officers and in a six-hour stand-off negotiators tried to persuade him to surrender, and also not to commit suicide, as he was threatening to do. At a certain point two officers fired tasers at him, apparently in an effort to prevent his suicide but he shot himself. This case has several features and a number of ramifications which have yet to be resolved. (At the time of writing the case is under investigation by the IPCC). Moat had a history of mental health problems and of aggressive behaviour and had requested help, which raises the issue as to why he had not earlier received adequate treatment. For some reason the prison warning about his threatened violence did not lead to police protection and did not prevent a death and two serious injuries (the police officer was shot in the face and blinded). Moat managed to evade capture for a week yet during that time he communicated with the media by phone-calls and correspondence. Moat made it clear that he had a grudge against police, had declared war on them and would shoot at them but not at civilians. When he was confronted there was a sustained effort to persuade him to put down the weapon and surrender before the operational decision was taken to employ tasers. It is not known if this happened almost simultaneously with Moat shooting himself, in a police attempt to prevent that happening. But friends and family have asserted that this assault by 'stun-gun' caused him to fire spontaneously in a reactive spasm as the shock of the two tasers hit him. Their criticism and that of others was to question why the negotiations did not continue, as it was claimed he was near to surrendering. Rather like the Stanley shooting in London (see below), this case elicited a great deal of sympathy for Moat as a victim of a police shooting. Controversy also arose because the YREP Tasers used were a model not yet approved by the Home Office and were being tried on an experimental basis by the Northumbria Police. This model is a cartridge which can be fired from a shotgun and does not have the wires attached to the prod as in conventional tasers; it delivers 1,220 volts for 20 seconds. But the Home Office announced that each police force had the discretion to choose any weapon within guidelines and providing that the use of force – here through 'tasers' – is 'legal, reasonable and proportionate' (BBC, 2010a, 2010b). In a way this was a case of someone who was clearly in need of psychiatric help and whose domestic problems suddenly escalated into serious and lethal violence. But it also raised questions about the choice and employment of police weapons and about tactics when confronted with a disturbed and armed person. Rather like the massacre in Cumbria the previous month, this extensive man-hunt turned into a mega-incident for a small, rural county force almost overwhelmed by a severe operational challenge combined with massive media interest. Eventually five other forces cooperated through a 'mutual aid' agreement, and armed officers came from Northern Ireland, the Met and elsewhere. What this case also conveyed was the image of heavily armed officers in helmets and body armour on the streets of Britain. This illustrates the contemporary reality of well-armed, specialist officers who depart dramatically from the stereotypical 'Bobby'.

This review of a range of scenarios for the police use of force and firearms indicates that they are extremely diverse, contain disparate risk scenarios, sometimes demand a quick response but at others require much patience, can challenge the command and control capabilities of senior officers, require a variety of training and a range of weapons and ammunition, and, with sudden incidents, can exceed the capabilities of the initial patrol officers at the scene to cope with them. A high level of professionalism and of equipment is needed as well as sometimes sound agreements with other agencies. The response to these scenarios depends also on whether special units (SWAT-style squads) or ordinary officers who are routinely armed are involved. Generally, however, the vast majority of the incidents covered by these scenarios pass off without a hitch and without a shot being fired.

The chance of matters going wrong, however, is potentially high, as with the multiple failures at the Stockwell shooting, which was potentially a 'mega'-incident in terms of the risk of a severe explosion with high casualties, while it was also quite exceptional in the ramifications surrounding the previously unknown tactics involved (see Chapter Five for more detail). Things can also go seriously wrong when the police encounter heavily armed opponents who take the initiative, fire aggressively, are determined to keep up the fight and are prepared to die (as in North Hollywood and Sunniland). Most police officers are trained minimally for self-defence; they typically react to violence and are not used to persistent, offensive firing. If they have body armour it will probably not be military-style, Kevlar-plated armour; given the 'increased firepower used on the streets you ought to be wearing that otherwise you'll be dead' (interview, Klinger). There are special police units like the SWAT squads that are better equipped than ordinary officers, are more assertive and can tackle tougher assignments. But even then those units will work very much within a paradigm of civil policing. For some particularly threatening situations, especially with a 'political' or terrorist connotation, the police and civil authorities may invite the military to run the operation as we have seen. This does raise a policy and demarcation issue about what incidents should be the responsibility of the public police or the military.

Difficulties with police using firearms: Tension, emotion and distortion

> Burrows wrote a fascinating (but unpublished) research thesis ... detailing experiments he had conducted with RUC officers. He concluded that in staged armed confrontations stress caused officers frequently to suffer severe perceptual distortion. Tunnel vision, time appearing to slow down, loss of hearing, difficulties in recall and visual impediments were common. Officers reported seeing people who were not present and failing to see those who were there. (Waddington, 2005: 14)

It is noteworthy that the stress and subsequent distortions mentioned by Burrows occurred during *staged* experiments; presumably real-life situations are even more stressful and even more open to distortion. Indeed, shooting at someone for most people, including most ordinary officers and even police firearms specialists, is not a cool, clinical, fully controlled matter. Using a firearm on a fellow human is an emotionally charged event – often accompanied by visual, aural and perceptual distortion – and even experienced officers who perform well on the exercise range can miss an apparently 'easy' target in real-life situations (Burrows, 2007; Collins, 2008). Officers have been known to miss a human target at a range of just 10 yards because of fear and tension. Fear in the face of a dangerous opponent or when confronted with the need to shoot a fellow human being should not be underestimated. I heard of an incident when a suspect slowly raised a gun concealed in a bag when taken by surprise by a firearms unit; he opened fire and one officer fired twice with a shotgun at close range but missed twice. This is despite the fact that it is much easier to hit someone with a shotgun than with other weapons. The problem is that everyone is trained on reticence and playing it long.[22] Also, while those who perform well on the range and in exercises will likely be seen as good material for a firearms unit, those who dare to fire at the right moment are often of a different sort; they are typically less disciplined and obedient than the stereotypically 'good' members (Collins, 2008). That explains why in accounts of firearms officers there is a lot of griping about those who do not deliver at the decisive moment (Collins, 1998; Gray, 2000). A firearms officer trains for years, but when he encounters the highly unusual event of having to use his weapon against a fellow human being and not a target in an exercise, he must instantly prove himself in decisiveness and alacrity, sometimes within seconds.

There is, however, a small 'warrior' class who seem cold and ruthless in killing, doing so without any apparent qualms of conscience. The South African policeman Eugene de Koch, known as 'Prime Evil', would be the archetypical example (Ellis, 1988). Professional hit men and some special forces soldiers may also be able to distance themselves from the consequences of killing by repetitive training and by focusing narrowly on the techniques and equipment of their trade (Collins, 2008). One SAS soldier when asked what he felt about killing a hostage-taker during the assault on the Iranian Embassy replied, 'Nothing. It was just like another exercise. Bang, bang, bang. Job well done' (BBC TV, 2003). Another said of that mega-incident

that if you train endlessly for Formula One car-racing then you want
to drive in a Grand Prix. The soldiers were all eager to take part in this
'Grand Prix' and were worried that they would be stood down.[23] A
somewhat similar 'gung-ho' attitude was expressed by Collins (1998:
121), who was champing at the bit to start a raid while in contrast
the negotiators were practising restraint:

> I smiled. It was funny in a way – here we were, both in the
> same job, trained to the highest standards, but with totally
> different ways of tackling a task. The negotiators were
> chatting quietly away with an armed and clearly totally
> deranged suspect. Their ideal solution was a peaceful
> surrender. I, on the other hand, was like a Rottweiler
> straining at the leash. All I wanted to do was storm in
> there and rip the little shit's head off.

Behind the hyperbole of such commercial and popular accounts there
is a glimpse of the diverse motivations of firearms officers in backstage
mode, and it must surely be the case that if one trains intensely year
in and year out there must be a desire, however strong the formal
restraint programming is, to be able to put one's skills into practice
at some time and prove oneself in action during a 'Grand Prix'.

When that does happen the evidence indicates that for most people
violence with weapons is rarely instrumental and clinical, but can
be exciting, distressing and also potentially depressing. It is typically
accompanied by adrenaline and tension; for the 'adrenaline junkies'
this gives a 'kick' while for others it is even erotic (Klinger, 2004: 71,
261).[24] The tension can be released in forms of exuberance during
or after the action. The two teenagers in the Columbine school
massacre in the US were laughing hysterically while shooting their
fellow students. Paramilitary hit men in Northern Ireland would
laugh uproariously after ruthlessly assassinating a man in front of his
family and go on to celebrate with a wild party, and the South African
Police death squad would return from a vicious, gruesome, murderous
raid to its base and indulge in much alcohol and an extensive '*braai*'
(barbeque). With such hard men of violence there is often bravado,
bragging, lewd humour, hard drinking and a resort to exploitive

or commercial sex, which echo the norms and behaviour of the criminals described by Katz (1988). The revelry, macabre humour and heavy alcohol consumption may, however, hide serious emotional problems. A number of officers who have killed, even legitimately and justifiably, will be pursued by demons and may end up with addiction, post-traumatic disorders or other psychiatric problems requiring treatment – assuming the condition is recognised and the treatment is available (Solomon and James, 1981; Haynes, 2006).

Klinger's (2004) assembly of accounts of shootings by 80 officers, for example, indicates that some have very little trouble, some have only short-term difficulties, but that others have considerable long-term problems. One officer had shot six people in his career, killing three, but had coped with this reasonably well. Much may depend on whether or not the shooting was seen as justified; on who the victims were – were they 'deserving' criminals or innocent bystanders or whether a fellow officer was involved – and if the officer himself was injured; and if the officer had made a mistake and/or felt guilt. Indeed, Klinger himself decided to leave policing after justifiably shooting a man dead in his first year as an officer with the LAPD; he shot a man who was wildly stabbing a prostrate colleague. An officer that he interviewed said you are never again quite the same person after you have killed someone (Klinger, 2004). One assumes that the two officers involved in the Stockwell shooting will have required considerable post-incident care.

In relation to coping with the after-effects, however, there is a fair amount of evidence that care for officers following a shooting often used to be primitive if not non-existent. This is well illustrated by Wambaugh's (1973) insightful and moving treatment in *The Onion Field* of a police officer suffering from Post-Traumatic Stress Syndrome (PTSS). He had his gun taken from him during an encounter and saw his disarmed colleague killed. But this was at a time when the police organisation in the US scarcely recognised this mental condition. Indeed, Waddington (1991: 66) writes of officers in Britain feeling 'abandoned' by their own organisation following involvement in a firearms incident with casualties. He refers to a Home Office report on post-shooting trauma by Manolias and Hyatt-Williams (1986: 11–14), which observes that 'Quite frequently little consideration seems to have been shown' to officers and mentions 'callous or even cruel treatment' in some cases. Generally nowadays officers involved in a firearms encounter will be put on sick leave and offered counselling. In Essex it became standard that the ACC Operations and ACC Personnel together took responsibility for ensuring that any officer involved in what could be defined as a potentially traumatic incident, including firearms, would receive strong institutional support and appropriate treatment (interview, Markham).

Using a firearm on a fellow human being is, then, never simply a technical, clinical and emotionally neutral matter. There is a wealth of evidence, for example, that even a high percentage of trained combat troops are reluctant to use their weapons in battle and are highly confused afterwards about how they have handled their guns. Muzzle-loading guns were retrieved from the Battle of Gettysburg with several bullets rammed down the barrel; the soldiers had carried on automatically loading the gun assuming they had fired it. This is clearly related to the 'fog of war' that surrounds the chaos, mayhem, noise and fearful apprehension on the battlefield as a 'place of terror' (Keegan, 1976; Collins, 2008). This is amply demonstrated in Beevor's (2009) description of the widespread psychological difficulties encountered by some soldiers fighting on the invasion beaches of Normandy in 1944.

Collins (2008), moreover, maintains that most people are loath to use individual violence and particularly that which involves face-to-face contact. It is easier to bomb or shell people at a distance or from the air, as the victims then remain a faceless group, or by using more technical means that take attention away from the grisly consequences of violence. According to Collins (2008), there have to be a number of facilitating contextual and group variables that make it easier for people to engage in close violence. But some people simply cannot cope with killing at close range.[25] In addition very few people, including experienced police officers and hardened soldiers, can shoot and kill another person and not be affected by it. Nearly every soldier or insurgent who is exposed to violence and death in combat for too long begins to deteriorate psychologically and in performance (Ellis, 1982).

In policing, moreover, firearms are sometimes employed in confusing and adversarial situations where officers feel threatened and anxious and are consequently emotionally aroused. Unlike a combat soldier in a conventional war – typically operating in a foreign country and trained to fight in a military unit against a defined, dangerous, depersonalised and even demonised opponent he does not know and whom he may kill on sight[26] – a police officer can be going about his or her routine business on the streets of their own city and be dealing with fellow citizens in a normal, non-confrontational manner. There may be an abrupt shift from relaxed routine to sudden danger. In Gray's (2000) account of policing the Met in ARVs, the crew of an ARV might just be sitting down to an ample and much anticipated breakfast when abruptly called away to deal with a demanding, tension-laden and highly dangerous confrontation. In Amsterdam an officer on routine patrol went to a reported disturbance in a house and was confronted with an aggressive woman attacking him in a confined space apparently with a knife; he shot her dead only to find it was a relatively harmless potato-peeler. Presumably the rapid conversion from routine to sudden danger unnerved him. In a split-second the officer at that moment perceived himself to be in danger. Under the pressure of the moment officers often mistake other instruments for a gun or interpret a sudden movement as reaching for a weapon. They are then often highly confused about what happened. Of course this perception of danger can also become part of post-encounter reconstructions based on formulaic defensive rationalisations and legally constructed justifications.

The 'split-second' decision is certainly not typical of most armed encounters involving police. Fyfe (1988), who was a former police officer and a respected firearms expert, even refers to it as something of a 'myth'. But such situations, however rare, do represent one of the toughest decisions a police officer may ever have to make. Many officers have told me about a time they almost fired a shot that could have been fatal or highly injurious and later would have been shown to be unjustified, and also about when they faced a gun, with one American cop pulling up his shirt to show me his gunshot wounds. One British officer told me of facing an armed suspect and suddenly realising that he was about to die and would never see his wife and children again; fortunately the suspect dropped his gun.

The conventional wisdom about such moments is that if the officer is too quick he lands in the dock, but if he is too late he ends up in a box. Perhaps in some societies this leads to an attitude, 'you can never be too quick and, if you are, we can sort it for you'. But this knife-edge moment between a correct judgement and a fatal error – literally between life and death – is well conveyed by a firearms officer entering an apartment to arrest someone wanted for a vicious murder and suspected of possessing a small handgun:

> Jimmy [fellow officer] immediately made his way to a double bed in the middle of the room. I could hear booming around the rest of the property, 'Armed Police! Armed Police!' and the heavy footsteps of officers running as they continued to enter…. Jim had located a man trying to hide under the mess of a bed I would normally call a duvet. Jim was screaming at him, 'Armed Police, show me your hands!' Everything seemed to slow down and my vision appeared to increase and focus as if I was looking through a telescope. If it was possible, the room had gone quiet although I knew Jim was shouting. The occupant of the bed fitted the description of the target but he wasn't showing hands, he was rummaging amongst the shit he slept in.
>
> My mind had decided what he was doing. I had judged him and now I was going to sentence him. I took the first pressure up on the trigger of my revolver and started to initiate a shot. His hands seemed to be moving in the direction of his bollocks and I had decided he was looking for the small firearm hidden down his Y-fronts. I was clinically going to shoot this individual. I started to increase the pressure on the trigger and acquire a sight picture, when my bubble was burst. Jim pulled away the bedclothes to reveal a naked male who was pissing himself with fright. 'Handcuff him,' shouted Jim….

We made our way back to Bootle Street and after a less than concise debrief we were told to take the rest of the day off. As I handed in my weapon, Jim winked and said, 'You did OK there, Andy.' OK? I nearly shot someone. Hadn't Jim noticed? (Hailwood, 2005: 99–100)

This is but one in a range of scenarios in which police decide to use firearms but when put in a situation of danger, even in set pieces where the officers are prepared for action, everyone involved is tense and under pressure. By issuing officers with firearms one is reliant on their subjective individual or group perception of danger; and one has to accept that *mistakes will be made*. Then one has to unravel genuine mistakes from negligent, over-hasty, poorly managed or even illicit shootings that may end with injuries and fatalities, internal inquiries, media scrutiny and criminal prosecutions.

Using firearms on the streets, moreover, has two specific and related difficulties at the delivery level. These are *over-penetration* and *ricochets* (stray bullets). A standard, 'full-jacketed' bullet from a high-powered rifle, for example, can pass straight through someone's body, hit other people and travel a considerable distance, say up to two kilometres. In addition, after penetrating a target, it may become distorted by hitting other objects, making it even more capable of causing injury. However, a high proportion of police bullets – at least half in the UK, if not far more depending on the circumstances – miss their target and carry on as stray bullets that can injure bystanders and other officers. In certain shoot-outs the vast majority of shots miss and go spinning around wildly, making the situation hazardous for bystanders and people in the vicinity. In the Gibraltar shooting of an IRA ASU by the SAS a full-jacketed bullet from a soldier's handgun passed through one suspect's (McCann's) body and hit a tourist; and in Northern Ireland the SAS occasionally shot bystanders during encounters with the IRA (Urban, 1993).

Added to over-penetration and ricochets is the possibility that officers will make mistakes and errors of judgement for a broad range of reasons. Mistakes will happen and people will die because of them (see Waddington, 1991; Squires and Kennison, 2010: 165–91).

'Mistakes' and their significance

'Mistakes' regarding shootings can expose inadequacies at various levels in the police use of firearms and management of firearms operations; can become scandals that deeply impact on the reputation of the police; can be important learning moments for the police; and can lead to changes in policy and practice. In such critical situations a great deal depends on the quality of those in command, the sophistication of the risk assessment and the willingness to negotiate before taking the decision to apply fatal force. Clearly controversy on shootings will be exacerbated if the victims are viewed as vulnerable (the young, the old, mothers with children) or with limitations (the mentally ill). The public, however, usually do have a collective sense of necessary and justified use of force by the police when the police are responding to obvious danger, are not the initiators, return what is accepted as an 'appropriate' level of fire and perhaps take casualties. But for any agency to put a bullet through the head of a mother holding a baby and presenting no threat to anyone, as at Ruby Ridge in the US, is an unmitigated disaster.

Indeed, of the various forms of deviance associated with policing – typically corruption, discrimination, manipulation of evidence to get a false conviction, invasion of privacy and so on – it is excessive, unjustified and illicit violence that can be the most controversial and emotive, if not explosive. All forms of police deviance represent how officials who are meant to uphold the law abuse their power to break the law. They can also lead to a loss of faith in the legitimate authority of those serving the state on behalf of citizens, and there is no more glaring test of the state's legitimacy than when its servants kill one of its own citizens. This often means that dubious and controversial police shootings – particularly when these are seen as unjustified, excessive or discriminatory (or all three) – can cause considerable social unrest and deeply affect the authority and credibility of the police.[27] The Federal Bureau of Investigation (FBI), for instance, lost a great deal of credibility and brought much opprobrium on itself by the mishandling of a siege leading to a shoot-out at Ruby Ridge.

Ruby Ridge (Idaho, 1992)

Police surveillance in a rural part of Idaho of a right-wing survivalist and warrant violator, Randy Weaver, led to the death of a US marshal, Weaver's wife and his 14-year-old son. The family carried weapons at most times as part of their lifestyle. At one stage in an attempt to serve warrants on Weaver, several US marshals were staked out around the cabin but were scented by the family's dogs, which chased them down a hill. In the confusion a marshal shot the son's dog, and the son returned fire hitting a marshal; the son was then fatally wounded. A siege situation developed and in an overreaction the FBI sent in its elite Hostage Rescue Team in full combat gear with an armoured personnel carrier and snipers. There was a stand-off that led to Weaver and a friend in his house being wounded when the FBI opened fire. But most damagingly for the entire operation and the FBI, Weaver's wife was by mistake fatally shot through the head by an FBI sniper while she was nursing her young baby, who was unhurt but covered in blood (O'Hara, 2005: 157).[28] Subsequently Weaver was only prosecuted for a few minor offences.

In documentaries about this incident some local police officers and the FBI negotiator are clearly distraught at the affair, and one former officer roundly calls it 'murder'. People like the Weavers virtually taunt the federal government, which they vilify, and in reaction there does seem to be a tendency in America to miscalculate situations and resort to extreme violence. For instance, on the way to Idaho the FBI operational leadership, in an unprecedented step, rewrote the standard rules of engagement, which allowed for a more aggressive approach to the incident (O'Hara, 2005).

Indian Embassy (London, 1973)

Particularly in the early days of police firearms use, from the 1960s onwards, there were a number of shootings that abruptly raised the hazards of police use of guns, but which were widely accepted as genuine mistakes under the circumstances. One example was at the Indian Embassy in London in 1973 at the time of the India–Pakistan war. Three young Pakistani men had entered the building, two brandishing firearms and the other a sword. Armed members of the Met's Special Patrol Group (SPG) were called to the scene and when confronted by the youths brandishing weapons and refusing to surrender, the officers opened fire killing two of them; they captured the third person. It was only then that it turned out the 'guns' were replicas. Replica and even toy weapons have become increasingly realistic and it is extremely difficult for an officer to see if the 'weapon' pointed at him is a genuine firearm capable of firing rounds, and if the person does not put it down and show a willingness to submit, then the officers will feel they have no alternative but to fire. This particular shooting was then widely accepted by the public according to Waddington (1991: 16).[29] That was certainly not true of the Waldorf shooting.

Stephen Waldorf (London, 1983)

Met officers were looking for a dangerous and resourceful armed criminal, David Martin, who had escaped from custody and had earlier shot and wounded a police officer. During his first arrest he had been tackled by a DC Finch; in the struggle Martin had tried to shoot another officer as well as Finch, who had to subdue Martin by hitting him with his service weapon. After Martin's escape, a Stephen Waldorf, who strongly resembled Martin, was seen in the company of Martin's acquaintances. Waldorf was subsequently followed by police through central London when the mini-car he was travelling in with two other people stopped at traffic lights. The same DC Finch as in the previous incident was asked to go up to the car to make an identification of the man. He thought that Waldorf was the suspect Martin, but then apparently panicked when Waldorf suddenly bent down as if reaching for something. Finch opened fire and other officers rushed up to fire into the car 14 times. Waldorf survived although he had been hit eight times in the body and head and seriously wounded (Waddington, 1991: 19–21). He was not only shot, but Finch leaned into the car and started beating him with his gun, fracturing his skull, and verbally abusing him. Eyewitnesses also claimed that Finch continued 'pistol-whipping' the seriously injured Waldorf on the pavement (Squires and Kennison, 2010: 72).

There are a number of critical questions about this operation. Was it sensible to intervene in the city centre amid busy traffic when the suspect could have been followed to a more suitable location? Was it advisable to send Finch of all people, given his earlier emotion-wrought encounter with Martin, up to the car without back-up to look in to identify the suspect? Was it sensible to fire shots into a mini-car with three passengers? In short, the focus on this debacle was the unprofessional, if not almost chaotic, manner in which the entire operation was managed (Waddington, 1991: 19–21). Who was in charge and who decided tactics; who gave the instructions; how much control did the supervisory officers have over their men; and what was the level of training and expertise of the unit? A serious mistake like this – which here almost cost an innocent man his life – leads to major reputational damage for a police force and can also mean payment by a force of large sums in compensation to victims. There was, however, a serious review of the incident leading to changes in firearms training and techniques emanating from the influential report of Commander Dear (Dear Report, 1983).

Harry Stanley (London, 1999)

In the Stanley case two Met firearms officers shot dead a man carrying something they took to be a firearm. The officers were responding to a call that an 'Irishman' in a pub had a firearm concealed in a bag; there was apparently also a suggestion that he might be a terrorist (Dodd, 2001). They challenged Stanley when he came out of the pub and told him to put down the bag; instead, according to the officers, he began to remove something from the bag and started to swing it towards them. The two officers opened fire fatally wounding him; he was first hit in the hand and then in the back of the head. They then discovered he had only been carrying a table leg. Not only was he not Irish and not armed, but forensic evidence also indicated he had been fatally shot with his back to the officers.

This is one of those difficult cases where officers believe there is danger based on information and handle the situation accordingly, only to later find that their perception – based, say, on seeing an authentic-looking replica weapon, something that could be a firearm, an object being removed from a bag or pointed in their direction or just a sudden movement – proves to be wrong. Of particular importance in this case are the prolonged repercussions for the two officers (Bennetto, 2005; and see Chapter Four). In short, the family of the victim, segments of the media and many members of the public in certain parts of London relentlessly kept up the criticism of the two officers and the Met almost up to the time of writing. They were incensed that the officers had resorted to shooting so quickly and especially that Stanley had been shot from behind when, it was assumed, he could then not have been forming a danger. It was only later that the American forensic expert Bill Lewinsky maintained that Stanley was probably instinctively turning when he saw the firearm pointed straight at him, which explained why they shot hit him in the back (Lewinski and Grossi, 1999). What also seemed to be completely absent in this case was any form of command and control structure to support the front-line officers. In a spontaneous incident with the crew of an ARV there will always be a lapse before a Silver Commander can get to the scene, due, for instance, to battling through the London traffic or over rural roads in a large county.

Mrs Bumpurs (New York, 1984)

In a tragic case in the US, with a long and complex background of inter-agency miscommunication, armed police burst into the apartment of a psychologically disturbed elderly woman who was holding a knife. Apparently she would no longer answer the door to diverse officials because she had perceptions of alien creatures invading her apartment; seemingly she held the knife more as a symbol of self-protection than for offensive use. Somehow the well-equipped team failed to disarm the woman and when she advanced towards an officer he fell down, leading another officer to fire twice with a pump-action shotgun at close range killing the woman. Presumably seeing a bunch of strange men in full combat gear bursting through her door was likely to make her more psychotic rather than compliant. Furthermore, the autopsy revealed that the first shot had hit the hand holding the knife and it was the second shot that proved fatal.

In this case, the reactions to this avoidable 'accident' – resulting from an amalgam of inter-agency failures – were exacerbated because the elderly woman was black and the officers were white (O'Hara, 2005). Here was an elderly, sick, black woman who had been hit twice and killed by a shotgun. The concern and dismay was further amplified by that second shot. Why the second round; why use this tactic; and why a shotgun? This and other cases raise the wider topic of how the police deal with the mentally ill who form a threat to themselves or others; and what is appropriate force in such situations (Stokes, 2001). Another factor is that when other agencies reach the limits of their powers, ability and resources to use force they call in the police to assist them; and the police may receive some slanted information. Much depends, then, on how adequately those agencies communicate and coordinate with one another – why had several agencies allowed this particular situation to escalate without finding a solution? – and also how the police are briefed about the level of risk involved.

Diallo and Bell (New York, 1998 and 2006)

Amadou Diallo was a young immigrant from Guinea who was apprehended as he was coming out of a house by members of an assertive NYPD plain-clothes unit for tackling street crime. The officers felt he fitted the description of a suspected rapist; when asked to raise his hands Diallo reached inside his jacket, and, thinking he was going for a gun, the officers started shooting. But Diallo was unarmed and had not been involved in any crime. He hardly spoke any English and may have misunderstood the officers and/or the purpose of the stop as he appears to have been reaching for his identity card (Skolnick, 2002). One officer opened fire, but Diallo was in a doorway and there was a ricochet from the wall behind him that caused one of the officers to fall over as he thought he was being shot at; the others thinking that their colleague had been hit then all started shooting and eventually 41 bullets were fired, of which 19 hit Diallo, killing him on the spot. Collins (2008: 112) sees this as one of those messy situations where a charged confrontation led to misperceptions that brought one officer to start firing, but once the other members of the team commenced shooting, they seemed incapable of stopping.

Another case involving the NYPD was the shooting of three unarmed, young black men who were hit with some 50 bullets. One of them was wounded and one was seriously injured but the third man, Sean Bell, died on what was to have been his wedding day. The men were at Bell's stag party when a scuffle broke out late at night between the stag group and two white men outside a club. This club happened to be under surveillance by an undercover police unit regarding criminal activities that were unrelated to these three young men. One of the police officers thought he heard someone call for a weapon and then the car of the stag group was said to have been driven at the officer and it also reversed and collided with the covert police vehicle. Perhaps the young men saw someone on the street and thought he was one of the original couple they were quarrelling with and did not realise he was a police officer. When the car hit the police van the officers jumped out and started firing. One officer fired 31 shots, which meant he had had to stop to put a new magazine into his pistol (*The Guardian*, 2006).

These two shooting incidents elicited prolonged protests both in the ethnic communities of New York and from many ordinary and prominent citizens.

Highmoor Cross (Thames Valley, 2004)

Often police are accused of being too 'quick on the trigger'. In the Highmoor Cross shooting in the Thames Valley Police (TVP) area they were pilloried for being too slow (IPPC, 2004). In a nutshell an armed man entered premises and shot three women, one of whom was his estranged wife; he then left the house with his firearm, a single-barrelled shotgun. The first call to the police reached a duty inspector in the TVP control room who responded by taking command of the situation, mobilising firearms officers and alerting the Ambulance Service. However, due to a cumulative combination of factors there was delay in handing over to a Silver Commander (roughly three hours), delay in effecting a rendezvous for firearms officers and delay in entering the premises (64 minutes after the initial report).

The IPCC evaluation, which was requested by the Chief Constable of TVP, Peter Neyroud,[30] was highly critical of how the incident was handled. This was investigated by officers from TVP under the supervision of the IPCC. The emphasis in the police response was judged to be 'over-cautious', according to the report, and was geared to eliminating risk rather than managing it. The delay was unjustifiable; there was a lack of clarity to act; and there was too little attention to the plight of the victims and those citizens who had come to their aid. Neighbours were desperately and repeatedly demanding help while two of the women lay dying and one lay seriously injured. One was declared dead at the scene, one died in hospital – but it is doubtful if she would have survived her injuries even with swift treatment – and the third women recovered from her wounds. The focus on carefully locating the armed suspect can be related to organisational memory in that TVP had dealt with the Hungerford massacre, which some officers remembered vividly, where TVP had had an officer shot dead when he intervened unarmed. At Highmoor Cross, the suspect was wrongly thought to be in possession of a high-powered rifle, which led to a fear that he might be able to 'outgun' the police armed with H&K MP5s (interview, Waddington).

Of significance here is that the incident occurred after national guidelines on firearms use had been issued in an ACPO manual, after the introduction of ARVs and long after the implementation of Gold, Silver and Bronze command roles. The report draws attention to examining force and national policy, clarity of command, communications, training and force culture. Highmoor Cross reveals how difficult it is to get it right in fast-moving incidents, as opposed to set-piece operations that can be prepared for; and, crucially, that all involved were convinced that they were operating within ACPO guidelines. Furthermore, the first emergency call will usually go to the duty officer in the control room, who not only has other calls to handle but also may have no experience with firearms operations. His or her task is to mobilise others and that inevitably takes time.

Comment: Guns and deaths: Controversy and learning

These varied incidents can be analysed at a number of levels and are open to multiple and contested interpretations. The Diallo shooting, for example, can be tied to racial profiling and discrimination, but it can also be related to institutional policy in that the NYPD had endorsed 'zero-tolerance policing', which had fostered a new, more assertive, form of policing the streets (Bowling, 1999; Punch, 2007). The elite Street Crime Unit (SCU) involved was meant to proactively and robustly tackle street crime such as robberies, muggings, burglaries and sexual assaults. Such units are frequently put under pressure to achieve results and the SCU was geared very much to 'stop-and-frisk' tactics on the streets in order to confiscate guns and drugs. Its members, who admitted later that they carried out far more stops than they recorded, claimed that they were working to reach an unofficial quota (Karmen, 2000: 137). Certainly in other cities, including Boston and Los Angeles, special units for tackling street crime had led to excesses against suspects and even ordinary citizens including shootings, beatings, theft and false charges (Punch, 2009a). In brief, departmental policies and crime-control strategies can affect weapons use and fatal force.

The examples presented and discussed here can be utilised to convey once more the inevitable confusion and tension that often surrounds shootings. 'Bad' shootings can be analysed at the individual, micro-level of diverse perceptions, of specific contextual factors, of enforcement policy and so on, but they can also have serious societal- and community-level impacts and consequences. In many high-crime areas of American cities, for example, the 'symbolic assailant' (Skolnick, 1966) for the police is a young black male, who the police believe is likely to be carrying a gun. However, high and volatile emotions and feelings are raised in the US, and in other countries, when the police shoot young black males who turn out to be unarmed or are killed in controversial circumstances. Rather like the widespread turbulence in reaction to the beating of Rodney King by the Los Angeles Police, the shootings of young blacks by officers, especially by white officers, have led to inquiries, court cases, media campaigns, serious riots, damages claims, demonstrations and prolonged community protests. In Cincinnati a white officer shot dead an unarmed black teenager in relation to a traffic violation; there followed several days of rioting with some 800 arrests. In London in 1985 seven officers forcibly entered the home of a Mrs Groce in Brixton in a search for her son, who was not found on the premises. By accident Mrs Groce was shot and permanently paralysed. The request by the lead officer for a special unit to make the entry had been turned down by a senior officer. There was outrage in the black community and two nights of heavy rioting followed with two deaths.

Hence police violence and especially shootings come to represent the repressive manner in which black people feel they are being under-policed in terms of service but over-policed with regard to violence in a racially biased society. In the case of the mentally disturbed Mrs Bumpurs, her death became a '*cause célèbre* for activists, was featured in a book-length rendering of "racial atrocities", and remains a main-stay in the literature of racially motivated police brutality' (O'Hara, 2005: 35).

Generally the public has some perception of 'deserved' and justified shootings, say against armed criminals refusing to surrender and brandishing or firing weapons, but also a strong condemnatory reaction to 'undeserved' ones. This tends to revolve around bad mistakes (shooting a five-year-old child); killing the vulnerable; and shooting at people, some with high 'social capital', who have no criminal background and are clearly temporarily behaving completely out of character. This was true in the case of Mark Saunders, a barrister who had been suffering from depression and who had been drinking heavily. He started an incident in London in 2008 that turned into a three-hour siege during which he fired a shotgun several times. Police negotiators felt that they were getting close to talking him into surrender when he shot wildly for the third time, after which police marksmen fired 11 shots hitting him at least five times (*The Daily Telegraph*, 2008a, 2008b). The criticism often focuses on why the police were so hasty in shooting, as in the Stanley case; could they not have done more to verify the information, and as the first shot had hit him in the hand, why then shoot him in the head? And why could they not have resolved the Saunders incident through negotiations or use of non-fatal force?

Furthermore, some confusion and delay in interpreting the situation and responding are often part and parcel of many spontaneous incidents so that a tardy response may also attract criticism. At the same time restraint and caution are often especially recommended in response to firearms. For instance, the predecessor of the IPCC, the Police Complaints Authority (PCA), reviewed police shootings between 1998 and 2001. The report and an article about it both placed 'considerable emphasis upon the armed police to *exercise caution*' (emphasis added). This reflects the shoot to prevent, restraint model. In essence the police should avoid tactics of confrontation; allow emotionally upset people or those who are under the influence of drink and/or drugs to calm down and sober up; use intermediaries and negotiators to seek a peaceful outcome; and 'most of all, allow time for the command structure to be established'. In short the conventional wisdom was to 'play it long'.

However, an IPCC Commissioner, Deborah Glass (2005), then wrote negatively of a 'culture of caution' in relation to the Highmoor Cross incident and she referred to 'the reluctance of firearms officers to actually use their weapons'. Waddington (2005: 15) reacted sharply in one of his *Police Review* columns and caustically remarked; 'the message [of the PCA report and accompanying article] was crystal clear: exercise caution. Yet, it is precisely the "culture of caution" that the IPCC now criticises. At the very least this represents mixed messages. At worst it amounts to being "damned if you do and damned if you don't"!' Indeed, 'damned if you do and damned if you don't' is the inherent dilemma regarding police use of firearms.

The comments of Waddington raise two further points. One is that shootings are open to multiple interpretations: there is the officer's subjective perception of the situation, say of the element of danger requiring the drawing and use of a gun, as opposed to witness statements and the evidence from forensics. Firing a weapon at a fellow human being is the ultimate judgement call for an officer. Investigators and oversight agencies, however, may interpret an incident quite differently in the cold light of day. The other is that an oversight agency is also not infallible. Waddington, an acknowledged expert on police use of firearms, is highly critical of the IPCC's report on TVP and Highmoor Cross and even calls it 'disgraceful'. How good are the oversight investigators? And how competent are they in the firearms area?

In brief, in assessing incidents involving police use of firearms a number of factors can be taken into account, including the individuals involved, the equipment and ammunition, levels of training and skill, 'programming' to fire in a certain manner, the specific context and the perceptions of the actors as the incident develops, but also organisational policies and societal values. There is also, it seems, an irreducible element of situational uncertainty, confusion and confrontational tension as events develop differently than anticipated or in a way for which the officers have not been trained. This may be compounded by personality factors, where an individual officer proves to be unduly hesitant or overly confident when tackling an incident. There is often an aggressive minority of officers in a police force who are responsible for a disproportionate number of violent incidents and citizen complaints about violence.[31] Much can also depend on departmental policy, standards of training, the weapons used, the quality and accuracy of the intelligence, the nature of the briefings beforehand, the assessed danger of the suspect(s) and the risk analysis made.

In effect, situational, personality and institutional variables can all make a major difference to outcomes influencing life or death. And in a form of 'tunnel vision' during incidents, officers may think they 'see' weapons that are not there. After a shooting incident officers often find it difficult to give a coherent account of what happened. As with some military encounters the officers can become so emotionally worked up that they cannot stop firing and do so with wild, inaccurate fire (Collins, 2008). Furthermore, the time dimension slowed down or accelerated in their perception; they were unaware of activities or sounds around them; they could not recall the fact that they fired or reloaded their weapon; could not say with certainty how many rounds they fired; and they were convinced they shouted a warning that no one else heard. After Stockwell the armed officers who entered the underground train at Stockwell stated that they had called out 'armed police' yet no one else in the carriage heard this. One of the highly experienced SO19 officers who fired his gun in the underground train at Stockwell could not say how many rounds he had fired. An American officer, who fired a CAR-16 (an eleven-and-a-half-inch barrel M16), which makes a deafening sound, said he heard nothing; and he 'didn't have a clue' how many rounds he had fired. He thought it was four, but it was actually 14; and he was a firearms instructor who taught officers to remain fully aware of the number of rounds they had fired (Klinger, 2004: 182). This confusion can play a role with regard to judging officers' testimony in an investigation after a shooting.

In summary, by issuing officers with firearms an organisation is always taking a permanent occupational risk:

- It is rarely possible to train every officer to a high standard of competency in firearms use (Waddington, 1991: 50; Waldren, 2007; interview, Timmer). In Baltimore in the 1980s, for instance, there was just one trip a year to the shooting range after basic training and this is blatantly inadequate (Simons, 2009).
- It is known that probably half, if not more, of the shots fired will *miss their target*; this raises the issue of ricochets, bystander injury, friendly fire and subsequent liability claims for injuries.
- Officers involved in shootings may be wounded or later develop post-traumatic stress syndrome, both of which can lead to compensation claims against the force if there is any suggestion of negligence, failures in duty of care or other health and safety violations.
- Where officers are allowed to take their weapons home, and in some American forces officers are required to carry their gun *at all times*, this increases the risk of accidents outside of work or the firearm being used in domestic violence. In the US police officers have a high rate of divorce, addiction, domestic violence and suicide (Crank, 1998). In the Netherlands an officer went home after work and shot his wife, three young sons and himself with his duty pistol. He should not have taken the weapon home, but it was known that he did so and no one raised the matter with him. It could be argued that if he was determined to kill his family he would have done it anyway; but it just so happens that here

his employer provided him with the murder and suicide weapon and allowed him to take it out of the station against the rules. Also in the Netherlands a young officer in training was showing his weapon outside of work to another trainee officer; he placed the gun against his friend's head, pulled the trigger and killed him. Another off-duty Dutch officer was helping to dress a young boy in some police attributes for the local school pantomime when a little girl saw his pistol in his open sport-bag; she took it out, held it in two hands and shot the officer through his calf (Timmer, 2005).[32] In fact there have been a number of accidental shots fired in classrooms when officers were giving presentations to young schoolchildren on policing (but fortunately without injury).

• This raises the issue of having a policy of keeping weapons in an armoury at work – which has now become the policy in the Netherlands – rather than allowing people to take them home. This is related not just to out-of-work accidents or misuse, but also to police suicides and to domestic violence. In some US forces there is a protocol that at least three officers will attend a police officer-related domestic dispute as it is considered that two of them will deal with the incident while it is vital that the third one locates and removes the officer's gun at the scene (O'Hara, 2005: 104). Where does the institutional responsibility for an officer's misuse or accidental firing of a weapon outside of work begin and end?

In short, in the 'fog', 'haze' or 'mist' of a seemingly dangerous incident, officers shoot themselves; shoot one another; get shot by their own weapon taken by an assailant; shoot bystanders; shoot people with replica weapons or toy guns (or cigarette-lighters that look like guns); shoot people who are unarmed; start shooting and cannot stop; shoot the hostage instead of the hostage-taker; and may shoot many times but haphazardly and without hitting the target (Collins, 2008 63–6). An American expert on the police use of violence, moreover, stated that officers were 'as likely to be killed by themselves, their acquaintances, or their colleagues as by their professional clientele' (Fyfe, 1978: 476).

This all simply illustrates that firearms are inherently dangerous and that accidents with them are inevitable; this can be during routine work, during a firearms operation or outside of work. On the one hand, there is an inevitability about accidents and also about mistakes and misses in shooting incidents; on the other hand, there is also a sense that legislation, policy and training can have an effect on reducing these negative features (Walker, 2005). The material presented here can only mean that policy, practices and procedures around firearms possession, firearms use and firearms operations must be imbued not only with a sound knowledge of the capabilities and dangers of guns, but also with the utmost need for safety and carefulness in the interests of the public – and the police.

Notes

[1] In Ottawa in 2000 I attended the impressive annual Memorial Service for fallen officers; this was conducted with much solemnity, and dignitaries and a large audience were present. There were police units from throughout Canada and some from the US marching in dress uniforms to pipes and bands. Before the parliament buildings those officers killed the previous year (all in accidents) were commemorated with a service, the last post, cannon shot and a lone piper sounding the lament 'Martyrdom' from atop a building. Also, a young female police officer was shot dead recently (2009) in the town where I live, Amstelveen, and there was a massive turnout of officers from all over the country, with many female officers, for the moving funeral.

[2] Klinger (2004: 270) reports that two officers conducting a routine stop were shot dead with their guns still in their holsters; and recently four Washington State officers were shot dead in a diner when they had almost no opportunity to defend themselves against someone who surprised them while they were sitting at the counter and was determined to kill them; only one managed to return fire (CBS News, 2009).

[3] In the early 1980s the American sociologist Al Reiss became interested in the idea of disarming the police and decided to try this with the small campus police force at his university, Yale in New Haven. His proposal foundered on an obdurate wall of resistance from the campus cops and stiff opposition from other institutional stakeholders.

[4] Roberts was in a car with two companions parked close to Wormwood Scrubs Prison in East London. Three plain-clothes officers in an unmarked so-called 'Q-car' considered this suspicious and decided to question the occupants. Roberts and an accomplice then opened fire killing all three officers. Among some people in London Roberts even became a popular hero; his name was chanted to taunt police at football matches I attended in London in the early 1970s. In other societies 'cop killers' can also achieve notoriety if not cult status, as with Larry Davis, who killed six officers and became a Bronx folk hero (Levitt, 2009: 156; see also Wambaugh, 1973).

[5] Moreover, PC Beshenivsky was a mother; she had been a police officer for only nine months, had three children and two step-children and was about to go off-duty and attend her daughter's fourth birthday party (Norfolk, 2007).

[6] English (2004: 117) describes the IRA gun-running activities, which brought 'hundreds of light, powerful, collapsible, concealable Armalite rifles' to Ireland in the 1970s.

[7] There are roughly 18,000 law-enforcement agencies including federal ones in the US, employing some 800,000 personnel.

[8] Remarkably, however, some early police officers in the US refused to carry guns and even to wear uniforms when the modern forces were founded in the 19th century (Klockars, 1985). It was demeaning to wear a uniform, they asserted, and a 'real man' was not cowardly and could cope without a gun (Miller, 1977)!

[9] It also reflected Hollywood's, and America's, fascination with violence and with guns. The weapon in the Dirty Harry films was in fact not a 'Magnum', but the ammunition was (Waddington, 1991).

[10] In the Netherlands there is in comparison a firearm in about 2% of households (Timmer, 2005).

[11] 'Recklessly spraying bullets at one another, they turned urban "wastelands" into "war zones" and "killing fields," mowing down innocent bystanders along with their intended targets' (Karmen, 2000: 173).

[12] Also, in Baltimore's Eastern District, the setting for the popular TV series *The Wire* on policing in a tough inner-city area, a recent ethnography based on participant observation as a patrol officer revealed relatively low levels of police violence and gun use although weapons

were often drawn. This might be related to the cautionary mantra repeated constantly in the training academy: 'The most important part of your job is that you go home. Everything else is secondary' (Moskos, 2008: 22).

[13] Rubinstein details the carrying of non-standard and non-approved firearms and ammunition. The latter included bullets the officers had altered themselves, carving the lead head to increase the wound to the victim, and 'hollow-point SuperVel bullets ... that are prohibited by international treaty', although several 'federal police agencies have made this ammunition standard'; but the officers' equipment was rarely checked by supervisors (1973: 288). He also mentions other illicit implements that a number of officers took with them on patrol.

[14] For firearms available to British officers see Waddington, 1991; Collins, 1998; and Waldren, 2007.

[15] Commissioner Robert Mark, who mounted an anti-corruption campaign in the Met in the 1970s, admits that as a young constable in Manchester he carried, as did everyone else, an illegal truncheon and during an arrest he broke a man's leg with it (Mark, 1978: 28). Blair Peach died following a demonstration in London when he was hit on the head by an object, believed to be a hand-held police radio. A Met unit of the Special Patrol Group (SPG) became involved in an altercation with demonstrators and it was assumed that Peach was hit by one of them, leading to his death. This has been confirmed by the recent publication of the confidential internal report of 30 years ago (*Guardian Unlimited*, 2010).

[16] Simon (2009: 138) mentions a Baltimore officer who was shot in the head twice but survived, although he was blinded and had to learn to speak again.

[17] For example, the UN's *Code of Conduct for Law Enforcement Officials* (United Nations General Assembly, 1979); the UN's *Basic Principles for the Use of Force and Firearms by Law Enforcement Officials* (United Nations Economic and Social Council, 1990); and Amnesty International's *Guns and Policing: Standards to Prevent Misuse* (2004).

[18] London Stansted is the 'preferred' airport in the UK for hijacked aeroplanes entering UK airspace. While the Essex Police and SAS have trained and prepared together for such an incident at that location,

presumably this has also been done at other major airports that might be forced to take a hijacked plane.

[19] On the Balcombe Street siege Commissioner Mark (1978) was crystal clear that in the event of an assault the hostages were expendable. [20] Allegedly he was denied medical aid and bled to death (Collins, 2008: 113). The police claimed the scene had to be safe before the ambulance could move in while there might have been a third robber. It is possible they were agitated and felt the robber did not 'deserve' treatment; he was still shouting aggressively on arrest. There can be much emotion and nervous tension at a shooting, especially with cops as victims, and this was an extraordinary experience, more like combat in a war-zone and unlike anything most officers had ever experienced; with continual radio despatches of 'officer down' they were doubtless considerably distraught and even not fully under control. As part of the reaction to a serious shooting it can be a form of reprisal to deny or delay medical aid to the wounded assailant.

[21] When President and Mrs Clinton visited Rotterdam and its harbour in 1993 members of the US Secret Service arrived weeks in advance, scoured the area and restricted possible lines of fire by strategically placing containers when the President and his entourage were in an open space on the harbour front.

[22] There is a banal element to 'playing it long', which is overtime; during extended incidents some mercenary cops are busily calculating their overtime payments (Collins, 1998); but I was also told of a unit pleading with the officer in charge of a firearms operation to get it over quickly so they could get away in time for a party.

[23] While waiting for the signal to go in they passed the time watching the World Championship Snooker on TV. On leaving the burning building they were warmly applauded and congratulated by police and others; amid the accolades one of the soldiers distanced himself from the intense violent event by quipping, 'by the way, who won the snooker?' (BBC Radio, 2009). This is typical SAS braggadocio.

[24] A Dutch officer from the Political Intelligence Branch became involved with the case of an IRA shooting in the Netherlands. He spoke of an IRA gunman who became sexually aroused and felt the need to masturbate after a shooting (presentation to visiting students of American University DC in the Netherlands in 1998).

[25] Some of the German reserve police officers who were asked to shoot Jews in Poland in WWII – the victims were men and women, the elderly and young children and they were shot at point-blank range in the back of the head – were repulsed by what they were required to do and could not bring themselves to take part in the gruesome slaughter of ordinary people. Even though this was wartime this inability of some to kill was accepted by their superiors and those who refused were never sanctioned (Browning, 1992). But it remained the case that the majority conformed, however reluctant some of them may have been and often with much intake of alcohol, and a minority learned to revel in the carnage.

[26] Klinger (2004: 14) served in Vietnam and says there were really no rules of engagement; the basic rule was 'you see the enemy, you shoot'. This bald statement conceals who was defined as the 'enemy', especially when it is estimated that it required a staggering 50,000 rounds to kill one 'enemy' in Vietnam (Collins, 2008).

[27] In the Netherlands a non-racial shooting in a small, relatively peaceful Dutch town which was seen as unjustified caused such consternation that there were three days of serious rioting (Timmer, 2005).

[28] The same set of factors – miscalculation and resorting to extreme measures – led to the disaster at Waco (Texas) where the defended complex of the Branch Davidians of David Koresh was assaulted with helicopters and armed personnel carriers and in an ensuing fire some 53 adults and 21 children died (O'Hara, 2005).

[29] The incident also revealed to the public for probably the first time that certain units, in this case the SPG, were routinely carrying firearms. This made some of the SPG vehicles forerunners of the later 'ARVs'.

[30] Neyroud had previously served in West Mercia, which had long been associated with coordinating firearms policy and practice and he was clearly concerned that the manual might encourage a rather rigid conformity to the rules. Boris Johnson, then a Conservative MP, wrote that officers were 'wrestling with procedures so rigid and so determined to stamp out risk that they left no room for individual initiative or even common sense' (*The Daily Telegraph*, 2004).

[31] The Christopher Commission (1991), which investigated the Rodney King incident, concluded that a significant minority of LAPD officers employed excessive violence, that among these were a group of 'repeat

offenders' who were not identified as such by the organisation and that there was a wider institutional failure within the LAPD's management in handling complaints and exercising accountability (Punch, 2009a: 6). [32] One assumes he learned from this painful error! That might suggest that firearms should never be taken into schools for safety reasons, but also to insulate children from the influence of deadly weapons. In interpreting these seemingly damning Dutch examples one would need to know how many accidents with police service weapons occur inside and outside of work in different countries.

FOUR

Rights, command and accountability

The material presented earlier indicates that the British Police during the last four decades – say from that crucial turning-point of 1966 (Waddington, 1991) – engaged in a continuous learning process regarding police use of firearms and the allied issues of rights, command, accountability, investigations and oversight. In wrestling with these complex and intertwined matters, police were driven by a number of factors that have culminated generally in a more professional and sophisticated approach.

The broader reform process in policing has not always been even, smooth and progressive, but rather has often been tardy, painful, contested and even at times retrograde. There have, for example, been highly critical moments eliciting considerable negative publicity with insistent demands for reform arising from major corruption scandals, miscarriages of justice, public order situations including the 1981 riots in Brixton and elsewhere, and from the profound repercussions of the murder of Stephen Lawrence. There can be no doubt, however, that policing has altered considerably in a number of areas and is continually subject to change and reform (Blair, 2003; Reiner, 2010).

Behind a number of these changes are several streams of influence combining to push the police to concentrate their minds on command, accountability, investigations and oversight (Jones, 2003). Here I shall touch on five key factors. The growing importance of human rights (HR) law and the pronouncements of the European Court of Human Rights (ECHR); the potential impact from the late 1990s of the proposed legislation on 'corporate manslaughter'; influential court cases and judicial pronouncements on police firearms use; developments in structures and practices of operational command and control; and problems with investigations and the rise of new oversight agencies.

Indeed, behind these particular impulses the police have been subjected in the last three decades more generally to a swelling stream of commissions, directives on procedures and legislation, which has cascaded onto them from both Conservative and Labour governments (Reiner, 2010).[1] Under the New Labour government from 1997, for instance, there was a flood of measures: 'During its first ten years in office New Labour passed fifty-three Acts containing criminal justice legislation and created 3,000 new or revised criminal offences' (Blair, 2009: 105). Of interest is that the escalating government pressure on the police focused on umpteen areas, but that 'maelstrom' of reform (Leishman et al, 1996) has, it seems, studiously avoided public attention to the use of firearms and fatal force.

In the wider environment a particular factor in relation to police use of force was the development and impact of international and HR law. HR law endeavours to limit the state's use of coercive and intrusive power while crucially it evinces the 'right to life' principle (Haas, 2008). In theory this body of law should infuse the entire approach to the application of potentially fatal force at the levels of the state, the institutions of law enforcement and even the front-line officers employing weapons (Crawshaw et al, 2006).

International HR law: The 'right to life' principle

The increasing destructiveness of armed conflicts during the 19th century with industrialised warfare causing mass casualties fostered a move to limit the use of certain types of weapons and ammunition in combat. The Hague Convention of 1899, for example, applied itself among other things to 'expanding bullets' (so-called 'dum-dum bullets'). Declaration 3 of the Convention stated that 'Bullets which expand or flatten easily in the human body, such as bullets with a hard envelope which does not entirely cover the core or is pierced with incisions' were prohibited. Their use has also been made a war crime under Article 8(b)(xix) of the 1988 Rome Statute of the International Criminal Court. Neither of these applies to police in peacetime.

In the 20th century, moreover, there has been a spate of conventions, directives and international laws, particularly in the wake of WWII. That ghastly experience, with massive military clashes, atrocities against civilian populations and the horrors of the concentration camps and the Holocaust, sponsored a post-war raft of initiatives on HR related to genocide and war crimes. These international conventions and directives and the development of human rights jurisprudence were and are of considerable significance for the police, but it remains the case that police actions are entirely regulated within domestic law.

However, governments of states that are party to the European Convention on Human Rights (EConvHR) need to ensure that their constitutions, laws, administrative guidelines, policies and practices are all in conformity with their treaty obligations. As governments are obliged to ensure the implementation of the rights in the treaties to which they are bound, this at least implies that within the police organisation there should be senior police officers with an awareness of the international legal context within which they operate. It would be myopic, to say the least, if ACPO developed policy and practice that ignored important judgments of the ECHR. There have also been a number of specific judgments of the ECHR that are highly relevant to policing and to accountability, as in the *McCann* case, which was dealt with in Chapter One.

Of pivotal importance in relation to force and firearms is Article 2 of the EConvHR, which protects the 'right to life'. This means that the UK is bound under international HR law to respect and protect the right to life. It further means that its law, ministerial guidelines, policies, practices and procedures must all be in compliance with its international legal obligations. This includes by definition policies and practices developed by ACPO. This obligation is expressed primarily, but not solely, in the EConvHR and through the jurisprudence of the ECHR.

In brief, Article 2(1) of the EConvHR requires that everyone's right to life shall be protected by law. Article 2(2) sets out those specific circumstances under which the taking of life will not contravene the Convention: 'when it results from the use of force which is no more than absolutely necessary'. Those circumstances are:

(a) 'in defence of any person from unlawful violence';

(b) 'in order to effect a lawful arrest or to prevent the escape of a person lawfully detained'; and

(c) 'in action lawfully taken for the purpose of quelling a riot or insurrection'.

In making these exceptions the Article purports to define exhaustively permissible grounds for deprivation of life. In order for lethal force to be justifiable in the circumstances set out in paragraph 2 of the Article, its use must be *proportionate* and *necessary*, as required by the term 'the use of force which is no more than absolutely necessary'. From interpretations of the Article by the ECHR it is now clear that Article 2 may be breached by the following: the actual application of unlawful force; force that is unnecessary and disproportionate; defects in the command and control of an operation involving lethal use of force; and failure to carry out prompt and impartial inquiries into killings by the state. All of these are patently relevant in relation to police use of force and police shootings.

Deliberations of the EConvHR and jurisprudence of the ECHR have shed light on the interpretation of the failure to protect the right to life. For example, the term 'absolutely necessary' is used to qualify the circumstances in which the use of force resulting in death may not contravene Article 2; this in turn is linked to the principle of proportionality. The Commission's opinion indicated that paragraph 2 did not primarily define situations where it was permitted intentionally to kill an individual, but it defined the situations where it was permissible to use force that might result, as the *unintended* outcome of the use of force, in the deprivation of life. The use of force, however, has to be no more than absolutely necessary and strictly proportionate to the achievement of the aims set out in Article 2. As mentioned in Chapter One, the landmark case in this respect is *McCann et al v The United Kingdom*, which arose out of the killing of three IRA suspects by four soldiers of the SAS in 1988 on Gibraltar. This has great significance for the police management of operations and for accountability.

For instance, the *McCann* case was cited, on this and other matters, in *McKerr v The United Kingdom*, where the applicant alleged that his father had been shot and killed by police officers in Northern

Ireland. The Court held that there had been a violation of the right to life because of a failure of the state to conduct a proper investigation into the circumstances of the death. It noted that, under Article 2, investigations capable of leading to the identification and punishment of those responsible had to be undertaken into allegations of unlawful killings. It observed that proper procedures for ensuring accountability of state agents were indispensable in maintaining public confidence and meeting the legitimate concerns that might arise from the use of lethal force.

It is crystal clear that various directives as well as HR law and jurisprudence have considerable import for policing regarding the use of force generally and the use of firearms in particular. British legal and judicial practice tends to rely on common law, and on acknowledging parliament as sovereign, but the UK was a signatory to the Convention in 1950 and it clarified the legal rights of UK citizens and the obligations of the state in the Human Rights Act (HRA) 1998.

Legal accountability

Alongside HR law and jurisprudence there was also a growing wave of laws, judgments, directives and developments from the early 1990s ostensibly steering the police to becoming more accountable and regulating their powers (Reiner, 2010).[2] In this flow the judgment in the 'Sussex' case with regard to firearms is crucial (see Chapter One for detail of the Sussex shooting incident). Let us recall in essence the parameters around police use of firearms in Britain. Philosophy, practice and legality were based on minimal and reasonable force; accounting for each shot fired; a self-defence plea for officers who had caused death or injury; that no one could give a direct order to fire to a police officer; and that each *individual* officer was responsible for any death or injury caused by a shooting.

What the Sussex case did, and this was reinforced later by the prospect of prosecutions against a police force for 'corporate manslaughter' under then forthcoming legislation, was effectively to point towards wider *organisational culpability* for the management of the operation leading to the death. In general the English legal mind tends to focus narrowly on the smoking gun, on the individual hand holding it or associated with it and on the specific incident, and it has a predilection for placing fault on the individual rather than on the collective (Wells, 2001). In contrast the statement by the presiding judge, Justice Anne Rafferty, at the trial for murder of the officer who fired the fatal shot in Sussex in 1998 displayed a growing legal consciousness about locating fault within the organisation, among higher management and over a period of time (Gobert and Punch, 2003).

The significance of Justice Rafferty's statement cannot be underestimated. Her pronouncement, and the subsequent trial for misfeasance of several Sussex officers, transmitted a powerful signal that deploying firearms in police operations must be embedded not just in the tradition of individual accountability, but also in a new awareness of institutional accountability. This has profound implications for senior police officers and for the police organisation. Her words should perhaps be engraved above the desk of every senior officer: 'Those having responsibility for implementing, seeing good compliance and monitoring good practice as to the use of firearms bear a heavy responsibility for the death' (Hopkins, 2001).

This is crucial because the deployment of firearms is the most serious responsibility in policing as such incidents are *always potentially lethal*. Justice Rafferty appears to be hinting that the law should be changed to locate fault at the appropriate level when firearms are used to kill or injure someone. But above all she was plainly stating that an operational command structure is also an accountability structure including legal accountability. Rafferty's words, and the two trials following from the Sussex shooting, indicated with glaring clarity that when operations go wrong it should be senior officers high in the chain of command who should also appear in court and not just those officers at the front-line who carried out the operation and, in this case, fired the fatal shot.

Justice Rafferty was saying plainly that one should not – to use martial imagery from the Flanders battlefields of WWI – solely blame the 'PBI' (Poor Bloody Infantry) in the myopic mire of the trenches, but should draw the trail of accountability back to the generals setting grand strategy in their comfortable chateaux far from the sights, smells and dangers of the front-line.

'Corporate manslaughter'

Another wider development moving liability from the individual to the institutional level was the growing pressure for legislation on what is referred to as 'corporate manslaughter'. Until recently this formally meant 'gross negligence manslaughter' and was thought of in relation to enterprises that could be held liable for the deaths of employees or members of the public as a consequence of their activities. This law did not apply to police forces. Although the concept of taking an organisation to court for a criminal offence has long been established, prosecutions have been sporadic (Slapper and Tombs, 1999). From the 1990s onwards, however, and partly in response to a number of major disasters, there was an increase in prosecutions. There were for instance several prosecutions against train operators and transport companies in relation to crashes (as at Southall); against hospitals for negligence in relation to the deaths of patients; and against P&O for the nearly 200 deaths at Zeebrugge following the capsizing of the ferry boat 'Herald of Free Enterprise' (Punch, 1996; Gobert and Punch, 2003). A number of legal difficulties in implementing the existing law meant, however, that there had been very few successful convictions of companies, and new legislation was proposed with the arrival of the Labour government in 1997 (Wells, 2001).

Of considerable interest here is that this raised the prospect of a prosecution for 'corporate killing' against a police force concerned in a fatality – say, a death in custody, during a high-speed pursuit or by shooting – as there was no longer Crown immunity under the new law on 'corporate killing'. Although the fresh Labour government had promised in 1997 to include corporate manslaughter in its legislative programme, the law was only passed in 2007 to be implemented in 2008 (Gobert, 2008). Several senior officers involved in the Stockwell shooting of 2005 were interviewed by the IPCC in relation to gross negligence manslaughter, but presumably this was done in case the Crown Prosecution Service (CPS) decided to prosecute them individually, as a corporate prosecution against the Met was not viable under the prevailing legislation. This may subsequently have influenced the CPS in turning then to a prosecution under health and safety (H&S) legislation. The Office of the Metropolitan Police was subsequently convicted and heavily fined for offences under H&S law in relation to failures in its 'duty of care'. It is debatable if legislation from 1974 designed for prosecuting labour-related offences in the workplace is appropriate for adjudicating a police shooting in 2005. Indeed, there were objections, from inside but also outside the police, against its use here as a diluted form of corporate manslaughter. A contributor to the *Safety and Health Practitioner* wrote that 'substituting a breach of the HSWA [Health and Safety at Work Act] for some form of charges for unlawful killing looks suspiciously like stable door-bolting' (quoted in Blair, 2009: 200), but the prosecution did raise the matter of organisational fault and liability in relation to 'duty of care'.

From the late 1990s, in short, there was the prospect of new legislation that could lead to a police force being prosecuted and convicted for the new offence of 'corporate killing' (Gobert, 2008). This legal trend to thinking more in terms of corporate rather than individual liability was evident in the trials following the Sussex shooting: Justice Rafferty spoke in the first trial about the 'heavy burden' of responsibility carried by the Sussex Police; and the prosecuting QC in the second trial spoke plainly of 'corporate failure' (Hopkins, 2001). It is clear that if the law had then applied to the police, the CPS would have had a strong case against both the Sussex Police and its senior officers for corporate manslaughter. Whether or not that would have led to a conviction is another matter.

Operational accountability

The complex and intertwined processes I am sketching have been enhanced by three largely internal developments. These are increasing professionalism around firearms, implementing new command and control structures, and moving towards a culture of accountability.

The evidence presented earlier in this book indicates that professionalism around firearms use and attention to the deployment of potentially fatal force has been taken increasingly seriously within the British Police Service. The last two decades especially have shown efforts to provide first-class equipment and training, to develop standard procedures and to establish an operational accountability structure for police firearms use. The descriptions of a number of firearms officers who served during this period portray an increasingly sharp learning-curve in this area (Collins, 1998; Gray, 2000; Hailwood, 2005; Waldren, 2007). There can be little doubt that firearms use is now widely approached in a highly professional manner, which was previously not always true of some segments of the Police Service. Part of that professionalism has been to formulate clear procedures and operational policy and practice in the ACPO *Manual of Guidance on the Police Use of Firearms*, which has been continually updated since the first one in 1983 (for example, ACPO, 1987, 2005). In general, firearms officers are carefully selected and monitored, well trained and equipped with first-class material.

An important building-block in this process involved paying serious attention to senior officer competency at, and accountability for, major incidents. For example, the officers in an ARV will normally only open the armoury in the vehicle to access their weapons following permission from a designated officer of senior rank. The exception is an ongoing situation where the crew believes immediate, independent action is necessary; but this would have to be fully justified afterwards. At such moments the police organisation is devolving the responsibility for taking the life of a citizen to those front-line officers acting on their own. This devolution is common in much policing, which is routinely based on decentralised functioning in small units with high autonomy. However, given the significance of firearms as always potentially fatal, efforts have been made to give rapid support to those front-line officers.

The 'command and control' structure commonly in use to achieve this was originally developed by the Metropolitan Police to cope with public order incidents. In larger set-piece or developing operations, including use of firearms, there will normally nowadays be a command structure based on the 'Gold, Silver and Bronze' model (Punch and Markham, 2004). Gold is for the strategic role, Silver for operational command and Bronze is for implementation. In a set-piece operation involving firearms, for instance, the Gold

Commander will be in overall control of the operation, setting the strategy, mobilising resources and contacting stakeholders; the Silver Commander is the key tactical figure in executing the operation; and he or she will have one or sometimes more Bronze Commanders to supervise the implementation of Silver's instructions. The standard deployment for the average pre-planned, armed operation in Essex was a firearms team of eight with additionally officers at the Gold, Silver and Bronze levels. At a major incident there might be 50 armed and other officers with several Silvers and Bronzes but always only one Gold Commander. There was always a Gold for firearms operations (interview, Markham). Of importance is that the 'Gold' role involves not only setting the strategic parameters, but also monitoring Silver's main decisions and keeping an operational audit of key decisions regarding communications with stakeholders and mobilising resources. A former officer with experience of the Gold role explained that at a firearms or other serious incident, Gold will 'work from the smoking gun backwards, consider scenarios and the legal implications, will think mostly risk averse and will keep a policy log in order to justify decisions; you wrap yourself around with loggists and runners and always do the log contemporaneously' (interview, Golding). At Essex all communications at the Gold level were as a matter of routine recorded; Gold was followed by a scribe and all briefings and debriefings were video-taped. There was a strong emphasis on the audit trail,[3] 'jotting down things early' and approaching the review process in an 'open, honest, self-critical' way whereby the lower ranks could comment on senior officers' performance and could also have an input in shaping policy documents (interview, Markham).

Often Gold will hold chief officer (ACPO) rank, but it is important to understand that Gold is a role that is not necessarily tied to rank. If the first officer on the scene of a major incident, say a train or a plane crash, is a constable then he or she is at that moment acting as an initial Gold until the command and control hierarchy can slot into place. Similarly the duty officer in the CAD room who takes a call about a calamity or shooting is temporarily a sort of 'holding Gold'.

With regard to armed operations the fundamental cornerstone is that the use of violence will be enmeshed in a command structure where all the officers concerned are trained to fit their respective roles; where there are standard procedures; and where the person who pulls the trigger has an institutional structure to support his or her decision (NPIA, 2007). Indeed, in some forces, as we have seen, there are certified firearms officers at the Silver level who provide 24-hour mobile cover for firearms incidents before a Gold Commander and other special units can be mobilised. This is to provide a swift response to the crews of ARVs or other officers responding to an incident that may involve the use of firearms. This recognises that the most important decision an officer may ever make in his or her career, taking the life of a fellow citizen while possibly also facing danger to his or her own life, may be made by someone ostensibly low in the hierarchy with a high measure of autonomy in a confusing and dangerous situation.

This in turn relates to the point made earlier that the Achilles heel of armed deployment was seen as the lack of 'cover' by senior officers during the 'unsocial' hours. This has been partly solved by the roving Silvers on a 24/7 roster. However, initial calls from the public, other forces and some officers often come into the control room and the duty officer there has to respond while taking other calls; and he or she may have little experience of firearms or of major incidents.[4] Taking this into account following the introduction of ARVs, all the inspectors working in the control room in Essex were retrained to play a role in which they could authorise deployment of weapons, mobilise resources, contact the mobile Silver Commander and inform the duty Gold Commander. This recognised that ARV crews sometimes needed quick authorisation and swift backing, and that the gravity of firearms deployment meant putting well-trained personnel in key positions throughout the rest of the organisation. In that sense, firearms have helped drive enhanced professionalism in the Police Service.

In recent decades there have been a series of incidents and pressures leading more generally in policing towards such command and control provision, but it was especially the routine arming of front-line officers in the late 1980s through ARVs that forced the Police Service to attend most seriously to issues around operational and institutional accountability. It also pointed ineluctably towards senior officers having to learn to accept accountability. Being held accountable became increasingly a central component of their occupational reality (Orde, 2003).

There remain two key issues, however. First, there will always be an 'accountability' gap in spontaneous, fast-moving situations where front-line units face the perceived need for immediate action before the wider command structure moves into gear. This can mean that armed officers find themselves in an operational vacuum. In essence the Police Service recognises that ARV crews are at times acting in the Gold role and that every effort has to be made to mobilise a command structure to support them. Furthermore, as a mechanism of 'quality control', the authorisation to arm has been located in officers of senior if not chief officer rank. In reality, though, during spontaneous incidents there is frequently a 'catch-up' phase before the command structure can be mobilised and Silver can get to the site; and everyone is highly reliant on the risk assessment made on site by the ARV crew. In other words, there is a 'world of difference between authorizing a deployment and pulling the trigger. Authority to arm is part of a wider risk assessment process ... killing someone in the "line of duty" is paradigmatically different' (personal communication, Gilmour). This is important in relation to the policy known as Kratos (dealt with in Chapter Five), because in the pre-Kratos model authorisation is granting authority to arm, but the decision to fire is taken by the individual officer on the basis of the threat and risk assessment he or she makes on location.

Second, it will always remain difficult to have senior officers, with diverse backgrounds and a broad palette of responsibilities, who will possess the ideal command experience and competencies specifically for armed operations.[5] This can mean that supervisory ranks are either reluctant to take a decision or else all too ready to accede to requests from the 'front'. During his research, for example, Waddington was in the Met Special Operations Control Room at New Scotland Yard during a royal ceremonial occasion when a request for authorisation to deploy firearms came in. The Gold Commander gave it 'without either much inquiry or hesitation', remarking 'What the hell do I know?'. He was not at the scene and was 'utterly reliant on the ARV crew's appraisal, and they knew better than him the risks they faced from a suspected armed man' (personal communication, Waddington).

Investigations

One recurring concern about police use of force and especially fatal shootings was the fact that the police investigated themselves. Unlike in the Netherlands, there was no external agency in the UK, nor in the US, to investigate such matters. In the UK, moreover, police chiefs zealously defended their independence, with the 'incorruptible' Robert Mark (1978) retiring early rather than countenance external encroachment on his authority in disciplinary matters. Also, in the US the police unions campaigned vigorously and often successfully against any whiff of civilian oversight. Indeed, US policing can be viewed as a virtual wasteland when it comes to effective oversight (Walker, 2005). Police shootings in the US, for example, were normally dealt with by the Homicide Squad of the same police force in which the officer under investigation served. In general, investigations of police shootings either by internal shooting review boards or by external, federal officials clear the officer of blame, and prosecutions are rare (Klinger, 2004: 203). It has repeatedly been suggested that the occupational culture demanded that the investigators should do their utmost to exonerate the officer in the spotlight. If not, the investigator was likely to become a 'pariah', according to Simon (2009: 392–3), who gives an example from his time as a journalist with the Baltimore Police Department of 'cosmetic' reporting with regard to two separate shootings by detectives:

> In the realm of American law enforcement the deceit has been standardized. Inside every major police department, the initial investigation of any officer involved in a shooting begins as an attempt to make the incident look as clean and professional as possible.... The bias at the heart of such an investigation is seen as the only reasonable response to a public that needs to believe that good cops always make good shootings.... Time and again the lie must be maintained.... When it comes to

police-shooting reports, the lieutenant is something of
an artist.... Rarely, if ever, has a shooting bounced down
the ladder after the lieutenant has put his mark on it. As
awkward and excessive as the use of deadly force might
have seemed out on that parking lot, it reads as squeaky
clean in the finished product.

There is no way of knowing how widespread this practice is, but we
do know that structures of oversight in American policing are either
weak or non-existent. There are a few exceptions, but then mostly
following federal injunctions for reform and auditing. In general,
there is a low culture of accountability with lukewarm compliance
if not resistance. This leads Walker (2005: 17) to observe: 'Many
cynics believe that the American police are incapable of reforming
themselves and that the police subculture is resistant to all efforts to
achieve accountability'.

In the UK the Police Service has traditionally investigated itself
and this applied also to firearms and fatal force. With no external
investigatory agency the practice was to 'invite' another force
to investigate the shooting in the force concerned. Critics and
disgruntled relatives of a victim frequently claimed that this could
lead to a cover-up of the sort described by Simon in Baltimore
(Waddington, 1991). Predictably, senior officers in Britain are
adamant that such investigations are conducted with the utmost
professionalism. The family of the man shot by the Sussex Police,
however, was convinced of a 'cover-up'. Yet in the investigations
by Hampshire and Kent Police into the Sussex shooting there was
certainly no cosy and collegial massaging of the facts, but rather bitter
and acrimonious exchanges between the two external forces and
the chief officers of the Sussex Police (Davies, 2001b). The outside
investigators had begun to explore wider disciplinary and criminal
offences beyond the shooting but the CPS declined to prosecute.
Indeed, the criticism is often aimed not just at the police, but also at
the CPS, as few police shootings lead to a prosecution and almost
none to a conviction. Shootings are often disputed and depend on
judging an officer's state of mind: if he sincerely believes that his life
was in danger then it is difficult to prove that his perception at that

moment was wrong and criminally liable. Also, it is most unlikely that a jury will convict a police officer on a murder charge unless the case against him is overwhelming. In many of the controversial cases of recent decades that were taken to court on serious charges the officer was found not guilty and was acquitted (Squires and Kennison, 2010).

However, if the critical view is that officers 'get off lightly', then that is not how those involved in a disputed shooting usually experience it, and training imbues them with the notion that they will be held to account. Waddington, who has been through the Met firearms training as part of his academic research on this topic, illustrated this:

> When I trained, we completed an assault on the 'killing house' at Lippitts Hill and were all congratulating ourselves on the well-executed plan. The instructors then appeared, carrying evidence bags. We were instructed to place our weapons into the respective bags. Our hands were swabbed and our coveralls removed. We sat in paper suits and were required to compose our statements. We were cautioned and told that we were each suspects in a murder inquiry. It was terrifying! But we were warned that if we pulled the trigger for real (this didn't apply to me, of course, I had the luxury of being an academic researcher), this is what would follow. That breeds a 'culture of caution'! Those guys embraced accountability – they knew only too well where the buck would stop! (Personal communication)

A bone of contention in this post-incident process has been the practice of officers jointly composing their statements. This opened the possibility of collusion in phrasing their accounts and raised the spectre of falsification and perjury. This collective consultation was common practice within the SAS in Northern Ireland with the Army's Legal Service acting as coaches to get the formulaic element of danger in the account plus consistency between unit members (Dillon, 1991). There was a similar practice within the RUC, where certain special units involved in controversial shootings were whisked away from the scene to be instructed by Special Branch in the appropriate wording of accounts. A senior officer from the mainland, Stalker (1988), who endeavoured to investigate three of those shootings was not only obstructed by the RUC but, in a *cause célèbre* of establishment chicanery, was removed from the inquiry and himself subjected to investigation. Next to possible collusion among officers – and what Glass (2007: 297) refers to as 'the artificial construction of an apparent consistency' – is the element of delay in writing the statements, which allows for consultation and reconstructing the events. Even if there is no ulterior motive there will almost certainly be a difference between a contemporary account, hot from the event, and what is written later. One factor that has to be taken into consideration, however, is stress immediately after a shooting. The post-incident process is now also geared to the welfare of the officer, with the notion that it may not be appropriate to write up notes into a statement until after rest and a medical inspection (Waddington, 2005). Moreover, ACPO has now issued guidelines that officers must not collude in report writing and have to write their statements individually and separately.

Indeed, the exercise at Lippitts Hill described by Waddington was designed precisely to reinforce the individual officer's responsibility. In practice it can happen that the firearms officers who fire a controversial shot that wounds or kills face suspension and several frustrating years of confrontational and persistent inquiries. In the Stanley case in London, for example, two Met firearms officers shot dead a man carrying a table-leg, which they took to be a gun (see Chapter Three for more detail). There followed several proceedings (criminal, disciplinary and civil) related to the incident, which took *over six years* before the two officers were finally cleared of any form of blame, although the shooting still remains a matter of some bitterness in parts of London and the media (Gilbert, 2005; Verkaik and Bennetto, 2005). There were no less than 10 reviews involving two inquests, the findings of which were set aside by the High Court; three investigative reviews by the CPS; a number of judicial reviews and two reports for the PCA by Surrey Police; and a final 'disciplinary decision review' by the IPCC (Squires and Kennison, 2010: 171).

This could be viewed as excessive and raises the issue as to whether or not there can be limits to investigative review. In response to the prolonged treatment of these two officers, Met firearms officers handed in their weapons authorisation in what some parts of the media called a 'strike'. A strike would have been unlawful, but this was virtually a form of industrial action expressing deep dissatisfaction. The seriousness of this can be gauged by the fact that the Commissioner, John Stevens, returned from holiday to douse the bush fire (Jay, 2004). There was a similar response after the Stockwell shooting, with firearms officers handing in their authorisation in protest at their colleagues' exposure to lengthy investigation.[6] Following Stockwell there was an investigation by the Met Professional Standards Department and by the IPCC, followed by a trial and an inquest.

No one would question the need for a thorough inquiry into any disputed shooting, but it must be galling from the officer's point of view to be trained to a high level; to take part in umpteen armed operations without firing in anger; and then, on the very rare occasion that he does shoot and hit someone, to face probably years of suspension and several investigations during which he cannot ply the craft that shaped his occupational identity. Also, for those facing criminal charges, as happened to several officers following the Sussex shooting, they have to face the particularly humiliating process for a police officer of arrest and possibly a criminal trial. Indeed, it was five years into the Stanley case before the officers were arrested 'on suspicion of murder, gross negligence manslaughter and conspiracy to pervert the course of justice' (Bennetto, 2005; Squires and Kennison, 2010: 172). As Waddington (2005) puts it, there are two victims of a fatal shooting: the suspect and the officer who shot him. And, of course, the family and friends of both.

Oversight

A central issue in the area of investigations and oversight is that when, after some 150 years of the controllers controlling the controllers, there was eventually an agency to oversee complaints against the police, it was seen as feeble and toothless. The founding of the

Police Complaints Board (PCB) in 1976 was a step forward, but it and its successor in 1985, the Police Complaints Authority (PCA), were both severely limited by being reactive, reliant on someone formally making a complaint, by needing the police to conduct the investigation and by possessing no independent investigatory capacity. They were both subject to loud criticism, and public confidence in them was persistently low (Punch, 2009a: 204–8).

As a result the Independent Police Complaints Commission (IPCC) for England and Wales was set up in 2003 and became operational in 2004. It provided for the first time an external, independent oversight agency with an investigatory capacity. An important dimension was that it could mount an investigation without a complaint if the case was deemed in the public interest. In practice the IPCC still remains highly reliant on the police to conduct investigations on its behalf. Like many regulatory agencies it is not particularly liked by the profession it oversees. Police officers tend to see themselves as possessing high expertise in investigations and look down somewhat on those who aspire to investigate them or to supervise their investigations. In fact the IPCC and Office of Police Ombudsman for Northern Ireland (OPONI) have recruited experienced police officers as investigators, while the investigatory capacity of both agencies was initially shaped by senior officers from the Met (Roy Clarke and Dave Wood, respectively). This in turn has led to critical questioning about impartiality. Like other regulatory agencies the IPCC has to chart continually a path between being too close to the institution it oversees – with the risk of co-optation, if not capture – and being too adversarial, which only elicits antagonism and non-cooperation (Hawkins, 2002).

The IPCC's mandate included the capacity to spell out some of the lessons learned from the incident and the operation. This approach constitutes a paradigm shift in police oversight from primarily seeking blame to also examining lessons learned. It was initiated by OPONI in Belfast from 2000 onwards and this ties in, according to Squires and Kennison (2010), with the thrust of New Public Management and the emphasis on organisational learning through establishing best practice (Leishman et al, 2000). A TVP officer, for example, said of the Highmoor Cross shooting: 'We did the actual investigation, but the IPCC provided us with a seal of approval while it was valuable on helping us with the learning points' (interview, Gilmour). For some, this brings the IPCC a bit too close to the police, almost in a kind of coaching role.

The key factor remains in relation to investigating and commenting on serious incidents – does the IPCC contain sufficient expertise and insight on police use of firearms and on aspects of command and control?[7] One former ACC spoke of the IPCC as not being 'up to speed on developments, lacking awareness and making some simply outrageous statements in reports; they don't fully understand policy and practice on command and control' (interview, Golding). Waddington (2005) was also most sceptical and strongly disputed the interpretation of the Highmoor Cross shooting by Commissioner Glass, who was the lead on firearms for the IPCC. As mentioned earlier, he was critical of the IPCC report on that shooting, calling it 'disgraceful', because he believed that there was insufficient attention paid to the risks and subsequent costs that are inevitable with regard to operational decision-making. The thrust of the report amounted to 'after-the-fact, cost-free solutions' and a demand for 'freedom for error'. In criticising the long-standing culture of caution, Glass was neglecting the fact that often it was those who opened fire who landed in hot water precisely for alleged lack of caution, as in the shootings of Stanley, Groce, Ashley and Waldorf (personal communication, Waddington; see also Glass, 2007, 2008).

Oversight agencies often attract hostile and discrediting remarks and it is evident that the IPCC does not have the resources to tackle more than a fraction of the cases that come to its attention (IPCC, 2006, 2007d, 2008a). It will remain highly dependent on the police to carry out investigations on its behalf or under its supervision. The Home Affairs Committee (2010), for instance, reviewed the record of the IPCC and was quite sharp in its appraisal. Only 1% of complaints were directly investigated by the IPCC, leaving 99% involving police investigating police. The system, it was further argued, was too officer-oriented and insufficiently complainant-focused. There were serious delays in processing complaints; inexperienced junior staff had to cope with supervising investigations involving senior police officers; and there was a tendency to lean towards the police interpretation of matters. Both complainants and officers under investigation – and a former Commissioner – were dissatisfied with its operating style and procedures (Home Affairs Committee, 2010: 23–5).

Whatever the limitations of the IPCC, however, it was crucial on grounds of governance that there was finally an external agency that could independently investigate serious police deviance. It will doubtless be continually engaged in mulling over the balance to be established in its relationship with the agency it is designed both to investigate and to advise and on which it is reliant for examining the majority of its cases.

Conclusion: A culture of accountability?

The architecture of policing has altered rapidly in the UK in recent years (Neyroud, 2004). One significant feature since 2000 has been the rise of police oversight agencies in Northern Ireland (2000), England and Wales (2003) and Scotland (2009). An important innovation was, as noted, the founding of the IPCC, which means that for the first time since the formation of the New Police in 1829 there was an independent, impartial, investigatory agency to examine complaints against the police, including the mandate to investigate any police use of firearms leading to an injury or death. Furthermore, police chiefs have become imbued, it is said, with the 'new professionalism' geared to change, the media, government fads and fashions, but have also started to take constant accountability to stakeholders as an essential if time-consuming function (Blair, 2003).[8] There is, however, a danger here that the latest developments make accountability complex if not intricate, multilayered, shifting and potentially opaque. Indeed, McLaughlin (2005: 477) remarked: 'What was notable by its absence during the First New Labour administration was any form of principled discussion about the forms of democratically constituted accountability and governance appropriate to the radically altered policing environment of 21st Century Britain'. Accountability is also something of a container concept that has different meanings in diverse contexts (Marshall, 1987); and not surprisingly every one favours it in their rhetoric. The Patten Report (1999: 22) stated that accountability should run through the 'bloodstream' of a police force. Clearly the wider 'governance' of policing is pivotal to enhancing accountability and getting it into the 'bloodstream' of a force, but here the emphasis has very much been on the primacy of operational accountability, for on its foundations rest all of the other forms of accountability.

In brief, there is an ostensible shift to strengthening institutional accountability with a stronger measure of external oversight through a battery of governmental agencies and through the IPCC. What is more difficult to establish is how far a new *culture* of accountability permeates policing in the UK. There are senior officers who strongly espouse accountability and advocate 'embracing' it (Punch and Markham, 2006); and anecdotal evidence from discussions with a number of senior officers indicates that there is a reform movement in this area, but, they add, there is as yet no unanimity on implementing it.[9] For example, there is a vitally important principle encapsulated in the command and control model – reinforced by the pronouncement of Justice Rafferty in the Sussex case and the ECHR's *McCann* ruling – indicating that accountability should be drawn *upwards*. Gold, for instance, devolves *responsibility* while accepting final *accountability*. Potentially within this structure and philosophy Gold should be prepared to face legal action for operational decisions.[10] I say 'potentially' because along with structure there needs also to be a culture of accountability where senior officers are imbued with an ethic of accountability as fundamental to their functioning. Structure alone is not enough; the members of a police force have to *want* to be accountable.

This is vital because next to genuine mistakes and errors of judgement there are highly sensitive aspects of policing involving deception, civil and human rights, invasion of privacy, racial and sexual discrimination, corruption and perversion of justice, as well as controversial, disputed and excessive use of force where issues of personal, organisational and criminal culpability arise (Marx, 1988; Kleinig, 1996; Neyroud and Beckley, 2001). In brief, I am reiterating the literature's persistent message: that policing is at unpredictable moments a risky if not hazardous enterprise; that this needs to be fully recognised; and that the organisation has to anticipate and institutionalise its response to major and critical incidents, but especially those involving violence. Indeed, the nature of the police organisation's response to dealing with violence and its repercussions is often a crucial litmus test in determining the legitimacy and credibility of the police in the eyes of the public. In the summer of 2005 the Metropolitan Police faced such a test and it proved to be severe one.

Notes

[1] Two important examples are the Public Interest Disclosure Act 1998, which gave more rights and protection to whistle-blowers, and the Freedom of Information Act 2000, which came into force for the police from 2005.

[2] 'Ostensibly' because others would argue that there has been a corresponding increase in powers in other areas driven by the security and counter-terrorism (CT) agenda (Reiner, 2007).

[3] The operational audit trail was accompanied by a wider institutional audit trail detailing training, selection and monitoring of personnel, choice of weapons and selection of ammunition, while all policy and certification was reviewed and signed for on a quarterly basis.

[4] Anecdotal evidence recounts that control rooms could become the preserve of the halt, lame and lazy, making them the last resting post of operationally inadequate officers perhaps with a personality, or drinking, problem. One former AFO told me that on occasion control room officers receiving an urgent call from a firearms unit would simply not respond while they tried to find out what they were supposed to do as they were loath to take responsibility and might then say 'You're at the scene so why don't you decide?'.

[5] Waddington in a personal communication argues that even a 'Silver' authorised for firearms early in his or her career would soon 'be out of touch with contemporary practices' and that it would be financially 'unsupportable' to keep training them up to the appropriate standard.

[6] In the early 1990s there was a shortage of AFOs as a number had surrendered their authorisation following the prosecution of fellow officers (Waldren, 2007: 188).

[7] An IPCC Commissioner informed me regarding competency in investigations on shootings that there are a number of ex-police

investigators with experience as AFOs at the IPCC, while several Commissioners have been involved in diverse capacities with firearms use, in investigating firearms cases and in campaigns related to guns.

[8] Chief Constable Orde of the PSNI (2003) stated publicly that he welcomes OPONI and is geared to working with it constructively, although he warns of increased bureaucracy and oversight becoming dysfunctional with 12 agencies overseeing the PSNI. He told me at a meeting in September 2005 that he spends a great deal of time on oversight while the domestic political parties expect ready access to him, as do some American politicians with an interest in Northern Ireland.

[9] For a detailed consideration of this area see Markham and Punch (2007a, 2007b) and Punch and Markham (2006).

[10] The Gold Commander in charge of public order policing during a campaign of animal rights demonstrations in Essex was taken to court for giving instructions to officers that led to breaking a local ordinance. Initial legal advice was to place liability on an officer low in the operational hierarchy, but he insisted that the Gold Commander who carries operational accountability should also face liability for his decision. After three days in the dock he was acquitted (interview, Markham).

FIVE

The military paradigm: Stockwell, Kratos and the aftermath

> Never go for the head and limbs.... Always go for the trunk. Never shoot to disarm or disable.... Hold your breath, squeeze the trigger, shoot to kill.

> No warning shots.... No cowboy stuff. It's too dicey. You might hit a passer-by. No shooting at arms or legs.... Go for the big target. Shoot to kill.

> (Firearms instructions to paratroopers in Britain and soldiers in Northern Ireland, respectively, in Asher, 2004: 31, 99)

The long-standing, traditional position of civil policing in Britain is based on restraint, avoidance of violence, the application of the minimum force considered necessary and proportionate and, if possible, the preservation of life. This 'restraint paradigm' contrasts strongly with typical military-style operations that function under an alternative 'military paradigm'. A central issue here is the extent to which British policing has shifted from the restraint paradigm and moved closer to the military paradigm. This is crucial to assessing the Stockwell shooting in London in 2005, the 'Kratos' policy underpinning it and the long-term implications of that incident for policing.

The military paradigm: 'Close combat-style' operations

As shown in the quotes above, soldiers are trained to 'shoot to kill' in combat during armed conflict in a conventional war, as in Iraq, or during counter-insurgency operations, as in Northern Ireland. Warfare is a gruesome, brutal and savage trade and front-line infantry are taught to kill other soldiers without compunction and with crude and ruthless violence by gun, grenade, bayonet, knife, spade, pick-handle or bare hands (Ellis, 1982). The grim reality of combat in warfare is a far cry from conventional policing in civil society.

This dichotomy is even more the case with Special Forces who are trained for certain high-risk and sometimes covert missions that include fighting behind enemy lines, Close Quarter Battle (CQB), ambushes, abductions, assassinations, rescue missions and attacking a stronghold (Asher, 2004, 2008). In the UK the SAS in particular has been central to training other military units for counter-insurgency and diverse other roles for four decades, but especially in Northern Ireland during the Troubles (Urban, 1993). It has also been influential since the early 1980s in policing with regard to preparing officers for certain types of tough operation such as 'rapid entry' to premises.

In Britain the military have no authority to mount any form of operational action, have no independent powers to use force outside of a number of secure locations and do not carry loaded firearms. Furthermore, in peacetime the armed forces are subject to the civil authorities, with the police having primacy on the use of force. In certain grave circumstances, however, the armed forces may be asked to assist the civil authorities, as with disasters, civil emergencies and matters of national security. This is known as 'Military Aid to the Civil Power' (MACP) and there are guidelines agreed on this between the Home Office and Ministry of Defence. MACP will be invoked when there are major incidents that exceed a police organisation's ability and resources to make an adequate response. This is likely to occur, say, with a siege with politically motivated hostage-takers or with a hijacked plane from abroad, where lives are in imminent danger from a person or group with weapons and/or explosives and where storming the building, oil rig or plane is deemed necessary. This form of military assistance at grave, counter-insurgency incidents of a 'political' nature – and involving what are considered externally generated 'terrorist' activities rather than domestic 'criminal' ones – typically means Special Forces and usually the SAS.[1]

In the Iranian Embassy siege in London in 1980, for instance, the Metropolitan Commissioner decided that an assault to free the hostages was beyond police capabilities and he approached the Home Secretary. The Cabinet Office Briefing Room (COBRA) was activated to deal with the crisis. COBRA is comprised of senior officials who coordinate information and activities at the governmental level. The Commissioner at the time of the siege, McNee (1983: 146–67), emphasises that the police alone were responsible for the conduct of the operation and, to preserve their operational independence, they were not members of COBRA. The key decision as to whether or not to negotiate with the terrorists was, however, taken at the cabinet level and this was a resounding 'no'. At the request of the Commissioner, the Home Secretary then called in the SAS; he doubtless had an arrangement on this with the Minister of Defence and presumably consulted the Prime Minister as well.[2]

When the military are invited in, the civil authorities and police formally 'sign over' the operation to the military. This signifies that the military are responsible for 'command and control' during their part of the operation. The military and the police will also draw up a 'Limits of Exploitation' agreement to establish the demarcation in roles and functions between military and police (Collins, 1998: 177). During the Iranian Embassy assault the military had primacy for about 45 minutes and then signed the operation back over to the police (McNee, 1983). This arrangement does not mean that legal responsibility for the use of force has changed. Ostensibly the same law continues to apply to the soldiers as to police officers, and the soldiers involved can be held to account in court for their conduct during the operation. For instance, although there was an emergency situation in Northern Ireland during the Troubles, martial law had not been declared and several soldiers were prosecuted and convicted for firearms offences including murder (McKittrick and McVea, 2001: 297). Soldiers can also be required to attend an inquest. In practice, however, other norms of accountability operate than with police officers. It is standard that immediately after an operation the soldiers will be rapidly removed to be debriefed and also coached by the Army's Legal Service; only then are they available to give statements to the police.

The SAS enjoys an especially fearsome reputation (Newsinger, 1997). The image is that few survive its operations, with republicans in Northern Ireland dubbing it the 'Special Assassination Squad' (Geraghty, 2000: 121). In fact, on a number of occasions where it was deemed appropriate, the SAS has taken prisoners and has exercised restraint in opening fire, and among police and others its members are respected as highly professional.[3] However, Urban (1993) refers to the SAS operating under a set of 'Big Boys' Rules', which means that when they go into action its soldiers are utterly determined and highly aggressive and at times the tactics and firepower they employ lead to 'collateral damage' with injuries to bystanders. It is plain, moreover, that when storming a building, ship or aeroplane containing insurgents with weapons and/or explosives, who are directly threatening the lives of those held captive and of those mounting the attack, the assault unit of soldiers is going to continue firing until all danger is eliminated. This practice was acknowledged by the ECHR in the *McCann* case. Typically there will be several shots to the head, taking into account that the suspect may be wearing body armour, and several to the vital organs of the body. This approach may mean that a hostage-taker who has put down his or her weapon and shows a willingness to surrender is shot dead; and the use of multiple shots at close range will clearly almost always result in death. The justification would be that an assault team entering a confined space with vulnerable hostages and armed suspects who are threatening the hostages and the assault team with danger, and who have perhaps already killed hostages or others, will not take the risk that a suspect will fake surrender and remain capable of firing a concealed weapon or setting off an explosive device by remote control. However, as mentioned regarding the Gibraltar shootings, the legality of this is somewhat questionable, although in the political and media euphoria following that mission the legality issue was not seriously raised in official circles.

The military-style, CQB operation was graphically illustrated when the SAS ended the Iranian Embassy siege in London, for the SAS units were clearly filmed by TV cameras when they spectacularly entered the Embassy of the Islamic Republic of Iran to rescue hostages being held by a separatist insurgent group demanding autonomy for a region within Iran and the release of prisoners (Asher, 2009: 1–21). After several days the negotiations had stalled and the hostage-takers had shot dead a hostage, thrown his body out of the door and were threatening to kill more hostages. Clad in black coveralls and with respirators over their faces, the SAS units attacked from several points including abseiling down on ropes from the roof to the balconies; they used explosives to gain entry through windows and threw stun-grenades to disorient the hostage-takers. They inadvertently set some curtains alight and a fire began to spread. As a result of the rescue action most of the remaining hostages were rescued unhurt and five of the six hostage-takers were killed.

Some 20 years after the embassy siege and the rescue, the BBC transmitted a TV documentary about the SAS operation with officials, survivors and SAS personnel talking of their experiences (BBC TV, 2003).[4] Generally the SAS is highly secretive and its operatives are not normally identified, but here some former members spoke openly about the operation while others did so incognito. They made it absolutely plain that they felt they had been given the green light from 'above' to kill the hostage-takers. One of them claimed that he was led to believe that Prime Minister Thatcher would be considerably embarrassed if her government had to deal with a hostage-taker in captivity who had survived the operation. Afterwards when the Prime Minister with her husband was congratulating the SAS troops on their successful operation her husband Denis is reported as saying with a grin, 'You let one of the bastards live' (BBC TV, 2003).

In the eyes of the assault troops, the mission was, first, to eliminate the hostage-takers, even if they had put down their weapons and were trying to surrender, and, second, to rescue the hostages. This conduct was confirmed by some of the hostages who saw two of the insurgents trying to surrender and being put against a wall and shot. Indeed, prior to that they had waved a white cloth out of the window as a sign of surrender, thrown away their weapons and were sitting with their hands on their heads.[5] One soldier said that there was confusion when the hostages were being rushed out of the burning building and he spied a hostage-taker escaping down the stairs. He was separated from the hostages and shot. Another hostage-taker escaped into the garden; a soldier thought of dragging him back into the building in order to shoot him, but was warned that there were too many witnesses and cameras present. Presumably the thinking was that these were armed and dangerous terrorists who had already killed and who had to be eliminated to erase any possible risk to the soldiers and hostages, such as someone pretending to surrender but then throwing a grenade. Indeed, the insurgent shot when trying to hide among the hostages coming down the stairs had a grenade in his hand, but luckily he had not removed the safety-pin and it did not explode.

There would doubtless have been no explicit orders to 'take out' the hostage-takers, while the formal assignment apparently spoke of '*minimum force*'. But the SAS unit clearly went in with their own operational assumption that they would take no risks and would eliminate the hostage-takers. Much would depend on the briefing they were given and the signals it conveyed; but obviously we are not privy to that briefing (which is classified: Asher, 2009). Due to surveillance those in command as well as the attacking units would have been fully aware of the conversations within the building, the nature of the arms available to the insurgents, their deliberations about resisting an attack and their threats to kill more hostages. The insurgents possessed an assortment of weapons, including machine guns and handguns, as well as grenades and explosives. During the assault on the building, 'minimum force' became translated into shooting the hostage-takers multiple times; apparently one was riddled with some 80 bullets although another source mentions 20 (Squires and Kennison, 2010: 73). As minimum force is nowhere defined, the SAS members could argue that this was the minimum force legitimately required under these extreme circumstances.

In short, military operations of a counter-insurgency sort in support of the civil authorities operate under a different operational 'paradigm' to that in policing. Unlike police officers, soldiers operate with the obligation to abide by specific orders, which will limit their individual autonomy; their authority to shoot comes from their position in a hierarchy of command and not from their individual authority (as with 'constables'); and they will also typically employ in counter-terrorism (CT) actions considerable firepower at close range and will continue to fire until the target has been hit in the head and/or vital organs many times. This is in a sense more than 'shoot to kill', which could be accomplished with less firepower; it is close-quarters shooting designed to *eliminate* any possible element of continuing danger.

Here the example of the Iranian Embassy siege has been used to illustrate the 'military paradigm' when the armed forces are employed in support of the police and civil authorities in major incidents with the use of almost certain fatal force. The Gibraltar operation involving the IRA and SAS is another illustration but, as we have seen in Chapter One, it has gained a wider significance through the ECHR's *McCann* judgment. For example, the ECHR argued that if the Gibraltar operation was primarily a police operation designed to arrest, then why were the military involved? This transmitted the message that such an operation was best handled by the police and not the military. It may well have been that soldiers had been used in such operations not just because of their specific skills, but also because their highly aggressive style attracted far less criticism than if the police were involved. However, there then followed the *McCann* judgment, concern among some politicians about too much involvement of the military in civil matters and the wish among the military only to be used for the most serious of scenarios. This led to setting clearer demarcation guidelines in 1989 (Waldren, 2007: 146). These factors doubtless helped shape police firearms policy in requiring that the police train for far more demanding operations, which took them at times closer to the military style, if not military paradigm.

Furthermore, some critics would say that the Iranian Embassy siege and the Gibraltar incident are both significant in revealing how the state cynically abuses its power in answer to threats and in ruthlessly eliminating its enemies. They would baldly call the Gibraltar shootings cold-blooded murder and the killing of unarmed insurgents attempting to surrender inside the Iranian Embassy a form of summary execution (Williams, 1989). In practice such incidents tend to elicit political, public and media euphoria at the 'successful' removal of a serious threat. Indeed, the global coverage of the televised assault on the Iranian Embassy turned the then relatively unknown SAS into a household name and its soldiers into instant heroes (Asher, 2009). But surrounding the understandable relief and predictable self-congratulation that envelops such operations, there does seem to be a wilful suspension of legality regarding the use of force by the military in certain anti-terrorist operations.

In contrast there can be no better example of the difference from the restraint paradigm than the conduct of PC Trevor Lock. Lock was on armed duty as a Diplomatic Protection officer inside the Embassy when the hostage-takers burst in. He learned later during the siege that if he had been standing outside and had resisted he would have been shot. Lock turned out to be a considerate, resilient and resourceful officer who managed to conceal his weapon during the entire siege. When it became clear that the SAS was launching an attack on the building, Lock courageously tackled one of the hostage-takers who was preparing to fire at the soldiers and held his gun to the man's head. By so doing he almost certainly saved the life of one or more of the rescuers. Lock was shouted at to move over and the by now unarmed hostage-taker was then shot by the SAS unit. Lock said he did not fire himself, which under those extreme circumstances he was perfectly entitled to do, because his training had instilled him with the guideline that an officer should only use minimum force to effect an arrest and also not to kill if that could be avoided (Waddington, 1991: 19). The shooting at Stockwell that I shall now examine was based on quite different values and premises than those held by PC Lock.

Stockwell: The external context

> Ian, find the fuckers. (Home Secretary to the Metropolitan Commissioner, Ian Blair, 2009: 10)

On 7 July 2005 the Met had to cope with four suicide bomb attacks on the public transport system of London with the blasts causing 52 deaths and more than 700 casualties. The shock to all in the city and beyond was immense and the searing images on global television networks of the wounded and dying emerging from the underground, and being carried away from the mangled bus, were horrifying. The scenes in the dark and narrow underground tunnels and in the wrangled tube carriages with the dead, dying and injured were appalling (Zimonjic, 2008). There was both a powerful public sense of resolve and a pervasive fear of more attacks; people who were there at the time said there was an eerie sense of tension in the city (interview, Janet Foster).

That traumatic day for the capital, the most violent since WWII, was followed by the second shock of four failed suicide attacks on 21 July. A fifth device was also located outside of the city centre (IPCC, 2007a). Again those four efforts were aimed at the public transport system with the likelihood of mass casualties; and, as in the previous incidents, they were conducted by young radical Muslims.

There had been a series of major attacks in previous years by radical Muslim groups in other countries on high-profile targets associated with Western states such as embassies, warships and international hotels. The most dramatic and bloody were the '9/11' attacks in the US in September 2001, with over 3,000 fatalities, which were carried out by radical Muslims using aeroplanes for their suicide mission. Britain's role in Iraq and Afghanistan and its support for the US in the 'Global War on Terror' had made the UK, and London in particular, a likely target. Indeed, experts had been saying 'it's not if but when'. The pattern elsewhere had been of large explosions at conspicuous locations causing many casualties and great damage. In Madrid in 2004, for example, several bombs had exploded on a number of trains in the morning rush hour to devastating effect, leaving nearly 200 people dead and hundreds injured in one of the worst terrorist attacks in Western Europe.[6] The Madrid bombings were not suicide attacks, but in the search for the terrorists, their associates and the possible bomb factory, the police approached suspect premises and those inside blew themselves up killing one officer and wounding others. British police had long been used to IRA violence and threats but the IRA became selective in its choice of targets, did not seek mass casualties, often gave a warning and never employed suicide missions (English, 2004). Also, the IRA had been infiltrated on a grand scale, and its operations and members were subject to intense scrutiny by the agents and technology of the British intelligence community.

This new style of terrorism influenced thinking on the approach to the suspects of 21 July, particularly as the '7/7' bombers had left a car at Luton Station on their way to London that contained powerful explosives, anti-personnel devices and a firearm with armour-piercing bullets. This indicated that any attempt to stop them in the car would probably have led to an attack on the police involved, if not to a massive explosion that 'could have blown the side off an armoured vehicle' (interview, Commander Carter). Complicating matters was the fact that in both London incidents the offenders were not to be found in the intelligence databanks and were not on the security services' 'radar'.

After the 7/7 bombings, London had been placed on the highest level of alert ever seen following the threat assessment of the Joint Terrorist Analysis Centre (JTAC).[7] This warned of the imminence of more serious attacks. What subsequently happened needs to be interpreted in the light of this extraordinary situation, which put all concerned under the most intense pressure. At one stage there was even a Chemical, Biological, Radioactive and Nuclear (CBRN) alert, and at another stage Buckingham Palace, Parliament and New Scotland Yard (NSY) were put on an unprecedented 'lockdown' for a short time. Everybody closely involved was working virtually around the clock, with 30 or even 40 hours on the go being the norm, and all were 'running on adrenaline' (according to the interview with Commander Carter, which informs this section).

There were four or perhaps five bombers on the run who could strike again and they almost certainly had accomplices, probably with a bomb factory. There was also a growing stream of calls from the public about young men with backpacks who fitted the descriptions and who were behaving 'suspiciously' on public transport or elsewhere. At the start of 22 July there were several suspected premises, but that rose to double figures during the day. This was, then, an unprecedented situation with four or more failed suicide bombers who were loose in London or elsewhere. No one anywhere had ever contemplated this scenario.

In brief, following the bombings of 21 July the Met had immediately mobilised a manhunt to locate the suspects and any associates who had not been apprehended and who were possibly planning further attacks. The resources of the Met were severely stretched. Intelligence pointed initially at several premises where the suspects might be residing. Armed police teams were on call from SO19 to make arrests. The aim of operation 'Theseus 2', hastily mounted after the events of 21 July and planned for 22 July, was explicitly to *apprehend and detain* the suspects.

One particular building was being watched because two suspects, one a Hussain Osman, had been traced to those premises. Initially everyone emerging from the flat under surveillance was to be apprehended and screened, but it turned out that the flat did not have a separate exit and there was a communal exit to the complex. A young male in his twenties, Jean Charles de Menezes, became viewed as a possible suspect after he left the building. He was followed, on the assumption that he might be Osman, on his journey to work and eventually onto an underground train at Stockwell Station. At no time was an effort made to apprehend him, as there was some confusion about identification. Nevertheless the urgent command was given by a senior officer at NSY to prevent him getting onto an underground train and possibly causing an explosion. On the assumption that he was positively identified and capable of setting off a bomb attached to his body, his arms were held by one of the surveillance team who had followed him on to the train. Two members of the SO19 firearms squad, which had rushed to the scene, shot him seven times in the head, neck and shoulder at point-blank range (1–8 centimetres). It later emerged that the victim, who died on the spot, was a Brazilian citizen who had worked legally in London for several years, had no links to terrorist activity whatsoever, had no bomb and was not armed. Mr de Menezes had been wrongly identified as one of the suspected bombers (IPCC, 2007a).

There can only be one consequence of shooting someone in the head seven times at close range and that is *death*. Indeed, the muzzle-blast by itself is usually fatal at that range (Bunker, 2005a; interview, Waddington). The intention was to incapacitate the brain and hence prevent the bomber from carrying out an explosion by triggering the device. Moreover, the police had used special 'hollow-point' ammunition designed to spread on impact. This was also meant to avoid penetration in a closed environment such as a plane or train or in a busy place with a 'backdrop' where bystanders would be vulnerable to a conventional round that had penetrated a suspect. This type of bullet, often colloquially referred to as a 'dum-dum' after a colonial Indian munitions factory, is banned in conventional warfare as covered by Articles of the Hague Convention (1899) because of the horrifying, gaping wounds it causes. However, rather incongruously, this ban does not apply to domestic law enforcement. Hollow-point ammunition is widely used in US policing, and in the UK individual police chiefs may decide which ammunition to employ, within Home Office specifications. In the early 1990s, however, hollow-point ammunition was viewed as 'illegal' within SO19 in London, and on occasion the Home Office had not approved certain ammunition precisely because it caused 'enormous injuries' (Waddington, 1991: 90; Squires and Kennison, 2010: 13). It seems surprising, then, that at the time of Stockwell some senior officers and the Commissioner were unaware of its existence within the Met.[8]

With Stockwell there can be no shadow of doubt that a *fundamental shift in policy* on police use of firearms in Britain had taken place, and this dramatically became evident to the press and public when the full details of the policy driving practice started to become known.

The 'Kratos' policy

This radical shift represents a formally legitimate policy, but one that has not been debated or made explicit in public for security reasons. It has been referred to as 'Kratos', the guidelines of which allowed officers to aim for the head at close range in cases of suicide attacks (Kennison and Loumansky, 2007). In fact there were two protocols, known as 'Kratos' and 'Clydesdale', for two separate scenarios. Clydesdale envisaged prior intelligence of a suicide attack at a large-scale event, which meant the command structure could be put in place for a pre-planned operation. Kratos was for spontaneous events involving possible suicide bombers, say, resulting from a call from a member of the public, and where there was the possibility of an explosive device being utilised. Previously at major public order incidents the role of 'Designated Senior Officer' (DSO) had been devised, which ensured that a senior officer was present who could grant authorisation for the use of baton rounds (colloquially known as 'rubber bullets'). That role was now adapted for the suicide bomber threat and a cadre of DSOs was trained for this function. For Clydesdale a DSO could be allocated in advance, and for Kratos there was a duty DSO available at NSY on a 24/7 basis. The essence of both protocols was that the DSO had the authority to authorise what is known as a 'critical head shot'. This was a shot or shots at the brainstem; aiming at the back of the head without warning and preferably at very short range from behind; and on the 'instruction' from the DSO. Within the Met both protocols became referred to collectively as Kratos, and I shall use that term.

Kratos had never been discussed openly because of the security considerations. It was a matter debated internally by the police, experts on use of firearms and officials from the Home Office (IPCC, 2007a), but ACPO would have retained primacy in the decision-making. The formulation of the policy commenced originally in the Met, which carries national responsibility for counter-terrorism, in a paper entitled 'Kratos people' in 2003 (IPCC, 2007a). Senior Met officers and others had visited some 20 countries to research this area, but Commander Carter was at pains to convey that the policy itself was formally shaped within ACPO in the 'Terrorism and Allied Matters' (TAM) Committee. This received input from the joint intelligence community and also from David Veness of the Met, who was then national head of counter-terrorism with extensive knowledge of Special Operations. The Committee had identified six areas related to threats defined as 'Deadly and Dangerous', referred to in TAM as 'DaDa', of which one focused on operations. There is always a Home Office representative on all ACPO committees to keep the Home Office informed; and on this sensitive topic Sir John Gieve, the Home Office Permanent Secretary, was fully informed. In London, moreover, the MPA was given a confidential briefing on Kratos. The policy was then routed to all forces from ACPO; given the formal autonomy of the separate forces, each police chief could decide whether or not to implement it. It was clear, however, that the Met faced the strongest likelihood of an attack and presumably a number of other forces faced more risk than others; but it is not known if other forces have ever issued an authorisation for Kratos.

Kratos indicated a fundamental change of direction with regard to the police use of firearms, which meant that operations, procedures, tactics, training, ammunition and firing position – inches rather than yards – had been indelibly altered. Crucially, the British police themselves had adopted the right to apply armed force in certain operations with only one possible and fully intended result – *killing people*.

Precisely how that decision to alter policy radically was taken is unclear, and exactly when the specific orders were given to change tactics, training and ammunition is shrouded in secrecy. At some stage experienced firearms officers, who had been brought up for years, and programmed, with a particular philosophy and practice on the use of their weapons, must have been told that they would have to learn and implement something new that contradicted everything they had previously practised. However, some details emerged at the Health and Safety trial, the inquest and in the IPCC report into Stockwell.

In brief, following the rise of suicide attacks in several countries, but particularly after the devastating 9/11 attacks in the US in 2001, governments and security forces in countries deemed at risk were confronted with the predicament of how to tackle suicide bombers utilising diverse methods. These included those bombers who had an explosive device on their person as was the case in both sets of attacks in London. Unusually they all carried backpacks, whereas most bombers have some form of 'waistcoat' or belt that contains the explosives concealed under their clothing. This can give off indicators that raise suspicions such as wearing overcoats even in warm weather, having a 'bulky' appearance and being seen to be labouring under the weight. The deployment of 'human bombs' had been used especially in Sri Lanka, Israel and Chechnya and it has spread to militants in Iraq, Pakistan and Afghanistan, where it has been employed to devastating effect.

All Western countries at risk were doubtless aware of this lethal practice and of the dilemmas of combating it. The notion of a fatal head shot, moreover, has long been commonplace in sniping and assassinations (Collins, 2008; interview, Waddington). This knowledge had been tied to CT tactics in relation to suicide bombers in the last decade by a number of sources, but most explicitly for law enforcement by Bunker in America (2005a, 2005b). It also emerged in the British media before 2005, but did not arouse much attention at the time (Orr-Munro, 2003). Legal advice was sought from a Treasury Counsel, who maintained that the method was legally acceptable within HR law and was compliant with Article 2 ('right to life') of the EConvHR. This was on the understanding that the deadly shooting was a 'clearly defined last resort approach' (IPCC, 2007a: 14, 40). The Hague Convention is not mentioned in this context in the IPCC report, presumably because, conveniently, it does not apply to situations outside of conventional armed conflict.

The Stockwell shooting: Key elements that shaped fault

The shooting of Mr de Menezes was highly controversial for two principal reasons. First, from Peel onwards there was a carefully nurtured mythology that the British police were unarmed and, if armed, would exercise restraint. Stockwell was a rude awakening for the nation, shocking them out of that comforting myth and confronting them with the harsh reality of contemporary firearms policy and practice. Second, it is crucial in a Kratos-type operation that you identify and shoot the right person. This plainly holds for all police use of firearms, but it holds even more so under Kratos because when police set out fully determined to kill someone they simply have to get it right because there is no hope of survival. Also, however, when dealing with a possible suicide bomber, police cannot afford to get it wrong. That excruciating dilemma was the burden pressing down on everyone that day.

Indeed, if the Met had got it right there would have been satisfaction at stopping a terrorist attack and preventing umpteen casualties. That was the initial positive reaction at NSY – that possibly a serious explosion with high casualties had been averted – before the sobering news of the victim's innocence arrived. For some officers this message only reached them the day after. There would doubtless have been some critical questions on method afterwards even if Mr de Menezes had been a suicide bomber. However, in getting it wrong the Met was exposed to a harsh spotlight focusing on the suddenly revealed method, and then this turned to a scrutiny of the issue of accountability: who could be held to account for this fatal error? What is clear is that Stockwell was a seriously flawed operation that was part of a wider institutional failure on the part of the Met surrounding the incident. Kratos, however, was not exclusively a Met policy, and other forces across the country had prepared for deploying it.

All police forces were on high alert, but the Met in particular was under intense pressure in an unprecedented situation. With little or no rest, officers were, during the evening and night of 21 July, planning an operation for the very next day. When reading the diverse accounts about the Stockwell shooting, one can see the traces, as in so many accounts of major accidents and disasters, of the accumulating errors, fatigue, miscommunications and misperceptions that build up to failure and in some cases lead to catastrophe. This may not be related to deficiency in the quality of those involved as it can be those who are well trained and with wide experience who inadvertently end up taking the path to disaster (Weick, 1990 ; Vaughan, 1996). Major incidents where the main players are confronted with unanticipated challenges are pressure-cooker events where decision-making is dependent on a range of variables including information, time, perceptions, planning, communication, personalities, prior training to test competencies and ability to cope with the unforeseen. They can cruelly expose personal and institutional weaknesses and vulnerabilities when they go wrong (Flin, 1996; O'Hara, 2005). Stockwell can be seen as what is known in impolite circles as a 'cluster-fuck', where all that could go wrong did go wrong (Collins, 1998). Indeed, the former Commissioner referred to it as a 'perfect storm' (Blair, 2009: 164).

Furthermore, one has to appreciate that things often *do* go wrong in operations. They can be replete with confusion, miscommunication, noisy control rooms, windows of opportunity that open and are missed, and errors of judgement. In the cold light of day some features of the Met response may seem messy and inadequate, but they were not unusual for some large, fast-moving events and certainly not for one of such an unprecedented nature.

The dramatic events of 22 July and the consequences arising from it have been extensively depicted and analysed. The material includes two IPCC investigations (IPCC, 2007a, 2007b); a report by the Metropolitan Police Authority (MPA, 2008); an inquest with its transcripts available on the internet; a trial in which the Met was prosecuted and convicted under Health and Safety (H&S) law; extensive media coverage in print and on TV, including a BBC TV (2006) *Panorama* documentary by Peter Taylor, entitled 'Countdown to killing'; academic commentary, including by Kennison and Loumansky (2007) and Squires and Kennison (2010); and memoirs by several leading officers including the former Commissioner, Ian Blair (2009), and a former senior Met officer, Brian Paddick (2008).

The purpose here is to examine specifically the processes leading to the manner of the shooting and the implications arising from that killing. It is not the intention to focus on individual fault, but rather on institutional failure. The key players have been subject to investigation by the IPCC; some appeared at a trial against the Metropolitan Police; and some were witnesses under oath at the inquest lasting several weeks, where they faced intensive cross-examination (including by the formidable QC Michael Mansfield). The trial was against the organisation, but the organisation was personified by key individuals, who in effect were put in the dock to face personal scrutiny, while the prolonged and detailed inquest virtually amounted to a muted form of public inquiry that replayed much of the testimony of the trial.

In particular I interpret from the material and interviews that Met officers had been preparing for a Kratos operation. Although Kratos was not formally announced, they collectively took the path that brought them to the implementation of Kratos practice in the meaning of a 'critical' shot to the head of an identified suicide bomber. Initially, Theseus 2 for 22 July was not viewed as a Clydesdale operation nor as a Kratos operation, but there appears to be a measure of ambivalence in the preparations and mindset of those involved. In brief the key elements were as follows:

- The Designated Senior Officer (DSO) for the operation, Commander Cressida Dick, was asked to report for duty early on 22 July. The two duty DSOs, one for night and one for day duty, had conferred late at night and decided that they were likely to be tied up on their respective shifts reacting to the anticipated high number of calls about suspicious people and that a separate

DSO was required for the 'proactive' search for the suspects. However, a DSO is precisely meant to take charge of a Kratos-type operation. Yet Dick never deemed it a Kratos operation and the two firearms officers who pulled the triggers never saw it formally as Kratos either.

- Implementing Kratos would have meant that the DSO formally authorised the SO19 members to use a critical head shot and they would have carried out that 'order' with stealth, no warning and no police identification. Unlike Clydesdale there was no codeword for Kratos.

- The operation focused on two residential properties. One of the failed bombers had been traced to a flat at the premises through a sports-club membership card in his discarded rucksack. When Mr de Menezes left through the communal door the observers could not know which flat he had just left or where he would go. In fact he then got on a bus, whereas the strategy had been to apprehend suspects away from the premises, but before they entered the public transport system, which was the most likely target.

- In turn that strategy depended on two key elements: one was the presence of SO19 units to conduct the arrest and the other was the identification of the suspect as a possible suicide bomber. It soon became plain that the strategy was not being implemented and, having set it, the Gold Commander took no active part in the operation, although Gold is essential to the command structure.[9]

- With regard to the first element, the firearms teams had not arrived at the premises and were hence unable to make an arrest. The fresh firearms team did not come on duty until seven o'clock and their briefing and kitting out would take some time. The team on duty during the night was in fact available and even at NSY, but was not sent as the control room was unaware of its presence elsewhere in the building. Surveillance had commenced just after six o'clock and three hours later both SO19 teams had still not arrived at the premises. The team members were in fact fairly close, but reported later that there was no sense of urgency.

- Second, with regard to identification there were flaws at the surveillance level. Images of the four suspects of 21 July had been recovered from CCTV and there was the sports-club membership card of Osman. Osman was a dark-skinned East African. Mr de Menezes was a white, European-looking Brazilian; yet he was described variously by the surveillance team as white and as North African. On his leaving the building, a soldier working with the police on surveillance duties was allegedly urinating and did not get a good look at him, but advised that it was worth taking 'another look' at de Menezes. He was recorded consistently in logs as not identified, with one log even stating he was not the suspect and the surveillance should be called off.

- However, de Menezes' movements – getting off and then on the same bus, busily phoning – started to become interpreted as counter-surveillance tactics, and his behaviour as 'furtive' and 'jumpy'.[10] Everyone was under increasing tension as what had been meant to be a standard operation to apprehend and screen suspects had turned into 'fast time' once this suspect had reached public transport. The conduct of de Menezes was increasingly being interpreted as suspicious and this built up towards jumping to a positive identification.

- Indeed, what pressurised everyone was that there had been a series of failures to identify the suspect positively from the moment he left the premises. This meant that the suspect started on a journey during which, without an identification of him having been made, a number of opportunities to apprehend him were consequently missed.

- The worst-case scenario was that a bomber would enter the underground system. Three of the 7/7 bombers and three of the 21 July bombers had taken the tube, and the latter had all commenced their journey at Stockwell Station; and this suspect was on a bus going towards Stockwell Station. The demands increased for identification as de Menezes approached the station, and officers started to use phrases like 'it's him, he's very jumpy', while another reported 'they can't give a percentage but they believe it's him'. The suspect got off the bus, walked towards the station entrance, picked up a free newspaper and used his pre-paid card to pass through the turnstiles. On the escalator he ran to catch the train, which was about to depart.

- The DSO in the control room at NSY had by now become convinced that she had received a positive identification although no one recalls giving one (IPCC, 2007a: 59):

> At this time our investigation has revealed that none of the surveillance team had positively identified the subject as Nettle Tip [the codename for the suspect]. Furthermore none of them agree that they heard anyone communicate that it was a definite positive identification. Conversely it seems that the Senior Officers in Room 1600 and the [SO19] team including DCI C all believed that a positive identification had been established. As [SO19] reached Stockwell, the Firearms Team Leader 'Ralph' heard over the radio that: 'it was definitely our man and that he was nervous and twitchy'.

- Consequently the DSO ordered that the suspect should be prevented from entering the station and getting on the train, saying urgently, 'Stop him'. Later she stated that by 'stop' she literally meant stop as an understood police term to intervene and prevent entry to the station; furthermore, she *never* indicated that a 'critical head shot' was appropriate.[11]
- Three factors shaped the response of the firearms teams. First, and this is fundamental, authorisation for firearms use had to be given prior to the operation otherwise the weapons could not be withdrawn from the armoury. Firearms officers have to withdraw their weaponry with the appropriate authorisation each time they go into action.[12] The firearms teams on the morning of the operation were issued with various weapons and equipment including hollow-point ammunition ('9 mm 124 grain h.p. bullets'; IPCC, 2007d: 79).[13] Kratos meant that if the officers fired their weapons with a critical shot to the head at close range *they would shoot to kill*. They could have done this with standard issue ammunition, which they had with them, but this would not only have risked blowing the head apart, but also would have endangered any others within the 'backdrop' due to over-penetration. This choice of ammunition must have influenced

their mind-set, however, as hollow-point ammunition was meant specifically for Kratos-type situations. They could perhaps have used that particular ammunition in other ways than at close range but their options had been considerably narrowed.[14]

- Second, the briefing of the SO19 teams informed them that they would be facing a deadly and dangerous opponent and that they might have to do something they had never done before. It is worth recalling the ECHR's *McCann* judgment, which pointed to the importance of the briefing in setting the mindset of firearms teams before a major operation. The briefing before Stockwell was not recorded or written down.

- Third, there had been no attempt to apprehend the suspect before he reached the station. The strategy was that SO19 units would be present at the premises, but this had not occurred and once de Menezes started his journey the firearms teams were running after events. They were battling through traffic to get to the station in time when they heard of a positive identification. These three elements must have heightened the tension in the teams and primed them for Kratos.

- At the command level there appeared to be no contingency plan for when the strategy was evidently seen not to be working. One possibility raised in the IPCC report was that part of the SO12 (Special Branch) surveillance team or the accompanying unit from SO13 (Anti-terrorism Branch) could have moved to apprehend the suspect.[15] This reticence to intervene and to apprehend became crucial once de Menezes entered the station and crossed the ticket-barrier.

- By now the firearms teams had become convinced by the messages on the radio and the urgent tone of the DSO that this was 'their man' and they were facing a genuine suicide bomber. Without waiting for their team leader to announce 'Code Red' – meaning move to intervention – several members jumped out of their cars and started to rush towards the station. When those firearms officers ran down the escalators at Stockwell Station they must have been ready to shoot the suspect without hesitation if the situation demanded it. Both testified at the inquest that they had still not yet formed that intention at that stage. A surveillance officer prevented the train from leaving by putting his foot in the door; with the SO19 officers running towards the train he pointed at de Menezes and called out 'That's him'. There was some shouting outside and de Menezes stood up and started towards them for the door as some other passengers were doing.

- The surveillance officer, thinking that de Menezes was 'closing him down' and might be about to explode a device, pinned his arms to his body, grappled with him and pushed him back into a seat. The first armed officer leaned over him and fired three bullets at de Menezes' head at point-blank range; the second armed officer rushed up, joined the melée and fired six times; one bullet missed and one misfired requiring the officer to clear the stoppage before continuing firing.

- Their firm belief, the two SO19 officers later stated, was that the suspect was a suicide bomber about to cause an explosion with ordinary members of the public as his victims and that, given the level of danger to all in the train, including themselves, they had no option but to open fire.[16] They had fired nine shots, of which five bullets entered the head, with one entering the neck and one the shoulder. They continued firing when he fell to the ground because they could not aim at his brainstem and had to make sure the danger was eliminated. The officers were besmirched with 'debris' and later they were in a state of some distress (IPCC, 2007a: 64f).

The two firearms officers at Stockwell were absorbed in the most serious incident they had ever encountered. Both were highly experienced and competent and had been on many operations, but neither had ever before fired a shot in anger. They reacted on the spur of the moment to their perception of what was happening on the basis of the information and briefing they had received and the training they had been given. Their part in the drama was over in a few seconds. They would have been completely unaware that they had rewritten policing history.

Kratos or not?

In retrospect the key factor in the flawed operation appears to have been ambivalence over the nature of the operation prior to its commencement. At the command level, moreover, there was ambivalence in the role of the DSO. This was an operation where the events were dictating the responses and there did not seem to be the controlled, strategic hand of a 'Gold' Commander at work. The standard practice in a firearms operation according to the ACPO Manual is that Silver is the key role in *tactical* decision-making. Certainly others during the incident perceived the DSO to be in the Silver role. The external designated 'Silver' with the firearms teams then acquiesced in functioning as the DSO's 'ground officer', thus effectively demoting himself to 'Bronze'. But in a fast-moving incident like this it is expecting too much from the DSO to somehow perform as a hybrid Gold–Silver. In effect the Gold and external Silver functions were taken out and the command structure was skewed towards a single command role, that of the DSO. This goes against acknowledged best practice on this matter, where there should be three distinct roles and functions. Everything indicates that the DSO and her staff were behaving at the tactical level. The number of people in the control room and the hustle and bustle are typical of tactics; there was the DSO herself; two SIOs (Senior Investigation Officers) from related operations; two Tactical Advisors on firearms; several people working the communications plus loggists; and a Forward Intelligence Cell with members of MI5 and SB feeding in information off-stage. In contrast, Gold Control, where Gold is located, tends to be fairly quiet, with Gold even being experienced as a 'lonely' role (interview, Golding).

Crucially, the DSO was totally dependent on the quality of intelligence reaching her from outside. The material indicates that 'espoused strategy' was to prepare to arrest any suspects, but when this was poorly implemented, the 'strategy in use', and the thought processes of the main actors, became to prepare to implement Kratos.[17] The DSO was asked to run a Kratos-type operation, but prior to this the firearms authorisation already shaped the likelihood that any armed response would probably be for a Kratos-style approach. The external context combined with the internal pressure appears to have created a mental picture in the control room at NSY that they were dealing with a confirmed suicide bomber and there was a transfer of this suspicion to the firearms team and others who were reliant on the information reaching them. The firearms teams must surely already have mentally primed themselves for the eventuality of a Kratos-style approach for the following reasons:

- Appointing a DSO to lead the operation would have generated an association with Kratos. The two officers who fired had never worked under a DSO before. They must at least have thought of the possibility of a head shot against a suicide bomber when they heard that a DSO was in charge. As a senior officer who had been involved in developing Kratos said at the inquest, 'You can't train that out of them' (Stockwell Inquest, 2009).
- A senior officer responsible for authorisation had led to them being issued with weaponry that is primarily associated with a fatal head shot. They had never previously been issued with hollow-point ammunition on an operation.
- At the briefing they were informed that that they might face immeasurable danger. The suspects they might encounter were likely to be 'deadly and determined', 'well prepared' and 'up for it'.
- They were further informed that they might have to employ unusual tactics that they had never used before.
- They were told that they had to trust the information they were to receive and that there might be no time to question instructions (Stockwell Inquest, 2009).
- Furthermore, they thought there had been an identification of a possible suicide bomber about to cause a large explosion on public transport.
- This all convinced members of an experienced firearms team that they had no other option than to kill someone when they saw the suspect in the bear hug of someone else. It was only then, they stated later, that they decided to shoot.
- In effect, they spontaneously 'authorised' Kratos on the spur of the moment (interview, Waddington, 2009).

Whether or not Kratos was formally announced is really immaterial and that dispute simply fudges the issue. This was indisputably 'Kratos' practice in the sense of a fatal head shot, because a number of choices had been made prior to and during the operation that left few options open other than to implement Kratos, if not in form then in procedure. A seemingly positive identification of a suspect of a bombing who might be on a mission to explode another device converted the suspect person to a real bomber providing a substantial threat who had to be 'stopped'.

All the accounts convey combined limitations of intelligence, coordination and communication that meant people were not fully in control of events in this complex and fast-moving operation. This inadvertently took them down a path that the actors believed they had formally not taken, and which led them to a result they had not wished. Officers had learned tactics and then been issued with ammunition that led them towards *shooting to kill* a suspect under the circumstances they encountered, and when an officer shoots to kill, he or she has to get the correct target because there is no doubt about the outcome. The chance of a fatal mistake is encapsulated in all police use of firearms, but it was multiplied extensively by Kratos because its method was 'shoot to eliminate' with no hope of recovery.

Where, then, should accountability have rested for this? With the surveillance officers who had difficulties with identification? With the soldier on surveillance duty who claims he had to urinate at precisely the wrong moment? With the two SO19 firearms officers who implemented Kratos practice although it was not formally in operation? With the SO19 Silver Commander who let himself become the 'ground commander' to a remote DSO? With the DSO who gave the ambiguous command 'Stop him' on the basis of an identification that had not been made and with a tone that conveyed the need for a decisive intervention against a suicide bomber? With the Gold Commander who set a strategy, but did not intervene when it was evident the strategy was not being implemented? With the Met Commissioner who is ultimately accountable for policy and for institutional mistakes within his force? With the Home Secretary who effectively designated the proposal to shoot to kill an 'operational' matter? With parliament, which is ultimately responsible for defining the limitations on the use of force and for protecting the lives of citizens? Or with the agency that approved the Kratos plan for the British police – ACPO?

The aftermath of Stockwell

Stockwell was one of the most serious blunders in British policing. On 22 July 2005 the Met indisputably failed on a number of standards, but not least on its own high standards as the 'finest police service in the world' (Blair, 2009: 135). First, the Met killed an innocent man; second, the operation itself displayed weaknesses at the command and operational levels; third, there was a failure of internal communication leading to confusion that impacted on the credibility and accuracy of external communication (IPPC, 2007b); and, fourth, the Commissioner tried to suspend the statutory obligation to allow the IPCC access to the scene at Stockwell Station (Punch, 2009a: 212–14).

In the aftermath of Stockwell and the IPCC investigation, the Crown Prosecution Service (CPS) decided not to pursue any individual on criminal charges, but it did prosecute the organisation, as the 'Office of Commissioner', under H&S law (O'Neill, 2007). The Met decided to contest the charges and it is debatable if this was a wise decision for a public police force to take. The then Commissioner plainly felt a principled obligation to defend his institution, and especially his personnel, and this position was also strongly supported by Commander Carter.[18] Blair felt that this prosecution was effectively putting the *operation* under a magnifying glass rather than the police as employers and that this 'opened up a complete nightmare' (Blair, 2009: 199). One can appreciate that this was a tough judgement call for him and his senior officers, but by contesting the case all the faults made on 22 July were itemised at length in the trial and in the media (*The Times*, 2007). Those multiple mistakes brought the judge to pronounce that there had been a grave series of errors amounting to 'a corporate failure'. He ruled that there had been 'a serious failure of accurate communication which has not been explained'. He criticised the delay in sending a trained firearms team to the building under surveillance. The briefing was 'inaccurate and unbalanced'. The police 'fell short to a significant and meaningful' degree; indeed, 'Some of these failures have been beyond explanation' (*The Guardian*, 2007a, 2007b; *Daily Mail*, 2007).

These court findings are, moreover, significant and send an important message for policy. The Met was found guilty on 19 points of putting the public at risk in relation to its 'duty of care'. It was convicted, fined £375,000 and ordered to pay costs of £530,000.[19] As mentioned earlier, it could be asked if dated legislation designed for labour-related offences in the workplace is appropriate for pursuing collective fault in the absence of an opportunity to use corporate manslaughter charges against a police force. The implication, however, was that any operation with an element of risk to the public, and by definition that is all firearms operations, had to take into account the 'duty of care' to the public.

Particularly disturbing was that the Commissioner tried to suspend the statutory obligation to allow the IPCC access to the scene of a police shooting. This decision was taken quickly after the incident – within an hour – and clearly reflects a standpoint taken earlier. The day before he had discussed with the Prime Minister and others the legal framework within which armed officers operate and was suggesting offering them a form of legal protection; he had also raised the difficulty of being subject to an IPCC investigation at the moment that the Met was conducting a massive and highly sensitive investigation against terrorists. He was working on a letter later on 21 July to back this up, but when faced with the Stockwell shooting on the morning of 22 July he rapidly reworded it to justify the IPCC exclusion and sent it straight to Sir John Gieve at the Home Office. This he now acknowledges was a mistake (Blair, 2009: 147). But in effect, at a crucial moment, the Commissioner, the head of a vital public service and the 'emblem of British policing' in his own words, was essentially saying, 'I and my organisation refuse to comply with compulsory oversight'. Furthermore, one of his officers bluntly refused to cooperate with the IPCC Two investigation (IPCC, 2007b).[20]

This stance by the Met can be interpreted as defensive, if not arrogant. Indeed, what appears to be missing in this episode is a culture of accountability when accountability is of the essence in policing. No doubt the higher echelons of the Met considered it necessary to defend their institution and personnel, and probably from inside NSY that was considered the right, if not the only, stance to take. However, the Stockwell affair would have had a far less charged aftermath if the Met had run a sound operation and got their command structure right; had handled their communications adequately; had not contested the H&S prosecution; had not contacted the Home Office to call off the IPCC; and had fully cooperated with the IPCC. This conduct not only goes against the common standards of sound crisis management, but also against the accepted practice of accountability in contemporary policing. None of this would have compensated for the death of Jean Charles de Menezes, but it would have made the aftermath less harrowing for his family and friends; and less damaging to the Commissioner and the Met.

One can see this as the tendency of organisations generally to resort to defensive mode when trouble looms and especially if there is any question of institutional or personal liability. This case might also be seen as 'typically Met behaviour'. The Met is so large and dominant that it cannot but distort relationships of scale and status in British policing and it attracts both hostility and admiration from its 'provincial' counterparts. There are long historical roots to this friction.[21] Squires and Kennison (2010: 186) point out, moreover, that many of the 'bad' shootings and mistakes over a period of 20 years have occurred within the Met, while a former chief officer said that he and his provincial colleagues often looked askance at firearms practice in the larger metropolitan forces (including Merseyside, the West Midlands and West Yorkshire): 'with an armed robbery we think prevention but the Met take out the bwaggers' (interview, Golding).[22] It could be that some of the larger, urban forces are more assertive and proactive with regard to force and firearms and this could be because of the nature of the policing problems they encounter (for example, violent drug gangs, gun crime and terrorism). But it just happens that we only have one case of Kratos being implemented and that was in London.

One should, however, bear in mind that the Met is a very large organisation in a busy capital city that presents the police with constantly shifting challenges on a scale and frequency that few other forces anywhere have to meet. On the law of averages things will sometimes go badly wrong. This should not shield the Met in any way from due criticism, but it also should not obscure the many excellent if not superb operations it successfully leads and the many highly competent officers it employs. The downside of size and dominance can, however, be a degree of arrogance and what one Commissioner called the 'defensive parochialism' of the Met (McNee, 1983). Moreover, the Met has had to operate in recent years in an increasingly adversarial political environment with a media that can be vile and vicious and that can feed off leaks both from politicians and from within NSY. The importance of this is to assess the willingness of the Met to account for its actions and the extent to which it slotted into defensive mode, for one assumes that if ever a police organisation should be held to account it is when it has killed an innocent person.

I raise this as illuminating the more general issue of police accountability in the aftermath of police shootings and we should not become mesmerised by the Met. Indeed, the value of the Stockwell case is that it raises wider, fundamental issues around who determined the Kratos policy and shaped its dramatic paradigm leap, and importantly the footprints in the sand leading up to Stockwell take us beyond the Metropolitan Police and towards ACPO. The IPCC report, for instance, contains a plethora of detail with a legalistic slant focusing on operational decision-making primarily on that one particular day, which was of course its primary remit and is standard for incident-geared investigating; but it is notably weak on tracing the policy trail back to ACPO's door. Yet at Stockwell all concerned – the SO19 officers, the DSO, the Gold Commander and the Commissioner – were implementing a policy determined not by the Met in London, but by ACPO. If one works from the 'smoking gun' backwards to follow the audit trail it leads clearly and indisputably to ACPO.

Notes

[1] The SAS are the Special Air Service, formally 22 SAS Regiment, of the British Army. There is also the less well-known SBS, or Special Boat Service, made up principally of Marine Commandos for interventions

on vessels at sea or at coastal installations (Urban, 1993; Asher, 2004, 2009).

[2] This is the then Commissioner's version, whereas Geraghty (2000: 125) says that Prime Minister Margaret Thatcher herself may have granted the authorisation, as does Asher (2009); it could be that this was confused with her expressing support for the decision. Geraghty also claims that she became 'as fascinated with the SAS as they were with her. Her combative spirit was exactly what they demanded of a leader. She was a regular visitor to their home base at Hereford'.

[3] Chief officers and other ranks involved in firearms both at the command and delivery levels will often spend some time with the SAS and SBS and are almost universally positive about their dedication, ability and hospitality.

[4] A police negotiator, hostages and a former SAS soldier – some of whom meet regularly in reunions – recalled the siege after nearly 30 years (BBC Radio, 2009).

[5] They were almost gentlemanly insurgents – polite on the phone to the negotiator and even considerate to some of the hostages – but who naively thought they could negotiate their demands and avoid violence; they also do not seem to have anticipated an attack. They started to get desperate when it became clear that they were dealing with an implacable government who would not accede to any of their demands including a safe passage out. If they had been a well-trained group determined to resist, like the radical Muslim insurgents in Mumbai recently, the result might have been very different. Given that they were armed, had killed and had threatened more deaths, the risk assessment would have had to take into account that they might resist. Initially, high casualties among the attacking group were anticipated (Asher, 2009).

[6] The explosion on a plane above Lockerbie in Scotland caused by a terrorist bomb killed 270 people on board and on the ground.

[7] Through the JTAC the Met could have close ties with the two British security agencies, M15 and M16, and GCHQ (Government Communications Headquarters), while M15 agents were posted full time to NSY during the period around the 2005 bombing campaign (Blair, 2009: 38).

[8] The then Commissioner and Deputy Commissioner (who, at the time of writing, is currently the Commissioner) took 'urgent legal advice' when they heard of this and were relieved when they heard the bullets did not break the 'Geneva' Convention, and also that they could not be 'accused of committing a war crime'; this is curious as the Metropolitan Police was not at war (Blair, 2009: 175).

[9] As mentioned earlier, for major incidents and set-piece firearms operations there will normally be an accountability structure based on the Gold, Silver and Bronze command and control model (Punch and Markham, 2004). Gold is for the strategic role, Silver for operational command and Bronze for implementation.

[10] It turned out they were perfectly normal actions related to his being late for work, to phoning his workmate about this and to having to change routes because of hold-ups on the underground service. In fact some suicide terrorists tend to be calm, serene and even trance-like rather than agitated and 'jumpy', according to Collins (2008: 440–6); but then others say they can be visibly nervous and sweat profusely.

[11] This may well have been the intention, but several officers with firearms and/or command experience have said that an armed unit would likely interpret 'stop' to mean employ any means to prevent a serious incident taking place. A former AFO felt the DSO's interpretation of the word was somewhat 'woolly' if not 'nonsense', while a former Met senior officer even referred to it as a 'death sentence' (Paddick, 2008: 275). The report of the IPCC (2007a) also stated that 'stop' must have meant something quite different to the officers than what the DSO meant to convey.

[12] When the firearms teams presented themselves they would have done so with written authorisation specifying the operation, appropriate weaponry and type of ammunition, otherwise the armourer would not have been empowered to release it. They would have shown their valid permit for that type of firearm; and their obligations in law would have been read out to them. Their legal position is also printed on the back of their 'pink-card' authorisation permit (Collins, 1998).

[13] Commander Cartersaid hollow-point bullets have 'been around for some years'; and they have been used by police with .22 rifles when killing animals (interview, Markham).

[14] If stealth is out of the question and a suicide bomber is confronted, then the tactic would probably be to isolate him or her and fire from a distance, which is why they had other ammunition. However, because of the point-blank range Kratos would mean using a handgun.

[15] 'Special Branch' (SB) in the UK is the police department responsible for intelligence and enforcement regarding 'political' activities and offences related to national security (Allason, 1983). The Met Anti-terrorist Branch (ATB) was founded in response to the constant IRA threat on the mainland and in the capital since the early 1970s. SB and ATB have now been combined as SO15.

[16] One of the firearms teams' leaders, 'Vic', stated: 'I heard who I believed to be [Trojan – meaning firearms tactical advisor] 84 say, "They've said he's to be stopped. Do not let him on the tube. Do not let him get on the tube", the tone of voice and urgency of this radio transmission, combined with the intelligence meant to me that he must be stopped immediately and at any cost. I believed that a bombing of the tube could be imminent and must be prevented' (IPCC, 2007a: 61).

[17] The Gold Commander should be held primarily accountable for this. He should have overseen the operation and realised that his expressed strategy was not being implemented. His options were to abort the operation or resort to a contingency plan; but it seems there was no 'Plan B'. Having set the original strategy, he seems to have stepped aside as nearly all the attention has become focused on the DSO. The DSO role appears somewhere in between Gold and Silver and was later designated as DSO Silver.

[18] In responding to the verdict the Commissioner was said to have been 'pugilistic and unapologetic' (The Guardian, 2007b). There were calls for his resignation, which he brushed aside; but alongside the aftermath of Stockwell (with the trial, two IPCC reports and the inquest) there was a damaging conflict with a former senior officer, Brian Paddick, and he then had to face a new Conservative Mayor of London, Boris Johnson, who expressed low confidence in him, which led him to resign in 2008 (Blair, 2009).

[19] The trial cost the public £3.5 million and witnessed a defence barrister trying to discredit Mr de Menezes, so that he had not only become a victim of police violence, but also had his character posthumously darkened by a lawyer on behalf of the Met, who had

killed him. There was mention of his drug use and possible illegal residence and these were tied to his 'defying' police instructions ,yet he was a legal resident and did not defy instructions because there were none. There was also a measure of misinformation and disinformation surrounding the case. In various leaks, briefings and reports, de Menezes was said to have been wearing a bulky jacket although it was summer, and hence perhaps concealing an explosive device, and to have jumped over the turnstiles at the station; neither of these were correct. Yet both of the SO19 officers involved referred to his bulky jacket in various statements. Also a police log had been deliberately altered, and officers claimed they shouted a warning to the suspect, but no one else heard it (IPCC, 2007a).

[20] Regarding non-compliance there is in Canada tort law relating to the statutory obligations of office that makes a police officer's failure to cooperate with an oversight investigation an offence of misfeasance in public office, with courts having judged non-cooperation as an 'unlawful breach of statutory duty' (Griffiths, 2007).

[21] The same dynamic is evident in the Netherlands, where the Amsterdam Police, the largest force that also polices the capital city, is viewed from outside as arrogant, wishing to dominate and always wanting to do things differently from everyone else. Also Amsterdammers typically refer to anyone from outside the city as 'farmers'. This attitude and stance is probably the same with the NYPD among US forces and with the 'leading force' in most countries.

[22] Golding also felt that the gung-ho tone of the book on a Met firearms unit, *The Trojan Files* (Gray, 2000), was 'outrageous' and not representative of many forces outside of the capital.

SIX

Conclusion: From Bobby to Robocop?

> Chief officers in Britain have increasingly felt it
> incumbent on them to develop policy, within the
> rule of law, independently of the wishes of local or
> central government. That may be wrong and may need
> changing.... (Blair, 2009: xv)[1]

This book has focused on policy and practice with regard to police
use of firearms. It delved into these matters principally with regard
to the UK, but also looked at the US and the Netherlands. The
police use of firearms is a perennial and central topic in a democratic
society because it involves representatives of the state being granted
the power and authority to deprive people of their lives. This pivotal
matter in policing helps to open up the consideration of a wider raft
of issues around law, policy, legitimacy, governance, accountability
and the demarcation line between police and government. These
complex and intertwined issues raise in turn three questions of great
importance: who actually decides policy on police use of firearms?;
why is there such a striking absence of debate on this topic?; and,
above all, what does the material and analysis in this book – and
especially the significance of Kratos – tell us about the direction in
which policing is moving?

In addition, what are the implications of that movement for the
relationship between the state, police and society – which was
traditionally based on a paradigm of consent – and for the role of the
police officer? Consent is based on the exercise of legitimate authority
and if the public doubts that legitimacy it can revoke consent. For
example, in Britain the approach to this fundamental topic – the
power of police to kill – was based on the philosophy and practice
of restraint. This can be traced back to 1829 with the founding of an

unarmed police force, Peel's assurance that the state was essentially benign, and his subliminal message that the citizenry need not fear the police officer. After 176 years, however, that traditional policy and practice evaporated on one day in 2005. The Stockwell shooting was a defining moment in police use of firearms – and indeed in British policing history – because it revealed a seismic paradigm shift.

It dramatically raised the question – is policing in the UK becoming more paramilitary in style, and can a constable take orders to shoot to kill someone without warning? Indeed, is the iconic Bobby, the very embodiment of the consent model, ineluctably turning into 'Robocop' without any consultation with the wider public on whom the consent paradigm depends? If that is the case then it would reinforce yet again that every time in the past when policy and practice on police use of firearms altered, it happened without any serious public and political debate. This has aided in obscuring the fact that a non-statutory, non-elected and largely unaccountable body – ACPO – made 'law' without any parliamentary debate and without the sovereign's signature.

There can be no better illustration of this than the policy referred to as 'Kratos', for it is patently clear that the pre- and post-Kratos policies on the police use of firearms are fundamentally different, if not incompatible. With Kratos ACPO fundamentally altered the ground rules on how police kill and in so doing covertly abandoned a long-standing paradigm of policing and altered the ethos and identity of policing in British society.

Pre- and post-Kratos policy

The term 'Kratos' is used here to refer to the policy developed to deal with suicide bombers carrying an explosive device on their person, in which police are trained to deliver a 'critical head shot'. I shall illustrate why this forms a dramatic turning point in British policing by itemising pre- and post-Kratos policy.

Pre-Kratos position:

- *Intention:* Stop the suspect from causing serious harm to others.
- *Point of aim:* Normally the body mass (but in a highly dangerous situation, anywhere, including the head).

- *Weapon of choice:* Generally an H&K MP5 carbine as the standard weapon.
- *Ammunition:* Standard round with low ability to over-penetrate; half-jacketed, soft-point bullets (Collins, 1998: 52).
- *Number of rounds:* One or just a few rounds, with the weapon set on semi-automatic to fire one round at a time and with each round having to be accounted for.
- *Warning:* 'Armed police!' shouted repeatedly to convince the suspect that he or she is in a hopeless position and should lay down the weapon (or other offensive instrument), desist from resistance, comply with instructions and surrender.
- *Range at firing:* It can be any distance, but typically it is a matter of yards, probably on average 10–20 yards, or 9–18 metres, unless a sniper is involved with a shot from a distance.
- *Goal:* The surrender of the suspect with no shots fired and no harm done to any of those involved.
- *Result:* Most suspects are apprehended and of those shot most will survive the shooting.
- *Likelihood of mistake:* Is always present, but the chance is reduced if all procedures embodying restraint, negotiation, warnings and minimum force are followed.
- *Legality:* Common law normally offers protection to firearms officers who pull the trigger and cause death or injury on grounds of self-defence based on an 'honestly held belief' of danger and assuming they employed what is adjudicated as 'reasonable force in the circumstances'. Section 3 of the Criminal Law Act 1967 requires the use of force to be 'lawful' and hence the police use of force could be challenged if it was held to be unlawful.
- *Discretion:* The assumption is that each individual officer makes a situational judgement on whether or not he or she is going to open fire based on an appraisal of the presence of danger in a situation. Training and operational accountability are hence geared to the principle of individual responsibility.
- *Orders:* An officer cannot be 'ordered' by a superior to shoot. He or she can be instructed or authorised to shoot but formally is not obliged to carry out that instruction. This power is in turn founded on the authority granted to the individual 'constable' in Britain.

Post–Kratos position:

- *Intention:* Stop the brain functioning in order to immediately cut off the suspect's ability to move even a finger and to carry out any offensive action that may lead to danger to police and bystanders by causing serious casualties in an explosion.
- *Point of aim:* Brainstem at the back of the head.
- *Weapon of choice:* A handgun such as a Glock pistol.
- *Ammunition:* 'Hollow-point' bullets, which are deemed illegal in conventional warfare and by extension also by national standards in a number of countries as unsuitable and undesirable in law enforcement. These bullets spread on impact with the body and remain within the body; when aimed at the head they will effectively 'mash' or 'cook' the brain (the terms used by diverse experts).
- *Number of rounds:* Multiple rounds with continued firing until the target is considered to be totally immobilised and the danger completely eliminated; perhaps until the officer's magazine is empty or even using a fresh magazine.
- *Warning:* None. It clearly makes no sense to announce your presence to a suicide bomber; it is appropriate to use stealth and creep up and shoot him or her in the back of the head.
- *Range at firing:* Point blank, within a few centimetres.
- *Goal:* Prevent the brain functioning.
- *Result: **All suspects hit will die.***
- *Likelihood of mistake:* Much depends on the quality of intelligence and the certainty of identification, but with no margin of error a mistake will always be fatal.
- *Legality:* The legality of Kratos is open to dispute, although following Stockwell, the single case so far, the CPS decided not to prosecute any individuals on criminal charges. Again the defence would be based on a plea of self-defence – with the danger not visible but imputed – but should in any future case the use of force under Kratos be adjudicated as unlawful, then, given it is based on the fully intended death of the suspect, the charge has to be murder.

- *Discretion:* The firearms officer acts under instructions to fire in a situation where the danger and 'reasonable cause' is imputed by others. This can be interpreted as a senior officer deciding when the officer should shoot and issuing what amounts to a direct *order*; the firearms officer is hence acting as the 'innocent agent' of a superior.

This sea-change, with immense significance for police use of firearms, and by implication for the nature and future of British policing, was a result of policy developed by ACPO.

ACPO and firearms

> ACPO ... has become the most powerful club in the country, promoting policies agreed among its members, resisting attempts to introduce measures for accountability and actively entering the political arena.... It reports directly to the Home Secretary, and has the capacity to become a centralized intelligence agency, without any charter to limit its operations. (Robertson, 1989: 24)

The prime mover in policing and firearms policy is plainly ACPO. ACPO is a non-statutory, non-elected body, which has been given the delegated responsibility by the state to decide how citizens will die at the hands of the police. This may seem surprising, but this sort of delegation by government to professional bodies and other agencies is not unusual, according to Savage et al (2000: 15):

> As policy-making has become more complex, governments rely increasingly upon professional associations, pressure groups, think-tanks and private sector companies for the formulation and implementation of policies.... Indeed Weir and Beetham (1999: 271) argued that 'organised interests and professional groups play a significant and often dominant role in government policy-making'.

187

Indeed, the authors add that at times ACPO was '*almost drafting government policy*' (Savage et al, 2000: 29, my emphasis). This might be viewed as appropriate on a range of instrumental, technical or non-controversial topics; but the issue of fatal force is related to one of the most important decisions a state can make: who is going to die at the hands of the state's agents and in what manner?

Perhaps the main actors involved feel they are part and parcel of an adequately structured and accountable process that concerns ACPO, the Home Office, HMIC and diverse experts (say, on firearms and latterly involving the intelligence agencies), but this does raise a number of important points. Is it acceptable that a matter of this gravity be devolved to ACPO; that the Home Secretary largely devolves the responsibility to the police as an 'operational matter'; and that public debate on how and when a police officer is going to take someone's life on behalf of the state and society is non-existent?

To whom is ACPO accountable? Indeed, what is ACPO and who are its members? Since the research of Savage et al (2000) there has been little scrutiny of ACPO in terms of composition and working style. The impact of New Public Management and the civilianisation of certain chief officer functions have almost certainly made ACPO more corporate and managerial. Also, with over 300 members of diverse plumage clearly the real work will be done in the specialist commissions where a few movers and shakers can be highly influential, but these internal processes are not visible as ACPO does not fall under the Freedom of Information Act. This means we do not know how long members sit on ACPO; how much continuity on key posts there is; who the influential opinion shapers on key areas such as firearms and counter-terrorism have been, especially since 9/11; what the level of compliance in the individual forces with ACPO guidelines is; and to what extent the Met engages or does not engage with ACPO in general or on particular issues. Of especial interest with regard to firearms is setting national standards, generating central expertise, establishing standards of aftercare, developing codes of practice and achieving universal compliance with them. The latter has often been problematic given the ostensible autonomy of the individual forces, but there has been a strong move within ACPO in recent years to become a form of '*police-led* national policing policy forum' with a presumption that all members will 'sign up' to ACPO policy (Savage, 2010), for there surely cannot be parochial diversity on how the police deploy potentially fatal weapons.

What we have seen is that ACPO took one of the most profound decisions in the nearly two hundred years of British policing. Police officers would under 'Kratos' effectively both *take orders* and *shoot to kill* a suspect. It can be maintained that this should never have been placed in ACPO's ambit. This non-statutory body took a decision to alter fundamentally the long-standing policy on police use of firearms, deeply engrained in the ethos of generations of officers, yet with no debate and no transparency. It has, moreover, compounded that covert policy decision by a degree of obfuscation and circumlocution; it avoids admitting that it has formulated a policy of 'shoot to kill'.

Indeed, the topic of firearms policy and use seems to be shrouded in a more than usually dense smokescreen of reserve, caution and even secrecy. This could be the legacy of the collective myth about the service being essentially unarmed that has led a long relay of chief officers and politicians to deny developments. In 2008, for instance, I wrote a position paper outlining some key points and drawing on the Stockwell incident that was shaped to contribute to an internal police debate on firearms. I sent it to ACPO and received an amicable email from the officer with the firearms portfolio (we had met previously). He promised to get back to me, but I never did receive a response. He was doubtless simply overburdened, which is quite understandable. It is not as if every chief officer replies to my occasional correspondence, but in general there is nowadays a culture of senior officers responding fairly swiftly. So this silence did spark speculation as to whether or not there was any fundamental debate taking place on this topic within the Police Service. Or perhaps this represented a degree of defensiveness that deflected anyone away who tried to penetrate the fog surrounding ACPO on firearms.

Squires and Kennison (2010) mention, for example, that the Home Office is noticeably uncooperative about access to data on the police use of firearms and has flatly refused to supply certain data. McKenzie (2000) also speaks of the secrecy on firearms policy in the UK and states that policy is not subject to informed debate. Even the leading scholar in this area, with excellent credentials with the police, remarked that senior officers are very 'tight-lipped' about the implications of the Stockwell shooting and especially the 'Kratos' policy on dealing with suicide bombers. He further stated, 'it must have been decided at the highest levels, perhaps even at prime ministerial level, but no one wants ownership' (interview, Waddington).[2]

It may well be that Kratos can be judged after due debate to be an acceptable and legitimate policy given the challenge of facing suicide bombers, but that is not so much the point as that the 'ownership' of this highly contentious issue is in the wrong hands, and the entire matter is replete with ambiguity if not confusion. It could be argued that this should have been a subject for parliament and that ACPO should not have been independently making 'law' in this particular area. Traditionally the police in Britain have remained politically impartial and were respectfully distant from the legislative process. This is doubtless something of a myth, however, in that policing is intrinsically 'political', while a number of police chiefs in the past have spoken out, sometimes quite forcefully, about societal issues and especially about aspects of criminal justice policy (Reiner, 1991).[3]

There were signs in the last decade, however, that some senior officers were actively promoting if not lobbying for changes in the law and this can be viewed as a symptom of the 'politicisation' of policing.[4] For instance, the government espoused a new security agenda after 9/11 and in 2005 was proposing legislation to allow the detention of suspected terrorists for up to 90 days. ACPO subsequently sent a letter to all chief constables 'urging them to lobby their local MPs in favour of 90 days'. This raised a 'storm of protest' – including from some police chiefs – and 'crossed the line of what was acceptable', according to Blair (2009: 183). Yet it was Blair himself as Met Commissioner who sent the senior officer responsible for anti-terrorism, Andy Hayman, to the House of Commons 'to try and persuade dissenting Labour MPs to vote with the government', according to Paddick (2008: 244).

There is a clear danger here of disturbing the implicit understanding that police autonomy was granted in reciprocation for impartiality. Indeed, Paddick goes on to say that this was 'a totally improper blurring of the distinction between law makers and law enforcers, between the legislature and the servants of the law' (Paddick, 2008: 244). It is highly debatable, then, whether Blair's statement (cited at the beginning of this chapter) that chief officers in Britain have increasingly turned to developing policy 'independently of the wishes of local or central government' is compatible with that distinction,. To what extent should developing policy be the role of police in a democratic society? One former senior officer is adamant on this issue:

> The police should stay out of the political arena. We hold the ring but we are apolitical and should stay outside of politics; we let others fight it out and decide and then we enforce the law. It's a false premise to think that the Police Service can devise a shoot-to-kill policy on its own; it must have it approved outside of itself. ACPO effectively changed the law and hence Kratos was formulated without the authority of the state through its elected representatives. ACPO shouldn't usurp that role as that undermines democracy. If Kratos is legitimate then why can't it be open? I suspect they don't have an answer and can't defend this. But a democracy should be strong enough to stand up to this threat. And the police should be seen to be protecting democracy by insisting on the democratic process within the rule of law. (Interview, Markham)

The 'democratic deficit', of devolving policymaking to agencies that are not democratically accountable, may well be tolerable in a number of policing areas, but not, I suggest, regarding police use of firearms and fatal force. What this has meant is that this pivotal topic has never been debated in an open forum and that the agency that implements the killing has also been given the responsibility for deciding the means of death (and until recently for investigating those deaths). In terms of governance, decision-making, transparency, debate and redress this must be a concern because the group taking that momentous decision is accountable only to itself. Scraton (1986: 4) previously raised this issue and argued for a rethink, 'to restore accountability to a system where ACPO is now accountable to nobody but itself'. He added that 'a state where in effect the police are only accountable to the police is a police State'.

In addition, it is customary for the Home Secretary to refer certain areas including firearms to ACPO and to individual police chiefs as an 'operational' issue. At one level this respects the long-standing assumption of police operational autonomy and constabulary independence (McNee, 1983: 66–7). But at another level one can perhaps be permitted a degree of scepticism about politicians 'passing the chalice' on this particularly crucial topic. Certainly in the last few decades 'law and order' has become the staple of adversarial political debate with something of an 'anything you can do I can do tougher' stance (Reiner, 2007). This has made the Home Office a key institution, but given the wide range of responsibilities in areas open to dispute on policy and with a vulnerability to controversy and scandal – such as policing, immigration and prisons – the role of the Home Secretary has become something of crisis manager reacting to incidents brought to his or her attention by a powerful if not predatory media. Indeed, Commissioner Blair faced four Home Secretaries within four years (2004–08) indicating that the length of tenure was disturbingly short and that the post had become a hot seat for politicians.[5] It may have been politically expedient in this climate to hand this 'no win' hot potato back to the police, for views on firearms generally are widely and irreconcilably divided and taking a firm position could bring electoral damage.

The Stockwell One report, for instance, refers to the authorisation to issue hollow-point bullets in the Met and that this had been referred not only to the HMIC – which informed the officer concerned that he was 'empowered to authorise such use' – but also to the Home Office. There it went to the Head of SC1, which is responsible for Public Order and Police Cooperation:

> Part of his responsibility is to support the Home Secretary in relation to a range of issues, including the police use of firearms. Section 53 Police Act 1966, as amended by the Police Reform Act 2002, gives powers to the Home Secretary in relation to equipment used by the police.

> To date the Secretary of State has not used those powers
> either generally or in relation to ammunition to be used
> by police forces. It therefore remains an operational
> matter for Chief Officers to decide which ammunition is
> appropriate for use in the particular circumstances faced
> by their officers. (IPCC, 2007a: 80)

In short there has been a relay of Home Secretaries who designated firearms as largely an 'operational' police matter.[6]

From that background one can perhaps understand why Michael Howard, when he was Home Secretary, parried calls in 1994 from the Police Federation and Paul Condon (the Met Commissioner) to arm the police more widely by defining it as an operational matter for chief constables (Squires and Kennison, 2010: 102). Yet this was from a prominent, law and order, 'prison works' Conservative, who was a hard-liner in almost every other area. This did not go unnoticed, however, with some seeing this side-step as putting operational issues beyond 'existing mechanisms of accountability', and with regard to police weaponry making a substantial change 'fundamentally altering the character of British policing' through an incremental process of 'stealth – as if "by the back door" – without effective parliamentary scrutiny' (Squires and Kennison, 2010: 102).

The negative consequence of this customary non-intervention in 'operational' matters was highlighted in the Patten Commission's Report (1999) on the reform of policing in Northern Ireland. It pointed out that the Northern Ireland Police Authority (PANI) received little response from the RUC because 'operational independence' is nowhere defined, and hence if a matter on the PANI agenda was not palatable to the police they simply hid behind the term to keep the issue out of public scrutiny.[7] The Patten Report (1999: 32) stated:

> In a democratic society, all public officials must be fully
> accountable to the institutions of that society for the
> due performance of their functions, and a chief of police
> cannot be an exception. No public official, including a
> chief of police, can be said to be 'independent'.

This vitally important statement is pertinent to examining the policy referred to as 'Kratos', where the police were trained to come up to a suspect from behind to shoot several times into his or her brainstem at point-blank range without warning. At its worst this can be viewed as the summary execution of a suspect who has not faced prosecution, trial by judge and jury, conviction and sentencing. How, therefore, can be this possibly be defined and dismissed as an 'operational' matter?

This reticence and dynamic of denial stands out starkly because for some 20-odd years governments have been frenetically trying to reform policing through a tsunami of measures that most commentators see as a concerted effort to increase central control over the police (Reiner, 2010). Furthermore, a number of recent Home Secretaries, including David Blunkett, were notoriously assertive and interventionist and not above harassing individual police chiefs on performance targets and other matters. This would seem to dent considerably the traditional notion of constabulary independence and even of operational independence (Williamson, 2006). Then when Blunkett pressurised the Chief Constable of Sussex to depart early following the Ashley shooting it was purely an expression of his and central government's wish to control chief officers in order to get them to do their whim (Allison, 2001a). Yet here was an opportunity to examine seriously issues of individual and institutional accountability around police shootings; but there was no attempt whatsoever to ponder the lessons for the Police Service arising from Justice Rafferty's highly significant pronouncement in court. It is glaringly noticeable, then, that in this crucial area – the killing of citizens by agents of the state – the government washes its hands of the issue by defining it as an 'operational' matter. If the somewhat demeaning metaphor bandied about by ministers in Whitehall is 'we steer and you row', then on police use of firearms it would appear to be 'you shoot and we hide'.

Where is the debate?

With regard to the changing features of police use of firearms, including the paradigm leap exposed by the Stockwell shooting, it is striking that this issue has but sporadically entered the public and political arena. In fact the history on this area reveals that change is largely incident-driven (Squires and Kennison, 2010). Policy, police practice and legislation are strongly influenced by dramatic events in the international environment and domestically by high-profile incidents like the shooting of Waldorf in London and by the Hungerford and Dunblane massacres. The last two deeply tragic incidents led to significant legislative change on firearms possession, registration and availability leading to the UK having relatively strict gun laws. This only occurred, however, after concerted efforts by grass-roots action groups, helped by sections of the media and in the case of Dunblane by the advent of the New Labour administration, and in the face of strong lobbying by pro-gun interests (North, 2000; Sampson and Crow, 2000: 160). It was also noticeable in the new Conservative–Liberal Democrat administration's reaction to the recent shooting massacre in Cumbria (June 2010) that the condolences to the families and praise for the police were balanced by support for the gun lobby, which remains influential in certain parts of British society. What is missing, however, is a fundamental debate about police use of firearms and fatal force and also about the place of guns in contemporary society.[8]

Yet in 2005 the Met Commissioner, in the prestigious *Richard Dimbleby Lecture* on BBC TV, argued that there should be a public debate on what sort of police the public wants. He additionally stated more specifically that he was in favour of a largely unarmed police force, but admitted that firearms policy had never been discussed in public:

> Until now, the police have discussed the strategy and tactics for using lethal force behind closed doors, open only to police authority members, Home Office officials, ministers and some specialist advisers. That has to change. An open debate is now required, not just about how the police deal with suicide bombers, but about *how, in a liberal democracy, a largely unarmed service uses lethal force in any and all circumstances*. (Blair, 2005, emphasis added)

This was an insightful presentation by the leading police officer in the country speaking for the wider Police Service to a national audience. *Five years on, though, where is that debate?*

There have been calls, for instance, for a Royal Commission (RC) on the role and functions of policing. There has not been an RC on policing for some 60 years. The Police Federation in particular has been demanding one for some time; Sir Ian Blair (2009) has recently advocated one; and ACPO has also called for some type of public forum on policing. After Stockwell the IPCC (2007a: 160) admitted that it had not examined the police response to suicide bombers or the concerns about a 'shoot-to-kill' policy and expressed the 'need for a wide and well-informed public debate on these issues'. The RC could do the following:

- Explore the roles and functions of the police and police accountability, with special attention given to the demarcation line between the professional autonomy of police through ACPO for policy and through police chiefs for 'operational' decision-making, and the rights and powers of the state through government in parliament within a democracy.

- Consider strengthening the remit of the parliamentary Select Committee on Home Affairs to focus closely on the police use of force and firearms. This is not meant to bring in political interference in operational policing, but to open up firearms and force to parliamentary scrutiny as in the Netherlands.[9] I can imagine that some police officers will be wary of anything that hampers their operational independence and fear the intrusion of a kind of rule-bound H&S regime. That seems to have shaped Ian Blair's thinking as Commissioner, that the level of regulation and post-incident scrutiny is excessive and burdensome; and he sought some lightening of this burden with the Prime Minister (Blair, 2009: 147). There should be limits to regulation and control as these can have negative effects on decision-making in organisations (Anechiarico and Jacobs, 1996), but I am working on the premise that accountability should not be able to hide behind 'operational independence' and that a non-partisan scrutiny of the parameters within which the police employ firearms and fatal force is essential in a democracy.

- Survey if the police and the public want a fully armed police.
- Debate what level of arming and weaponry is appropriate in policing.
- Examine the positions of the public, other stakeholders, ACPO, police authorities, the DPP and CPS, the IPCC, the Home Office, the Police Federation and the political parties on a 'shoot-to-kill' policy and on the use of hollow-point ammunition.
- In lieu of a written constitution and a Bill of Rights, scrutinise the possibility of a Charter of Citizens' Rights (as in Canada) espousing the state's commitment to the right to life principle and to the integrity of the body (as in the Dutch Constitution). The UK is a signatory to the EConvHR and has passed the HRA, 1998 and all firearms policy should be infused with HR compliance; indeed, the ACPO firearms manuals begin with the need to conform to Article 2 of the Convention. Yet a leading authority on the area writes: 'For whatever reason, criticisms of police operations delivered by the Court [ECHR] are not being translated into policy and practice by the UK authorities. This is to our cost and possibly to the cost of lives of victims' (personal communication, Crawshaw).
- Establish how to move away from the incident-driven nature of firearms policy – and of possession of weapons – to a more generic, principled, anticipatory position on the whole issue of guns in society, police responses to gun possession and gun crime, and police use of firearms. Too often policymakers have been forced to react to developments arising from incidents rather than crafting forward-looking policy.

From Bobby to Robocop?

Britain's most senior counter-terrorism officer has called for armed police to be equipped with high-powered assault rifles to enable them to cope with a Mumbai-style terrorist attack.... He warned that the risk to the 'unarmed bobby on the street' meant that armed officers should be given 'heavier ballistic weaponry and heavier ballistic ammunition'. (*The Daily Telegraph*, 2010)

What is sorely needed in this area is clarity. Since the casual negligence of the early days, with revolvers in pockets and instructions to avoid using them, the police have gone through a long learning curve to increased professionalism and enhanced expertise. The question now is, echoing Blair in his Dimbleby Lecture, what sort of police does society want? And in particular here, to what extent does society want an armed police and what should be its powers on the use of force and firearms? Is the current situation with most officers unarmed, a limited mobile response through ARVs and specialist firearms squads with a relatively small number of AFOs and SFOs, the preferable solution? Should the plea from the 'gun lobby' within policing for heavier weaponry, as earlier raised in 1994, be heard?[10] Would that fundamentally alter the nature of policing in Britain? These are vital matters at a time when the boundaries between police, military and intelligence agencies are becoming increasingly porous, as with the formation of SOCA (Serious Organised Crime Agency), and when the traditional operational independence of the police is more than ever under threat (Bowling and Newburn, 2006; Hoogenboom, 2010).

Police use of firearms is, it cannot be stressed enough, *always potentially fatal*, and there will always be a certain number of irreducible misses and mistakes. Also, more guns and more powerful guns will mean more strays, more bullets that over-penetrate, more mistakes, more casualties and more deaths.[11] This must be a powerful signal for caution. To what extent, crucially, has policing already been altered by Kratos and the Stockwell shooting? Does it represent the danger of a slippery slope towards more aggressive, paramilitary policing entering daily policing and altering the relationship with the public.[12] Waldren (2009: 16) warns that high-velocity weapons are already increasingly being used for '*routine patrol purposes*' in parts of Britain (my emphasis). Also, is there a risk in the covert world of counter-terrorism of fostering extra-judicial killings? The latter are not remote and unthinkable in democratic Europe because they have already happened in Spain in the 1980s and within the UK in Northern Ireland, where many of those illicit shootings went unpunished.[13] The unaccountable abuse of authority and force with no redress is the antithesis of all that democracy represents and promises; and accountability for the exercise of power and force is precisely what distinguishes democratic society from undemocratic and totalitarian societies.

The ultimate in police decision-making is killing a fellow human being. Pondering this awesome responsibility leads inevitably to paying serious attention to internal and external accountability and sound, credible oversight. Furthermore, the policing profession needs continually to seek improvement in leadership, command and control structures and procedures, competencies for handling major incidents, the link between these factors and those who deliver front-line policing, and the relationship with and communication to the public on policing policy. In that sense the discussion on firearms is a vehicle for generating high professional standards throughout policing as well as forcing us to examine the nature and future of policing.

In essence, civil policing in a democracy is geared to reaction, restraint, minimum force, negotiation and 'playing it long'. The ethos in Britain, moreover, was strongly based on the preservation of life, the minimisation of risk and the promotion of public safety within the rule of law. It then becomes problematic if policing becomes proactive, aggressive and 'plays it short'. The Chandler's Ford shooting in Hampshire in 2007, for instance, when a Met armed squad lay in wait for an armed raid on a security van transporting cash, and in which two of the armed robbers were shot dead, raised the issue of why the police allowed the raid to take place and essentially mounted an ambush when the aim of the operation was to 'prevent and apprehend' (Carson, 2008; IPCC, 2007c; Yeebo and Fresco, 2007; Squires and Kennison, 2010: 184–90).

The need for clarity on these matters was greatly amplified by Kratos and the Stockwell shooting. Kratos can be viewed as a tactical answer to a strategic issue – how to deal with suicide bombers – that was not adequately thought through.[14] Indeed, an 'insider' admitted that the policy was 'knocked together, in haste, with relatively little wider consideration of potential contexts or possible consequences, 'it was real seat-of-the-pants stuff,' he noted, 'making it up as we went along' (Squires and Kennison, 2010: 32). It may well be that at times policymaking is hasty, improvised, narrowly reactive and unsophisticated in reaction to dramatic events, But this then tends only to produce *lex imperfecta* whose defects are rudely exposed on implementation (Reisman, 1979).[15] The question is whether or not that is acceptable when dealing with how police officers will kill fellow citizens in the name of the state.

What ACPO did with Kratos was to alter two fundamental domain assumptions underpinning police use of firearms. First, it moved from a 'shoot-to-prevent' paradigm to a 'shoot-to-kill' paradigm – and even to 'shoot to eliminate' – where the result can only be death. Several academics and practitioners I talked to have questioned the legality of this. In Sussex, for instance, an officer was prosecuted for murder for shooting an unarmed suspect. Yet after Stockwell the CPS decided not to prosecute any individual police officers, although there was a prosecution and conviction under H&S law of the Office of the Metropolitan Police.[16] It may well be that the DPP, CPS and judiciary might interpret the law differently if another killing of an innocent person under Kratos takes place. What would be Justice Rafferty's stance if a police force was prosecuted in her court under the corporate killing law for a Kratos-style shooting? Indeed, one commentator felt that the IPCC far too readily accepted the legal advice that such shootings are compatible with Article 2 of the EConvHR (interview, Waddington).[17]

It would obviously have been interesting to know what sort of judgment the ECHR would have come to if it had deliberated on a clearly intentional killing of the sort that led to the death of Mr de Menezes in London. The de Menezes family could have appealed to the ECHR as their relative was resident in the UK, but they were relatively poor people from a Brazilian province without the financial and social 'capital' to pursue the matter. If the victim had been a young British man of, say, Asian or African origin whose killing elicited outrage in the respective ethnic community and whose parents were tenacious and articulate, with the capacity to generate media and political support, then this could easily have become a *cause célèbre* equivalent to the Stephen Lawrence affair. So there remains a nagging, underlying legal doubt surrounding Kratos. This is of considerable significance for the officer pulling the trigger, who in the past could assume that more than half of those shot would survive, but who now knows that his actions can have only one result – death. Kratos seems almost naively to assume that there will be no error.

Second, the Kratos policy brings into question the legal status of 'constable' in Britain as an independent law enforcer. In theory a police officer cannot be given a direct order; and regarding firearms this means he or she cannot be told when to fire a weapon. Unlike the military in combat this does make the individual officer responsible for the use of firearms and can bring him or her to court on criminal charges, including murder. Kratos would seem, however, to contain the element of an officer being given a direct 'order' to open fire. It moves the threat assessment away from the shooter to the commander. Some argue that nothing has really changed and that under Kratos the DSO gives an 'authorisation' to an officer, who still retains the independence to fire or not. But this is not how many commentators and one a former Met leading firearms experts understand it. Waldren (2007: 221) plainly states, 'for the first time, they [Kratos provisions] included provision for a senior officer to order when shots will be fired'. In the briefing at Stockwell the SO19 officers were primed to perhaps not take the time to question 'instructions', while the DSO herself spoke of giving an 'order'. Who then is accountable for those shots under Kratos?

Does this change the historic legal status of the constable in British policing, making him or her 'the paramilitary arm of the state' (Squires and Kennison, 2010: 41)? The armed officer is often in an unenviable position where he or she can be found guilty of unreasonable force for opening fire or else for neglecting duty on failing to open fire. Added to that, he or she is personally responsible for each shot fired and cannot fall back on the 'acting on orders defence'. In principle, Kratos allows precisely for that defence with the DSO taking responsibility from the shoulders of the armed officers pulling the trigger. What happened in London on 22 July 2005, however, was precisely the opposite. The DSO did not call Kratos into operation and did not authorise a critical head shot. If the DSO was convinced that there was a positive identification of a suspected suicide bomber then that presumably should have happened. That was the whole point of having a DSO, and in fact two authorisations were granted that same day by other DSOs in response to highly suspicious behaviour on public transport. This is not intended in any way as a criticism of a well-respected officer who took a decision in unprecedented circumstances and under intense pressure; indeed, she was exonerated from any personal blame both at the trial and the inquest. Rather the aim is to examine the significance of that decision.

What this meant was that the two firearms officers who entered the train had to take the decision whether or not to implement Kratos themselves. This was essentially old-style authorisation leaving the ultimate decision to the officers at the scene based on their threat assessment before firing, except that here the threat was not visible and was imputed by others. Indeed, in Kratos the officers are supposed to act at the behest of a remote senior officer who should be in possession of sufficient information to get the threat assessment right. Somehow at that crucial moment accountability was not drawn to the appropriate level. If Kratos authorisation had been given, then it could have proved a test case on the legal validity of a superior officer giving orders to open fire when there is no directly evident 'reasonable cause' apparent to the shooter. In fact, Ian Blair (2009) has suggested that the police force should take the responsibility under Kratos and not the individual officer.

This reinforces my plea for clarity, and there surely has to come some legal clarification for the position of firearms officers operating under the supervision, if not the 'orders,' of senior officers. Will they remain the legal scapegoats for wider failings? Were the words of Justice Rafferty in the Sussex case in vain? Have they fallen on deaf ears within the police hierarchy? Are there, indeed, senior officers who since Stockwell draw back at the thought of being held accountable for a killing they have ordered under Kratos?

Finally, the thrust of this book – drawing on historical developments in policing in Britain and abroad, Justice Rafferty's pronouncements, the *McCann* and other ECHR judgments and the reports and rulings emanating from key cases, but especially the watershed Stockwell affair – points indisputably to a number of fundamental building blocks for major police operations. They apply particularly to those carrying a risk to life, and I have consequently focused on police use of firearms as the decision to shoot is the ultimate judgement call in policing. In short all firearms operations should have the following principles solidly embedded:

- A premise and ethos that accountability will be located with those who are responsible for setting up and managing the operation.
- The command and control functions staffed with officers who are qualified in firearms and have been tested in the leadership qualities and competencies for their respective roles. This applies particularly to the Gold function, and senior officers should be tested on competencies with consequences for promotion to high rank and for their operational duties.[18]
- Any deaths or injuries through police behaviour to be followed by a highly professional and impartial investigation.
- Accepting accountability be a core institutional value in terms of auditing, reporting and communicating to outside stakeholders. This involves the construction of a full audit file with recorded briefings and cooperation with oversight agencies. The police organisation also owes a duty of care both to its personnel and to the public.
- Crucially, that the operational accountability structure is also a liability structure. When things go wrong, *accountability is drawn upwards* and ultimately Gold 'carries the can', internally and externally.

These are the fundamentals of an institution based on the sound principles and healthy tradition of civil policing in a democracy and geared to an ethic of service to the community, competent leadership, self-critical professionalism, investment in the primary processes and delivery of quality and embracing a culture of accountability and transparency. Furthermore, there emerged a long-standing philosophy and practice of policing in Britain where firearms use was firmly embedded in 'shoot to prevent' and the responsibility of the individual officer. At Stockwell, in contrast, police officers implemented a policy that could only have one possible outcome – this was 'shoot to kill', which could only lead to death – and they did so on the basis of 'orders' from a superior. From a paradigm of restraint, British policing covertly moved to officers creeping up to a suspect and shooting him – without identifying themselves as police and without issuing a warning – multiple times in the back of the head at point-blank range with ammunition banned in warfare. This may be the only answer to the unprecedented and excruciating dilemma for law enforcement on how to tackle suicide bombers within the norms, values and laws of a democracy. But this was far more than a paradigm shift. It can be viewed from the way policy was formed on the hoof as leading to paradigm abandonment with eyes wide shut, exacerbated by myopic denial. Or perhaps the appropriate metaphor is of a paradigmatic backwards somersault.

My argument is that the police should not be allowed to decide such matters on their own as this crucial issue has profound ramifications for the future and the identity of British policing. This in turn carries great societal significance because in the consent model police seek their legitimacy in the wider society, and there is no area that requires legitimacy, institutionally and individually, more than when police deprive someone of their life. This book, then, argues for parliamentary, professional and public debate to bring the policy and practice on police use of firearms and fatal force firmly into the public domain.

Notes

[1] The last sentence in full is, 'That may be wrong and may need changing, but not by one politician on a political whim'. This refers to the role of the new Conservative Mayor of London, Boris Johnson, who was more interventionist in policing matters than his predecessor, Ken Livingstone, who also had a Labour Party background.

[2] It is not known what and whether the Prime Minister (PM) knew. Apparently on the morning of 22 July a government liaison officer present at an NSY briefing was unaware of Kratos when it was raised and said he would immediately inform the PM, although the Home Office was certainly kept informed through the Permanent Secretary, while the Commissioner had met the PM the day before (Blair, 2009).

[3] Early in the 1990s the Met Commissioner, Condon, and others were highly vocal about more routine issues of firearms to the police

(Campbell, 1994a, 1994b; Clarke, 1994; Connett, 1994a, 1994b; Hooley, 1994).

[4] The Labour government from 1997 onwards was keen to impose a highly centralist measure of control from above the ministries through the Cabinet Office. One step was to use COBRA during crises, and after 7/7 Blair (2009: 13) attended a meeting under Whitehall with the heads of MI5 and MI6, the Foreign Secretary, the Home Secretary, the Defence Secretary and several high-ranking military officers in attendance. Another step was to invite the Commissioner and the President of ACPO to attend cabinet meetings to discuss policing and criminal justice issues. This can clearly have advantages, but the key is to retain operational independence and, while this may have been respected, there was a danger of being drawn too closely into the governmental domain. It was the assumed closeness to the Labour administration that made Ian Blair vulnerable to criticism from the Conservative opposition and the media.

[5] I heard Jack Straw on a BBC radio programme discussing his time as Home Secretary and saying he woke up every morning thinking about what headlines and what controversies were going to confront him that day.

[6] Within, it should be said, guidelines laid down by the Home Office and overseen by the HMIC. On at least two occasions the Home Office turned down requests for a particular type of ammunition including hollow-point ammunition and the 'Glaser safety slug', which causes 'enormous injuries', as they were considered 'ethically unjustifiable and inconsistent with the Hague Conventions' (Waddington, 1991: 90).

[7] There have been police chiefs who did not take their police authorities very seriously – when Hermon led the RUC he treated PANI with open contempt (Ryder, 2000) – or else could rely on a tame, compliant authority.

[8] Due to constraints of time and space I have not dealt with policing and gun crime nor with gun control in the UK and in the US, where it is a key societal issue, nor with the allied campaigns and subsequent legislative change in both societies. These are dealt with to a certain extent by Squires and Kennison (2010), while McLaglan (2005) focuses specifically on gun crime in the UK.

[9] The level of ministerial involvement in operational decision-making in the Netherlands, and other countries with a strong central steering of policing, seems to me to be excessive, and it makes that decision-making often cumbersome and even ineffective.

[10] There were also insistent demands in the early 1990s for more police firepower (Byson, 1994; Campbell, 1994a).

[11] Waldren (2009: 16), for example, draws attention to the danger of over-penetration as the H&K G36, in use by some specialist units, is a 'fully fledged 5.6 mm caliber assault rifle with a muzzle velocity of 3000 feet per second' and the chance of finding a bullet that eliminates over-penetration at close range is 'nil'.

[12] This contemporary debate on paramilitarism goes back to the 1980s (Waddington, 1987; Jefferson, 1990). Indeed, the Metropolitan Police were being accused of being too 'paramilitary' in the middle of the 19th century (Emsley, 1996).

[13] A covert unit, GAL (*Grupos Antiterroristas de Liberación*), was responsible for the abductions, torture and assassinations of suspected ETA Basque insurgents (Punch, 2009a: 49).

[14] One commentator whom I prefer to keep anonymous stated that Kratos was 'an unholy fudge, like trying to pin something on jelly, that was cobbled together under a fog manufactured by ACPO that then led predictably to an almighty cock-up'.

[15] In Golding's interview he sketches Whitehall as something of a frenetic village where policies and proposals are sometimes hatched in indecent haste. He describes being present at one policy meeting where he gave some off-the-cuff comments on an issue and to his amazement these went straight into the draft proposal being typed up to be sent off post-haste.

[16] The new corporate killing Act (Corporate Manslaughter and Corporate Homicide Act 2007) also only recognises collective fault and has removed individual fault (Gobert, 2008).

[17] The two Stockwell inquiries formed a mega-case for the IPCC so soon after starting operations and it was perhaps reluctant to probe too deeply in this early phase of its existence, where it was trying primarily to establish its investigative credentials. Both inquiries must also have drained resources and attention away from other cases and I was told informally by someone from the IPCC that people got 'really tired

and fed up' with the predominance of the two Stockwell inquiries. In the confrontation with the Met Commissioner on access to the Stockwell shooting, moreover, the IPCC Chairman even felt that the very future of the IPCC was in the balance, so the stakes where high and this might explain the degree of reticence and not probing too assertively (Hardwick, 2010).

[18] Generally Bronze and Silver Commanders are competent and well groomed for their roles; but as Yardley and Eliot (1986: 26) put it: 'Any senior officer who is to command marksmen cannot do that job effectively unless he [sic] has some degree of proficiency in, and understanding of, the tactical use of firearms himself. This cannot be accomplished in a course lasting a couple of days'. Also, as a former AFO said, 'in order to understand where the boundaries are on a firearms operation, and the team is often exploring those boundaries in practical situations, the commander has to have experienced the boundaries or he or she won't have the credibility to lead and to control the team' (interview, Gilmour).

APPENDIX

Types of firearms

For the types of firearms available to the police in Britain see Waddington (1991), Collins (1998) and Waldren (2007).

Air guns and 'BB' guns. Air guns fire a pellet projected by compressed air, whereas 'BB' guns fire ball bearings.

Assault rifles. These are shorter, lighter weapons than the standard rifle and with a smaller calibre and high muzzle velocity; they are very effective at short range. Probably the most renowned is the Russian AK47 Kalashnikov.

Automatic weapons. Automatic weapons are designed to fire a number of shots rapidly without having to be manually reloaded after each shot. Several techniques have been developed that allow the spent round to be ejected and a fresh round to be moved into the breech 'automatically'. They are also referred to as 'self-loading' weapons. People also speak of a 'semi-automatic' weapon, which means a firing mode where the shooter has to pull the trigger for each individual shot, while an 'automatic' weapon can be fired continuously until the pressure is released from the trigger. Some weapons are configured for only for semi-automatic firing while others are capable of being fired on semi- or fully automatic modes.

Carbine. The carbine is a lighter form of rifle with a shorter barrel originally designed for use by cavalry. The H&K MP5, for instance, is referred to as a carbine and not a rifle.

Heckler and Kochs (H&Ks). 'H&K' has become a prominent weapons manufacturer, with certain of its handguns, such as the MP5 carbine, enjoying a prolonged product lifecycle. Since the mid-1970s, Heckler and Koch and its MP5 have come to dominate the choice for a close-quarter combat weapon that is also widely used in law-enforcement. The MP5 came into prominence in SAS hands during the Iranian Embassy assault in 1980. It is a reliable and versatile weapon that is manufactured in a variety of models. H&K also produces assault and sniper rifles and sub-machine guns. British police officers normally carry their H&Ks on single-shot, semi-automatic mode; for other purposes they usually can be configured for short bursts (3–5 bullets) or for full-automatic firing.

Machine guns. These weapons are capable of firing a large number of rounds rapidly, usually through an ammunition belt, with Maxim's model of 1883 being viewed as the first fully automatic version. There are heavy, medium and light versions and some models require a tripod and a crew of two or three soldiers.

Revolver. The handgun evolved from the single-shot pistol to the revolver, pioneered by Colt's 'six-shooter' of 1836 in the US. It has a revolving chamber that typically holds six bullets (but can hold up to 10) and it requires pulling the trigger to rotate the chamber to fire each individual round. Revolvers are relatively simple and cheap to produce and are reliable weapons, but have, for a variety of reasons, often been replaced in recent years within law enforcement by 'automatic' pistols.

Rifle. This is a weapon with a long, rifled barrel that greatly enhances muzzle velocity, firing distance and accuracy in the flight of the bullet compared to smooth-bore guns. The development of bolt-action, breech-loading versions increased the speed of reloading and later there were 'automatic' or 'self-loading' models (see below). A considerable variety of rifles has been produced for a wide variety of purposes.

Self-loading pistols (SLPs). These handguns are typically flatter and less bulky than most revolvers and allow for ease of firing and considerable firepower. Some models take a 17-round magazine which, with a swift magazine change, makes 34 rounds available to the shooter compared to the six of most revolvers. The Glock 26 pistol is configured to take a 33-round magazine. The SLP is sometimes coupled with a reputation for unreliability in certain models through jamming, as with a 'stove-pipe' blockage when a round is not fully ejected. The British police have used mostly Browning and Beretta pistols and latterly the Glock 17 (9 mm, with 17-round magazine).

Self-loading rifles (SLRs). This type of 'automatic' weapon can be used on semi- or full-automatic mode, depending on the model and configuration. They can carry large magazines that can be quickly changed, including 100-round drum magazines.

Shotgun. This is a smooth-bore gun, with single- or double-barrels, firing diverse sorts of ammunition.

Sub-machine guns. This refers to one-person, hand-held, compact automatic weapons with a short barrel, between that of a rifle and a pistol, and a high rate of fire (such as the British Sten-gun or the Israeli Uzi). This term is often used inappropriately for other weapons such as the H&K carbines on semi- or full-automatic mode.

References

ACPO (Association of Chief Police Officers) (1983) *Guidelines for the Police on the Issue and Use of Firearms*, London: Home Office.

ACPO (1987) *Guidelines for the Police on the Issue and Use of Firearms*, London: Home Office.

ACPO (2001) *The Manual of Guidance on the Police Use of Firearms*, London: Home Office.

ACPO (2003) *Code of Practice on the Police Use of Firearms and Less Lethal Weapons*, London: Home Office.

ACPO (2005) *The Manual of Guidance on the Police Use of Firearms*, London: Home Office.

ACPO (2006) *The Manual of Guidance on the Police Use of Firearms*, London: Home Office.

Alison, L. and Crego, J. (2008) *Policing Critical Incidents*, Cullompton: Willan.

Allason, R. (1983) *The Branch*, London: Secker and Warburg.

Allison, R. (2001a) 'Blunkett urges sack for Chief Constable', *The Guardian*, 26 June.

Allison, R. (2001b) 'Whitehouse leaves Sussex police early', *The Guardian*, 26 June.

Amnesty International (2004) *Guns and Policing: Standards to Prevent Misuse*, London: Amnesty International.

Anderson, D.M. and Killingray, D. (1991) *Policing the Empire: Government, Authority and Control 1830–1940*, Manchester: Manchester University Press.

Anechiarico, F. and Jacobs, J. (1996) *The Pursuit of Absolute Integrity*, Chicago: Chicago University Press.

Ascoli, D. (1979) *The Queen's Peace*, London: Hamish Hamilton.

Asher, M. (2004) *Shoot to Kill*, London: Cassell.

Asher, M. (2009) *The Regiment: The Real Story of the SAS*, London: Penguin Books.

Bayley, D.H. and Skolnick, J.H. (1998) *The New Blue Line: Police Innovation in Six American Cities*, New York: Simon and Schuster.

BBC Radio (2009) 'The reunion: Iranian Embassy siege', 6 September.

BBC Radio (2010a) 'Armed police seal off town in hunt for Tyneside gunman', 7 July (from www.bbc.co.uk/news).

BBC Radio (2010b) 'Tasers fired at gunman Raoul Moat "not approved"', 13 July (from www.bbc.co.uk/news).

BBC TV (2003) 'SAS embassy siege', documentary by Bruce Goodison, 3 October 2002.

BBC TV (2006) 'Countdown to killing', *Panorama* documentary by Peter Taylor, 8 March.

Beevor, A. (2009) *D-Day: The Battle for Normandy*, London: Viking.

Belur, J. (2010) *Permission to Shoot: Police Use of Deadly Force in Democracies*, London: Springer.

Bennetto, J. (1994) 'Police seek wider use of armed patrols', *The Independent*, 7 July.

Bennetto, J. (1995) 'Police reject guns on the beat', *The Independent*, 16 May.

Bennetto, J. (2005) 'Officers arrested over Stanley shooting', *The Independent*, 3 June.

Blair, I. (2003) 'Leading towards the future', Speech at Future of Policing Conference, London School of Economics, September.

Blair, I. (2005) *Richard Dimbleby Lecture*, London: BBC TV.

Blair, I. (2009) *Policing Controversy*, London: Profile Books.

Bootsma, P. (2001) *De Molukse acties*, Amsterdam: Boom.

Boston Globe (2009) 'Police getting more firepower', 29 May.

Bowling, B. (1999) 'The rise and fall of New York murder', *British Journal of Criminology*, 39 (4): 531–54.

Bowling, B. (2010) *Policing the Caribbean*, Oxford: Oxford University Press.

Bowling, B. and Newburn, T. (2006) 'Policing and national security', Paper presented at Columbia University – IALS Workshop: Police, Community and the Rule of Law, London, March.

Brodeur, J.-P. (1981) 'Legitimizing police deviance', in C.D. Shearing, (ed) *Organizational Police Deviance*, Toronto: Butterworth, pp 127–60.

Browning, C. (2001) *Ordinary Men*, London: Penguin.

Bunker, R. J. (2005a) *IACP: Training Key 581: Suicide (Homicide) Bombers: Part I*, New Washington, DC: International Association of Chiefs of Police.

Bunker, R.J. (2005b) *IACP: Training Key 582: Suicide (Homicide) Bombers: Part II*, New Washington, DC: International Association of Chiefs of Police.

Burrows, C. (1996) *A Review of the Discharge of Firearms by Police in England and Wales 1991–1993*, Joint Standing Committee on the Police Use of Firearms in consultation with the PCA, unpublished.

Burrows, C. (2007) 'Critical decision making by police firearms officers: A review of officer perception, response and reaction', *Policing*, 1 (3): 273–83.

Byson, N. (1994) 'PCs to pack pistols on city streets', *The Sun*, 17 May.

Campbell, D. (1994a) 'Police to get guns for routine patrols', *The Guardian*, 17 May.

Campbell, D. (1994b) 'Condon calls for tougher gun laws', *The Guardian*, 2 August.

Campbell, D. (2009) 'Police apologise for fatal shooting of innocent man', *The Guardian*, 5 March.

Campbell, D. and Travis, A. (1994) 'Police Chief says shootings bring armed force closer', *The Guardian*, 11 March.

Carson, W. (2008) 'Chandler's Ford shooting: Deadly end to robbers crime spree', *Southern Daily Echo*, 4 October.

CBS News (2009) '4 Wash. State police officers gunned down', 29 November.

Christopher Commission (1991) *Independent Commission on the Los Angeles Police Department*, Los Angeles: City of Los Angeles.

Clarke, M. (1994) 'Arming the police: Time for a change', *Police Review*, 14 January.

Clinard, M. (1978) *Cities with Little Crime*, Cambridge: Cambridge University Press.

Collins, R. (2008) *Violence: A Micro-sociological Theory*, Princeton/Oxford: Princeton.

Collins, S. (1998) *The Good Guys Wear Black: The True Life Heroes of Britain's Armed Police*, London: Random House.

Commissioner's Annual Report (1974) *Report of the Commissioner of Police of the Metropolis for the Year 1973*, London: HMSO.

Connett, D. (1994a) 'More police firepower urged', *The Independent*, 16 May.

Connett, D. (1994b) 'Police to carry guns openly on London Streets', *The Independent*, 17 May.

Cramphorn, C. and Punch, M. (2007) 'The murder of Theo van Gogh', *Journal of Policing, Intelligence and Counter Terrorism*, 2 (1): 34–53.

Crank, J. P. (1998) *Understanding Police Culture*, Cincinnati: Anderson.

Crawshaw, R. and Holmström, L. (2006) *Human Rights and Policing* (2nd edn), Leiden/Boston: Martinus Nijhoff.

Crawshaw, R., Cullen, S. and Holmström, L. (2006) *Essential Cases on Human Rights for the Police*, Leiden/Boston: Martinus Nijhoff.

Critchley, T.A. (1978) *A History of Police in England and Wales*, London: Constable.

Cullen Report (1988) *The Public Inquiry into the Circumstances Leading Up to and Surrounding the Events at Dunblane Primary School on Wednesday 13th March 1996* (Inquiry chaired by Lord Cullen), London: HMSO.

Daily Mail (2007) 'A man without honour' [this was the lead headline, with a four-page spread entitled 'Blunders from start to finish' plus an editorial comment on the Stockwell trial and the Commissioner's position], 2 November.

Daily Telegraph, The (2004) 'Safety phobia isn't funny – it can be fatal', 7 October.

Daily Telegraph, The (2008a) 'Mark Saunders shooting: Wife speaks of love', 8 May.

Daily Telegraph, The (2008b) 'Mark Saunders shooting: Lawyer shot dead by siege police "came close to giving up"', 19 May.

Daily Telegraph, The (2010) 'Give us more firepower to stop terrorist attacks, says police chief', 15 April.

Davies, N. (2001a) 'Armed and dangerous: The police with their fingers on the trigger', *The Guardian*, 23 May.

Davies, N. (2001b) 'Inquiry into shooting provoked three-way row among police', *The Guardian*, 23 May.

Dear Report (1983) *Report of the Working Party on the Training and Selection of Authorised Firearms Officers*, London: Home Office.

de Volkskrant (2005) 'Theo van Gogh vermoord', 2 November; internet edition.

Dillon, M. (1991) *The Dirty War*, London: Arrow.

Dodd, V. (2001) 'Police who shot unarmed man will not face criminal charges', *The Guardian*, 14 December.

Edwards, C. (1988) 'Was Hungerford "a basic failure of the police"?', *The Listener*, 14 January.

Ellis, J. (1982) *The Sharp End of War*, London: Corgi Books.

Ellis, S. (1988) 'The historical significance of South Africa's Third Force', *Journal of South African Studies*, 24 (2): 261–99.

Emsley, C. (1996) *The English Police: A Political and Social History*, London: Longman.

Emsley, C. (2009) *The Great British Bobby*, London: Quercus.

English, R. (2004) *Armed Struggle: The History of the IRA*, London: Pan.

Flin, R. (1996) *Sitting in the Hot Seat*, New York: Wiley.

Foster, J., Newburn, T. and Souhami, A. (2005) *Assessing the Impact of the Stephen Lawrence Inquiry*, London: Home Office.

Fyfe, J.J. (1978) *Shots Fired: An Examination of New York City Police Firearm Discharges*, unpublished PhD dissertation, State University of New York at Albany.

Fyfe, J.J. (1988) 'Police use of lethal force: Research and reform', *Justice Quarterly*, 5: 164–205.

Geller, W. and Scott, M. (1992) *Deadly Force: What We Know*, Washington, DC: PERF.

Geraghty, T. (2000) *The Irish War*, London: HarperCollins.

Gilbert, H. (2005) 'Firearms officers avoid misconduct charge', *Police Review*, 30 September.

Glass, D. (2005) 'Judgement call', *Police Review*, 1 July.

Glass, D. (2007) 'Getting the balance right: The use of firearms in British policing', *Policing*, 1 (3): 293–9.

Glass, D. (2008) 'Firearms officers "slur" disappoints IPCC', *Police Review*, 11 January.

Glenny, M. (2009) *McMafia: Seriously Organized Crime*, London: Vintage Books.

Gobert, J. (2008) 'The evolving legal test of corporate criminal liability', in J. Minkes and L. Minkes (eds) *Corporate and White-Collar Crime*, London: Sage, pp 61–81.

Gobert, J. and Punch, M. (2003) *Rethinking Corporate Crime*, Cambridge: Cambridge University Press.

Goldsmith, A. (2009) 'Policing: The new visibility', Presentation at Conference on Police Governance and Accountability, University of Limerick, December.

Gray, R. (2000) *Armed Response: Inside SO19 – Scotland Yard's Elite Armed Response Unit*, London: Virgin Publishing. Reprinted as *The Trojan Files* in 2001.

Green, P. and Ward, T. (2004) *State Crime: Governments, Violence and Corruption*, London: Pluto.

Greenwood, C. (1966) *Police Firearms Training*, London: The Forensic Science Society.

Greenwood, C. (1972) *Firearms Control: A Study of Armed Crime and Firearms Control in England and Wales*, London: Routledge.

Greenwood, C. (1979) *Police Tactics in Armed Operations*, Boulder, CO: Paladin Press.

Griffiths, C.T. (2007) *Canadian Criminal Justice*, Scarborough, Ontario: Nelson Education.

Guardian, The (2001a) 'Poor planning led to tragedy', 22 May.

Guardian, The (2001b) 'Family of shot man to sue police', 22 May.

Guardian, The (2006) 'New York on edge as police kill unarmed man in hail of 50 bullets on his wedding day', 27 November.

Guardian, The (2007a) 'Met police guilty over de Menezes shooting', 1 November.

Guardian, The (2007b) 'Guilty, but Blair refuses to go', 2 November [this was the lead headline, with a two-page spread and an editorial on the Stockwell trial].

Guardian, The (2010a) 'Death of Blair Peach: The truth at last', 28 April.

Guardian, The (2010b) 'Cumbria shootings: 12 dead as gunman goes on killing spree', 3 June.

Haas, M. (2008) *International Human Rights*, London: Routledge.

Hailwood, A. (2005) *Gun Law: Fighting Britain's Deadliest Gangs: Inside an Elite Police Firearms Unit*, Reading: Milo Books Ltd.

Hardwick, N. (2010) Unpublished review of M. Punch (2009) *Police Corruption*, forthcoming in *Policing: Journal of Research and Practice*.

Hawkins, K (2002) *Law as Last Resort*, Oxford: Oxford University Press.

Haynes, C. (2006) 'Firearms incidents are as stressful to recall as when they happen', *Police Review*, 8 December.

Hillas, S. and Cox, T. (1986) 'Stress in the police service', Occasional Paper, Police Scientific Research and Development Branch, London: Home Office.

Hilliard, B. (1987) 'The Hungerford massacre', *Police Review*, 9 October.

Hinton, M.S. (2005) *The State on the Streets*, Boulder/London: Rienner.

Hinton, M.S. and Newburn, T. (eds) (2009) *Policing Developing Democracies*, Abingdon: Routledge.

Home Affairs Committee (2010) 'The work of the Independent Police Complaints Commission', House of Commons, London: TSO.

Home Office (1986) *Report by the Home Office Working Group on the Police Use of Firearms*, London: HMSO.

Hoogenboom, A.B. (2010) *The Governance of Policing and Security*, Basingstoke: Palgrave Macmillan.

Hooley, P. (1994) 'Our brave officers need guns', *Daily Express*, 11 February.

Hopkins, N. (2001) 'Policeman cleared over killing', *The Guardian*, 3 May.

Hopkins, N. and Davies, N. (2001) 'Top officers condemned over fatal police raid', *The Guardian*, 23 May.

Huggins, M. K. (ed) (1991) *Vigilantism and the State in Modern Latin America*, New York: Praeger.

IPCC (Independent Police Complaints Commission) (2004) *Highmoor Cross Report*, London: IPCC.

IPCC (2005) *Report to the Independent Police Complaints Commission Regarding: The Fatal Shooting of Henry Bruce Stanley* [by Surrey Police], London: IPCC.

IPCC (2006) *IPCC Annual Report 2005/06*, London: IPCC.

IPCC (2007a) *Stockwell One: Investigation into the Shooting of Jean Charles de Menezes on Stockwell Underground Station on 22 July 2005*, London: IPCC.

IPCC (2007b) *Stockwell Two: An Investigation into Complaints about the Metropolitan Police Handling of Public Statements Following the Shooting of Jean Charles de Menezes on 22 July 2005*, London: IPCC.

IPCC (2007c) *Chandler's Ford: Interim Report into the Police Shootings in Chandler's Ford on 13th September 2007*, London: IPCC.

IPCC (2007d) *IPCC Annual Report 2006/07*, London: IPCC.

IPCC (2008a) *IPCC Annual Report 2007/08*, London: IPCC.

IPCC (2008b) *IPCC Concludes Investigation into Double Fatal Shooting – Hampshire*, London: IPCC.

IPCC Press Release (2004a) 'IPCC Commissioner Deborah Glass speaks following Harry Stanley inquest verdict', 29 October, London: IPCC.

IPCC Press Release (2004b) 'IPCC comments on Thames Valley Police's review into Highmoor Cross incident', 6 October, London: IPCC.

IPCC Press Release (2006) 'Harry Stanley – IPCC publishes decision and report', 9 February, London: IPCC.

Jay, A. (2004) 'Armed police call off gun strike: Suspended officers receive backing of Metropolitan Police Commissioner', *The Guardian*, 3 November.

Jefferson, T. (1990) *The Case against Paramilitary Policing*, Milton Keynes: Open University Press.

Jones, T. (2003) 'The governance and accountability of policing', in T. Newburn (ed) *Handbook of Policing*, Cullompton: Willan, pp 603–27.

Josephs, J. (1993) *Hungerford: One Man's Massacre*, London: Smith Gryphon Publishers.

Karmen, A. (2000) *New York Murder Mystery: The True Story behind the Crime Crash of the 1990s*, New York: New York University Press.

Katz, J. (1988) *The Seductions of Crime*, New York: Basic Books.

Keegan, J. (1976) *The Face of Battle*, London: Jonathan Cape.

Kennedy, D.B. (2006) 'A precis of suicide terrorism', *Journal of Homeland Security and Emergency Management*, 3 (4): 1–9.

Kennison, P. and Loumansky, A. (2007) 'Shoot to kill – understanding police use of force in combating suicide terrorism', *Crime, Law and Social Change*, 47: 151–68.

Kitchin, H. (1988) *The Gibraltar Report: Inquest into the Deaths of Mairead Farrell, Daniel McGann and Sean Savage, Gibraltar, September, 1988*, London: NCCL.

Kleinig, J. (1996) *The Ethics of Policing*, Cambridge: Cambridge University Press.

Klinger, D. (2004) *Into the Kill Zone*, San Francisco: Jossey Bass.

Klockars, C.B. (1985) *The Idea of Police*, London: Sage.

Klockars, C.B. (2005) 'The Dirty Harry problem', in T. Newburn (ed) *Policing: Key Readings*, Cullompton: Willan, pp 581–95.

Kraska, P. (1999) 'Questioning the militarization of US police: Critical versus advocacy scholarship', *Policing and Society*, 9 (2): 141–55.

Kraska, P. (ed) (2001) *Militarizing the American Criminal Justice System: The Changing Roles of the Armed Forces and the Police*, Boston: North Eastern University.

Kraska, P. and Cubellis, L.J. (1997) 'Militarizing Mayberry and beyond: Making sense of American paramilitary policing', *Justice Quarterly*, 14 (December): 607–29.

Kraska, P. and Kappeler, V. E. (1997) 'Militarizing American police: The rise and normalization of paramilitary units', *Social Problems*, 44 (1): 1–18.

LAPD (Los Angeles Police Department) (2000) *Board of Inquiry into the Rampart Area Corruption Incident*, Los Angeles: LAPD.

Lee, M. and Punch, M. (2006) *Policing by Degrees*, Groningen: Hondsrug Pers.

Leishman, F., Loveday, B. and Savage, S. (eds) (1966) *Core Issues in Policing*, London: Longman.

Leishman, F., Loveday, B. and Savage, S. (eds) (2000) *Core Issues in Policing* (2nd edn), Harlow: Longman.

Leppard, D. (1994) 'Police set to use machine guns to fight UK crime', *The Sunday Times*, 15 May.

Leppard, D. (2006) 'Police get "licence to kill" without questions', *The Sunday Times*, 12 March.

Leppard, D. and Prescott, M. (1994) 'Thousands of police to carry guns openly', *The Sunday Times*, 1 May.

Levitt, L. (2009) *NYPD Confidential*, New York: Thomas Dunne Books.

Lewinski, B. and Grossi, D. (1999) 'The suspect is shot in the back – is your shooting clean? Understanding the limits of survival psychology', *The Police Marksman*, XXIV (5): 23–5.

Manning, P.K. (1977) *Police Work*, Cambridge, MA: MIT Press.

Manolias, M. and Hyatt-Williams, A. (1986) 'Study of post-shooting experiences in firearms officers', Scientific Research and Development Branch, London: Home Office.

Mark, R. (1978) *In the Office of Constable*, London: Collins.

Markham, G. and Punch, M. (2007a) 'Embracing accountability:The way forward – part one', *Policing: Journal of Research and Practice*, 1 (3): 1–9.

Markham, G. and Punch, M. (2007b) 'Embracing accountability:The way forward – part two', *Policing: Journal of Research and Practice*, 1 (4): 485–94.

Mars, J. R. (2002) *Deadly Force, Colonialism, and the Rule of Law: Police Violence in Guyana*, Westport, CT: Greenwood Press.

Marshall, G. (1987) 'Police accountability revisited', in D. Butler and A. Halsey (eds) *Policy and Politics*, London: Macmillan, pp 51–65.

Marx, G. T. (1988) *Undercover: Police Surveillance in America*, Berkeley: University of California Press.

Mason, G. (1988) 'When communications fail:The HMI's report on the lessons of Hungerford', *Police Review*, 5 August.

McCulloch, J. and Sentas, V. (2006) 'The killing of Jean Charles de Menezes: Hyper-militarism in the neo-liberal economic free fire zone', *Social Justice*, 33 (4): 92–107.

McKenzie, I. (1996) 'Violent encounters: Force and deadly force in British Policing', in Leishman, F., Loveday, B. and Savage, S. (eds) *Core Issues in Policing*, London: Longman, pp 131–46.

McKenzie, I. (2000) 'Policing force: Rules, hierarchies and confidence', in F. Leishman, B. Loveday and S. Savage (eds) *Core Issues in Policing* (2nd edn), Harlow: Pearson.

McKittrick, D. and McVea, D. (2001) *Making Sense of the Troubles*, London: Penguin.

McLachlan Report (1988) *The Hungerford Incident*, London: HMIC.

McLagan, G. (2005) *Guns and Gangs: Inside Black Gun Crime*, London: Allison and Busby.

McLaughlin, E. (2005) 'Forcing the issue: New Labour, new localism and the democratic renewal of police accountability', *The Howard Journal*, 44 (5): 473–89.

McNee, D. (1983) *McNee's Law*, London: Collins.

Miller, W. (1977) *Cops and Bobbies*, Chicago: University of Chicago Press.

Millward, D. (1994) 'Hungerford massacre led to quick change in the law', *Daily Telegraph*, 3 August.

Ministry of Home Affairs (2007) *The Police in the Netherlands*, The Hague: Ministry of Home Affairs.

Moore, B. (1997) *Victims and Survivors*, London: Arnold.

Moskos, P. (2008) *Cop in the Hood*, Princeton: Princeton University Press.

Moysey, S.P. (2007) *The Road to Balcombe Street*, London: Haworth Press.

MPA (Metropolitan Police Authority) (2008) *MPA Stockwell Scrutiny: Final Report*, London: MPA.

Mulcahy, A. (2006) *Policing Northern Ireland*, Cullompton: Willan.

Muller, E.R., Rosenthal, U., Zannoni, M., Ferwerda, H. and Schaap, S.D. (2009) *Strandrellen in Hoek van Holland*, Den Haag: COT.

Newburn, T. (ed) (2003) *Handbook of Policing*, Cullompton: Willan.

Newburn, T. (ed) (2005) *Policing: Key Readings*, Cullompton: Willan.

Newsinger, J. (1997) *Dangerous Men: The SAS and Popular Culture*, London: Pluto Press.

Neyroud, P. (2004) 'Closer to the citizen? Developing accountability and governance in policing', Presentation at British Society of Criminology Conference, Birmingham, July.

Neyroud, R. and Beckley, P. (2001) *Policing, Ethics and Human Rights*, Cullompton: Willan.

Nicholl, C. (1994) 'Ease off the trigger we don't want to be armed', *The Observer*, 7 August.

Nollkaemper, P.A. and van der Wilt, H. (eds) *System Criminality in International Law*, Cambridge: Cambridge University Press.

Norfolk, A. (2007) 'Beshenivsky suspect is captured in Somalia and flown to Britain', *The Times*, 2 November.

North, M. (2000) *Dunblane: Never Forget*, Edinburgh and London: Mainstream.

NPIA (National Police Improvement Agency) (2007) *Practice Advice on Critical Incident Management*, Bramshill: Leadership Academy.

O'Hara, P. (2005) *Why Law Enforcement Fails*, Durham, NC: Carolina Academic Press.

O'Neill, S. (2007) 'Met Police on trial for shooting of de Menezes', *The Times*, 1 October.

Orde, H. (2003) *Working with an Independent Investigation Agency*, Presentation at OPONI Conference, Policing the Police, Belfast, November.

Orr-Munro, T. (2003) 'Police issued with guidance on dealing with suicide bombers', *Police Review*, 24 January.

Ottawa Citizen (2010) 'Braidwood inquiry finds officers' use of Taser not justified', 20 June.

Paddick, B. (2008) *Line of Fire*, London: Pocket Books.

Patten Report (1999) *A New Beginning: Policing in Northern Ireland. Report of the Independent Commission on Policing for Northern Ireland*, London: Home Office.

PCA (Police Complaints Commission) (2003) *Review of Shootings by Police in England and Wales 1998 to 2001*, London: TSO.

Penglase, B. (1996) *Final Justice: Police and Death Squad Homicides of Adolescents in Brazil*, New York: Human Rights Watch.

Polk, K. (1994) *When Men Kill: Scenarios of Masculine Violence*, Cambridge: Cambridge University Press.

Pretoria News, The (2008) 'Kill the bastards, minister tells police', 10 April.

Punch, M. (1979) *Policing the Inner City*, London: Macmillan.

Punch, M. (ed) (1983) *Control in the Police Organisation*, Cambridge, MA: MIT Press.

Punch, M. (1985) *Conduct Unbecoming: The Social Construction of Police Deviance and Control*, London: Tavistock.

Punch, M. (1996) *Dirty Business*, London: Sage.

Punch, M. (2007) *Zero Tolerance Policing*, Bristol: Policy Press.

Punch, M. (2008) 'The organization did it: Individuals, corporations and crime', in J. Minkes and L. Minkes (eds) *Corporate and White-Collar Crime*, London: Sage, pp 102–21.

Punch, M. (2009a) *Police Corruption*, Cullompton: Willan.

Punch, M. (2009b) 'Why corporations kill and get away with it: The failure of law to cope with crime in organizations', in P.A. Nollkaemper and H. van der Wilt (eds) *System Criminality in International Law*, Cambridge: Cambridge University Press, pp 42–68.

Punch, M. and Markham, G. (2000) 'Policing disasters', *International Journal of Police Science & Management*, 3(1): 40–54.

Punch, M. and Markham, G. (2004) 'The gemini solution: Embracing accountability', in M. Amir and S. Einstein (eds) *Police Corruption*, Huntsville, TX: OICJ, pp 493–509.

Punch, M. and Markham, G. (2006) 'Police accountability: Never ending quest', Paper presented at Columbia University – IALS Workshop: Police, Community and the Rule of Law, London, March.

Reiner, R. (1991) *Chief Constables*, Oxford: Oxford University Press.

Reiner, R. (2007) *Law and Order*, Cambridge: Polity.

Reiner, R. (2010) *The Politics of the Police* (4th edn), Oxford: Oxford University Press.

Reisman, D. (1979) *Folded Lies*, New York: Free Press.

Reuss-Ianni, E.R. (1983) *Two Cultures of Policing*, New Brunswick, NJ: Transaction Books.

Reuters (2010) 'Gunman kills 12 in Lake District rampage', 2 June.

Robertson, G. (1989) *Freedom, the Individual and the Law* (6th edn), London: Penguin.

Rollo, J. (1980) 'The Special Patrol Group', in P. Hain (ed) *Policing the Police, Volume 2*, London: Platform Books, pp 153-208.

Rose, D. (1996) *In the Name of the Law*, London: Jonathan Cape.

Rostker, B.D., Hanser, L.W., Hix, W.M., Jensen, C., Morral, A.R., Ridgeway, G. and Schell, T.L. (2008) *Evaluation of the NYPD Firearm Training and Firearm-Discharge Review Process*, Santa Monica, CA: Rand Corporation.

Royal Commission on the Police (1962) *Final Report*, London: HMSO.

Rubinstein, J. (1973) *City Police*, New York: Ballantine.

Ryder, C. (2000) *The RUC*, London: Arrow.

Sampson, P. and Crow, A. (1997) *Dunblane: Our Years of Tears*, Edinburgh: Mainstream.

Savage, S. (2010) 'The British policing elite: The Association of Chief Police Officers'; this paper is published as 'ACPO: *Elite de la police britannique*', in *La Tribune Du Commissaire*, 114 (March), pp 23-29.

Savage, S., Charman, S. and Cope, S. (2000) *Policing and the Power of Persuasion*, London: Blackstone.

Saville Report (2010) *Report of the Bloody Sunday Inquiry* (inquiry chaired by Lord Saville), London: Northern Ireland Office.

Scraton, P. (1985) *The State of the Police*, Pluto: London.

Simon, D. (2009) *Homicide: A Year on the Killing Streets*, Edinburgh/London/New York/Melbourne: Cannongate (originally published in 1991 with Houghton-Mifflin).

Skolnick, J.H. (1966) *Justice Without Trial*, New York: Wiley.

Skolnick, J.H. (2002) 'Code Blue: Prosecuting police brutality means breaking the rule of silence', *American Prospect*, 27 March–10 April: 49–53.

Skolnick, J.H. and Fyfe, J.J. (1993) *Above the Law: Police and Excessive Use of Force*, New York: Free Press.

Slapper, G. and Tombs, S. (1999) *Corporate Crime*, Harlow: Longman.

Smith, G. (2005) 'A most enduring problem: Police complaints reform in England and Wales', *Journal of Social Policy*, 35 (1): 121–41.

Solomon, R.M. and James H.H. (1981) 'Post shooting trauma', *National Symposium on Police Psychological Services*, Quantico, VA: FBI Academy.

Squires, P. and Kennison, P. (2010) *Shooting to Kill?*, London: Wiley Blackwell.

Stalker, J. (1988) *Stalker: Ireland, 'Shoot to Kill' and the 'Affair'*, London: Penguin.

Stevens, J. (2003) *Stevens Enquiry 3: Overview and Recommendations*, London: Home Office.

Stockwell Inquest (2009) *Inquest into the Death of Jean-Charles de Menezes: Rule 43 Report*, Coroner, Sir M. Wright, Coroner's Court, Southwark Street, London. Transcripts available at: www.stockwellinquest.org.uk

Stokes, P. (2001) 'Police shoot dead man brandishing samurai sword', *The Daily Telegraph*, 14 July.

Tendler, S. (1994a) 'Police step up gun patrols to protect London officers', *The Times*, 21 February.

Tendler, S. (1994b) 'Police could show guns on the street', *The Times*, 28 March.

Tendler, S. (1994c) 'Police chiefs seek more firepower', *The Times*, 16 May.

Tendler, S. (1994d) 'Public happy to see police armed', *The Times*, 18 May.

Tendler, S. (1994e) 'Condon calls for new laws to curb gun culture', *The Times*, 2 August.

Thames Television (1988) 'Death on the Rock', documentary on SAS shooting of three IRA members on Gibraltar, 28 April.

Thames Valley Police (2004) *Review of the Practices and Procedures Adopted by Thames Valley Police in Connection with the Fatal Shootings at Highmoor Cross on Sunday 6th June 2004*, Oxford: TVP.

Times, The (2007) 'Met chief urged to quit over shooting' [this was the front-page headline but there are four further pages devoted to the de Menezes trial, a comment column and an editorial], 2 November.

Timmer, J. (2005) *Politiegeweld*, Alphen aan de Rijn: Kluwer.

Timmer, J., Naeyé, J. and van der Steeg, M. (1996) *Onder Schot*, Deventer: Gouda Quint.

Travis, A. (1994) 'Armed patrols loom, says police chief', *The Guardian*, 7 July.

Travis, A. (1995) 'Police hold referendum on carrying firearms', *The Guardian*, 21 March.

United Nations Economic and Social Council (1990) *Basic Principles on the Use of Force and Firearms by Law Enforcement Officials*, adopted by the Eighth UN Congress on the Prevention of Crime and Treatment of Offenders, Havana, Cuba, 27 August–7 September.

United Nations General Assembly (1979) *Code of Conduct for Law Enforcement Officials*, adopted December, New York: UN.

Urban, M. (1993) *Big Boys' Rules*, London: Faber and Faber.

Van Maanen, J. (1988) *Tales of the Field*, Chicago: Chicago University Press.

Vaughan, D. (1996) *The Challenger Launch Decision*, Chicago: Chicago University Press.

Verkaik, R. and Bennetto, J. (2005) 'Shot dead by police 30, officers convicted 0: No charges for policemen who killed man carrying table leg', *The Independent*, 25 October.

Waddington, P. J. (1987) 'Towards paramilitarism? Dilemmas in policing civil disorder', *British Journal of Criminology*, 27 (1): 37–46.

Waddington, P. J. (1991) *The Strong Arm of the Law: Armed and Public Order Policing*, Oxford: Clarendon Press.

Waddington, P. J. (1999) 'Armed and unarmed policing', in R. Mawby (ed) *Policing Around the World: Issues for the 21st Century*, London: UCL, pp 151-66.

Waddington, P. J. (2005) 'Our risk-averse society dislikes violence', *Police Review*, 23 September.

Waddington, P. J. and Wright, M. (2007) 'Police use of force, firearms and riot control', in T. Newburn (ed) *Handbook of Policing* (2nd edn), Cullompton: Willan, pp 693-724.

Waddington, P.J., Adang, O., Baker, D., Birkbeck, C., Feltes, D., Gabaldon, L.G., Paes Machado, E. and Stenning, P. (2009) 'Singing the same tune? International continuities and discontinuities in how police talk about using force', *Crime, Law and Social Change*, 52 (2): 95–110.

Waldren, M. J. (2007) *Armed Police: The Police Use of Firearms since 1945*, Thrupp/Stroud: Sutton Publishing.

Waldren, M. J. (2009) 'Take the bullet', *Police Review*, 4 September.

Walker, S. (2005) *The New World of Police Accountability*, Thousand Oaks, CA: Sage.

Wambaugh, J. (1973) *The Onion Field*, New York: Dell.

Ward, D. (2003) 'Police chief apologises to family of man killed in bungled raid', *The Guardian*, 14 November.

Weick, C. K. (1979) *Social Psychology of Organizing* (2nd edn), Reading, MA: Addison-Wesley.

Weick, C. K. (1990) 'The vulnerable system: An analysis of the Tenerife air disaster', *Journal of Management*, 16 (3): 571–93.

Weir, S. and Bentham, D. (1999) *Political Power and Democratic Control in Britain*, London: Routledge.

Wells, C. (2001) *Corporations and Criminal Responsibility* (2nd edn), Oxford: Oxford University Press.

Williams, M. (1989) *Murder on the Rock*, London: Larkin Publications.

Williamson, T. (2006) 'Who needs police authorities?', *Police Review*, 20 January.

Yardley, M. and Eliot, P. (1986) 'The case for special units', *Police,* XVIII (June), pp 26–31.

Yeebo, Y. and Fresco, A. (2007) '"Bloodbath" as armed robbers are shot dead in bank raid', *The Times*, 14 September.

Zimonjic, P. (2008) *Into the Darkness: An Account of 7/7*, London: Vintage.

Index

Note: Names of organisations are mainly indexed under the full form. For a list of abbreviations and acronyms see pages xii–xiv. Numbers are filed as though spelled out, e.g.'7/7' bombings appear under S as 'seven'. Page numbers followed by *n* refer to information in a note.

Bumpurs, Mrs (victim of police
shooting) 109-10, 114
Bunker, R.J. 162
burden of responsibility *see*
accountability
Burrows, C. 45-6, 97-8

C

Cabinet Office Briefing Room
(COBRA) 151, 205*n*
call management and armed response
40-1, 112, 135
carbines 34, 79, 209
Carter, Commander 158, 161, 174
Chandler's Ford shooting 199
Charter of Citizens' Rights proposal
197
Christopher Commission 123-4*n*
'citizen-armies' and weapons in home
78-9
'civil policing' ethos and minimal
force 2, 199
'Bobbies' and historical background
25-6
move away from 4, 203-4
Clarke, Charles 8
Clegg, Private 48-9
Close Quarter Battle (CQB)
operations 150, 152-6
Clydesdale protocol 160-1
COBRA 151, 205*n*
Collins, R. 101, 110-11
Collins, S. 39, 99
collusion in post-incident reports
139-40
military procedure 139, 151
colonial police as armed 27
Columbine high school massacre 99
command and control systems 3, 125
and accountability 21-3, 129-37
'corporate manslaughter' as offence
131-2
Gibraltar shootings 17-21
as institutional value 203
and military involvement 151, 154
operational accountability 132-7,
145, 194, 202, 203
problems of distance from situations
136-7
Stockwell shooting 171, 173-7,
201-2
Sussex shooting 12-14, 20, 21, 129-
31, 138-9, 194
see also orders to shoot

inability to keep pace with arming of
police 37, 39-42
inadequate authorisation of weapons
use 40, 41
and individual responsibility to shoot
49-50, 63, 64, 129, 201-2
military involvement and
responsibility for 151, 154
and 'mistakes' 108, 109
delays in deployment of armed
police 111-12
in Netherlands 51-2, 54-5, 56, 62
office hours and lack of cover 40-2,
135
professional competence and
qualification 203
Stockwell shooting and 'Kratos'
policy 160-3, 165-74, 177, 187, 200
communication
failures in Stockwell shooting 174-5
lack of clarity in commands 168,
201-2
lack of inter-agency communication
109-10
Computer Aided Dispatch (CAD) and
armed response 40-1, 112, 135
Condon, Sir Paul (Commissioner
MPS) 193
confusion in fatal force incidents
116-17
consent and police legitimacy 5, 25-6,
183-4, 204
'constabulary independence' 64, 185,
192, 194, 201-2
control room and armed response
40-1, 112, 135
'corporate manslaughter' legislation
14, 125, 129-30, 131-2, 206*n*
see also institutional responsibility
counter-terrorist operations
and human rights law 17-19
'Kratos' policy formation 160-3, 190,
191, 194, 200
see also Gibraltar shootings; Stockwell
shooting; suicide bombers
Crank, J.P. 63
Crawshaw, Ralph viii-ix
Criminal Law Act (1967) 48, 185
criminals
access to guns and array of weapons
80-1, 90-1
denial of treatment when injured
122*n*
shooting of unarmed officers 72
see also violent crime